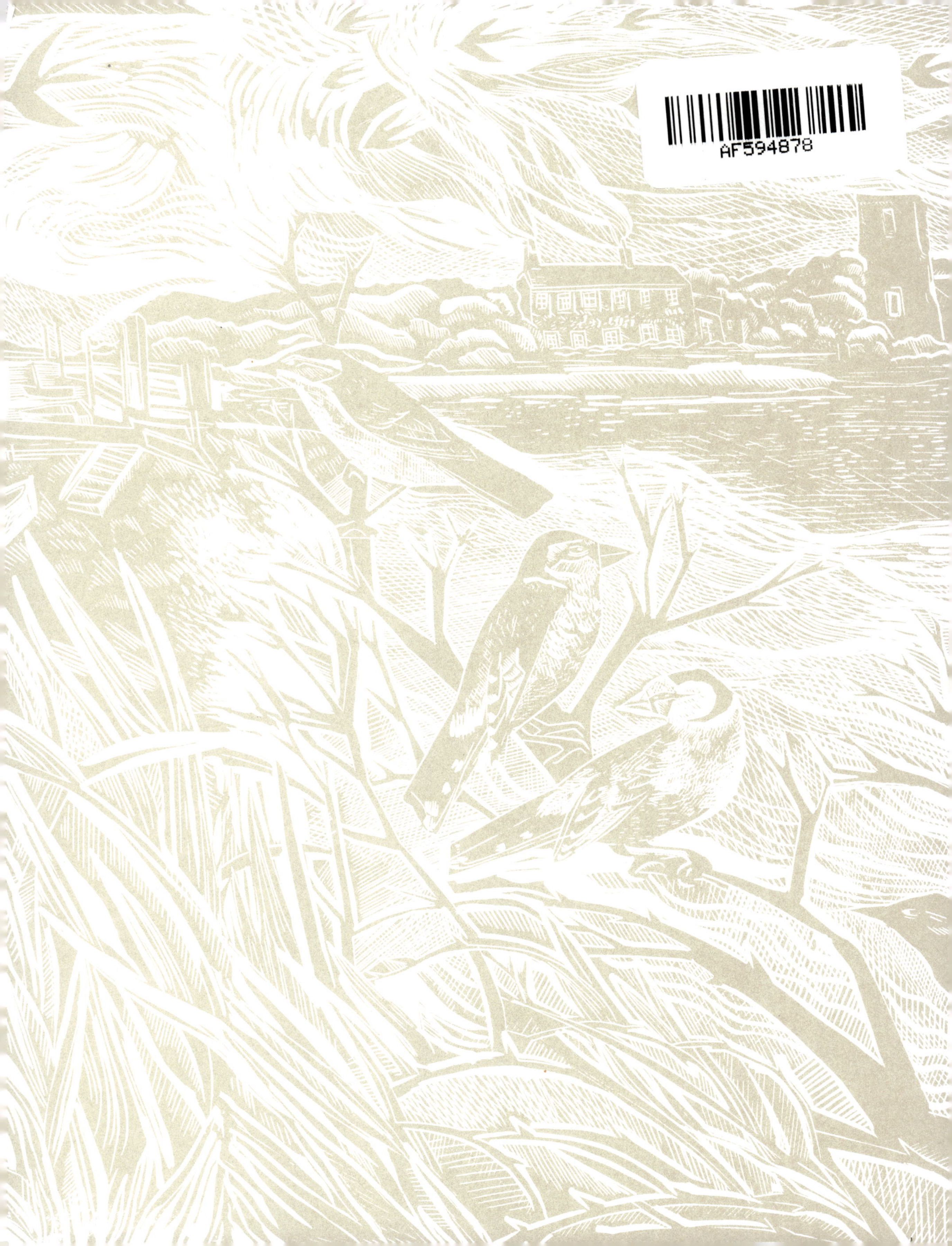

A Year Unfolding

Angela Harding

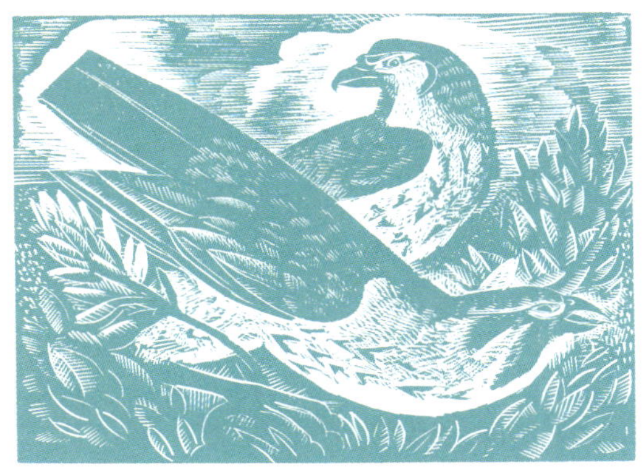

A Year Unfolding

SPHERE

First published in Great Britain in 2021 by Sphere

7 9 10 8 6

A CIP catalogue record for this book is available from the British Library.

ISBN 978-0-7515-8433-2

Senior Commissioning Editor: Fiona Rose

Managing Editor: Nithya Rae

Production Manager: Abby Marshall

Cover design: Sean Garrehy

Interior design: Nathan Burton

Typeset in Capitolium 2
Printed in Italy by Printer Trento Srl

Papers used by Sphere are from well-managed forests and other responsible sources.

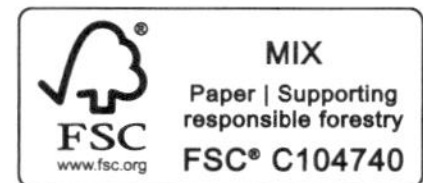

Sphere
An imprint of
Little, Brown Book Group
Carmelite House
50 Victoria Embankment
London EC4Y 0DZ

An Hachette UK Company
www.hachette.co.uk

www.littlebrown.co.uk

CONTENTS

Introduction:

A Printmaker's View 7

Background 11

Bikes, Birds and Boats 13

Studio and Techniques 15

Early Spring 16

Spring 44

Early Summer 66

Summer 94

Autumn 118

Winter 144

Acknowledgements 182

Index 184

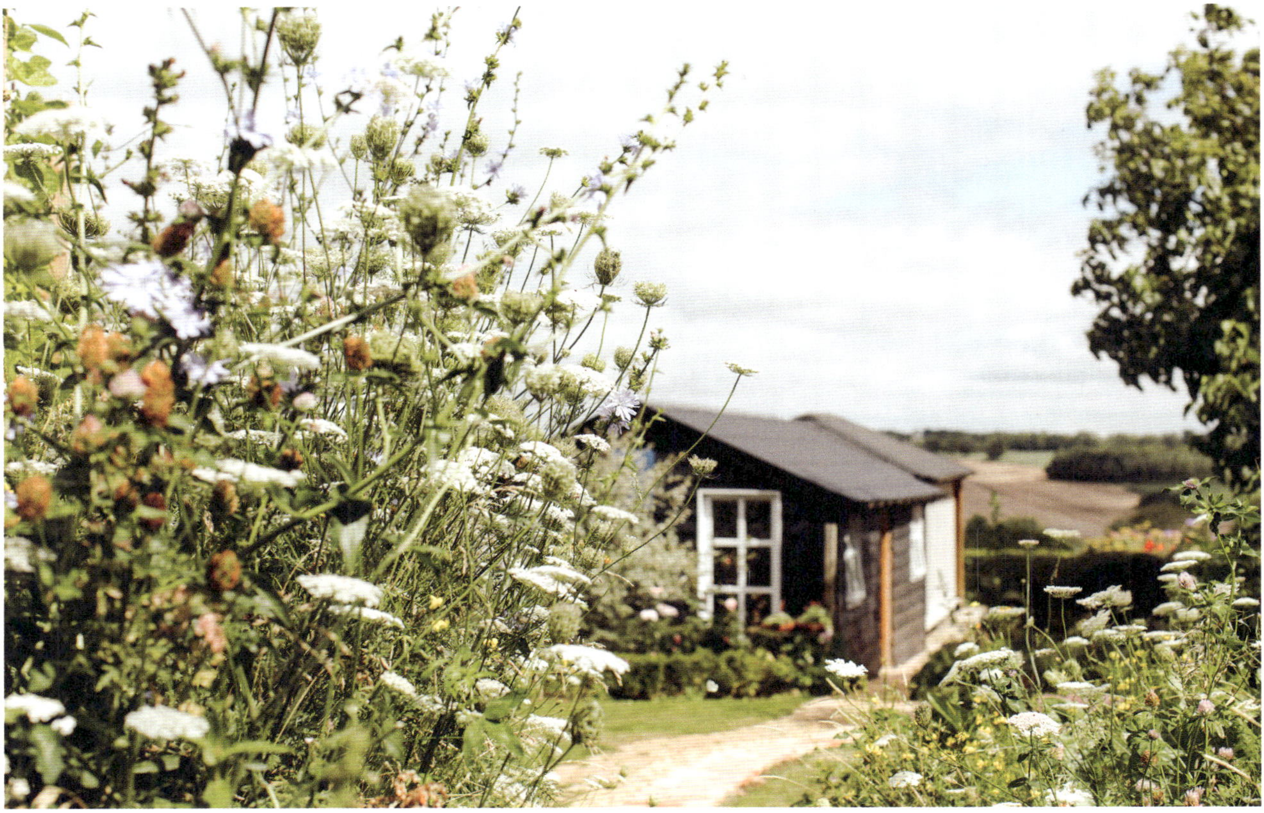

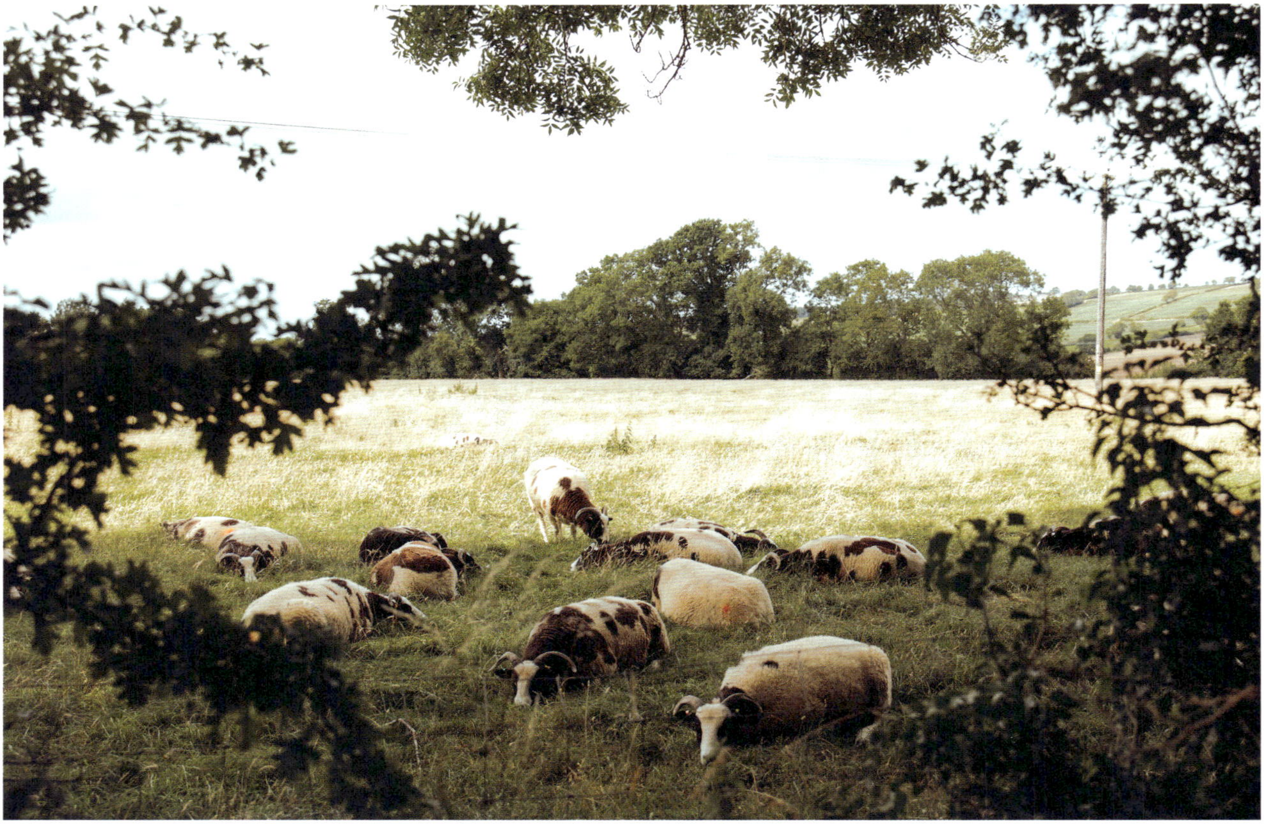

A Printmaker's View

Fields, skies, sea-waves and still water are the backdrops I use in my prints; birds and other wildlife the characters I place upon them to make my artwork. I have always lived in the countryside – even in my youth as a student in Leicester in the 1980s I lived out of town. I rented a small cottage in the market town of Melton Mowbray, which is about 13 miles from Leicester. Rather than get the train I would cycle to college. The route took me through the countryside and I would often stop to do observational drawings and collect roadkill! The creatures I found would be strapped to my handlebars to study and draw. These anatomical drawings then became prints, at that time mainly etchings. Today I use the medium of lino and silkscreen and my imagery is much more stylised but drawing still remains very important – drawing for me is the key element to a successful print or illustration. So, for over forty years, printmaking has been my passion and from a child, wildlife has fascinated me. The artwork I create brings these two inspirations together in my prints.

Today I live in Wing, a small village in the smallest county of England – Rutland. Birds have always been a very strong element in my work, so my home village of Wing is aptly named. The landscape here is not dramatic; it has gentle rolling fields topped with spinneys of native trees. The hedges are a mixture of hazel, hawthorn and blackthorn; they divide the fields into pockets of brown and green. In winter I can watch flocks of fieldfares and redwings stride across the fields pecking at the ground in formation like synchronised swimmers; in spring hares box and in summer swallows swoop and dive. This is the view from my studio window, a view of the English countryside which I often use as a backdrop for my prints.

Much of the inspiration for my artwork comes from watching this view and from watching the year unfold from winter to spring to summer and autumn while I work at my desk.

I am lucky to earn my living from my artwork. I am also very lucky to have my studio at the bottom of the garden. This allows me not only to make prints but also to take time out to tend to the garden, birdwatch and enjoy being at home. Perhaps this year more than any other many people have this in common. Due to lockdown and the pandemic we have valued nature from our own homes in a new way. Many of us have been able to enjoy its sounds, its smells and its beauty – whether that is in a small garden, a wilderness, a park or watching an indoor plant flourish over the course of time. It gives us a connection to nature that is cherished. This year more than any other I have noticed the changing seasons. Snowdrops pushing through the winter soil, snake's-head fritillaries bending their elegant heads in the wildflower bank, and the ever-deepening richness of birdsong as the seasons progress.

The illustrations in this book are my response to nature and a reflection of what I see around me. Some of the images have been commissioned by publishers but they always stem from a personal experience of watching, drawing and printing. I hope you will enjoy a printmaker's view of watching a year unfolding.

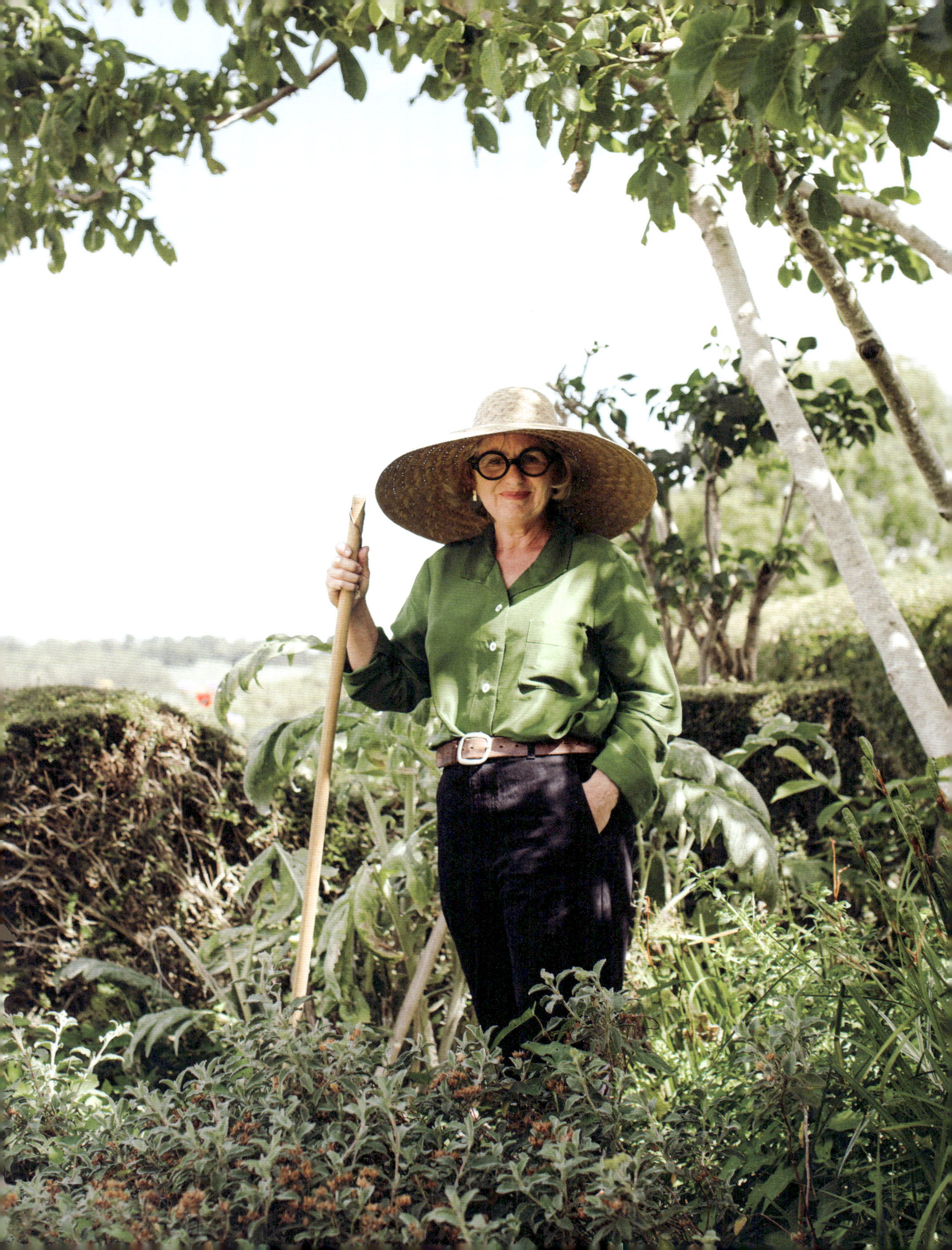

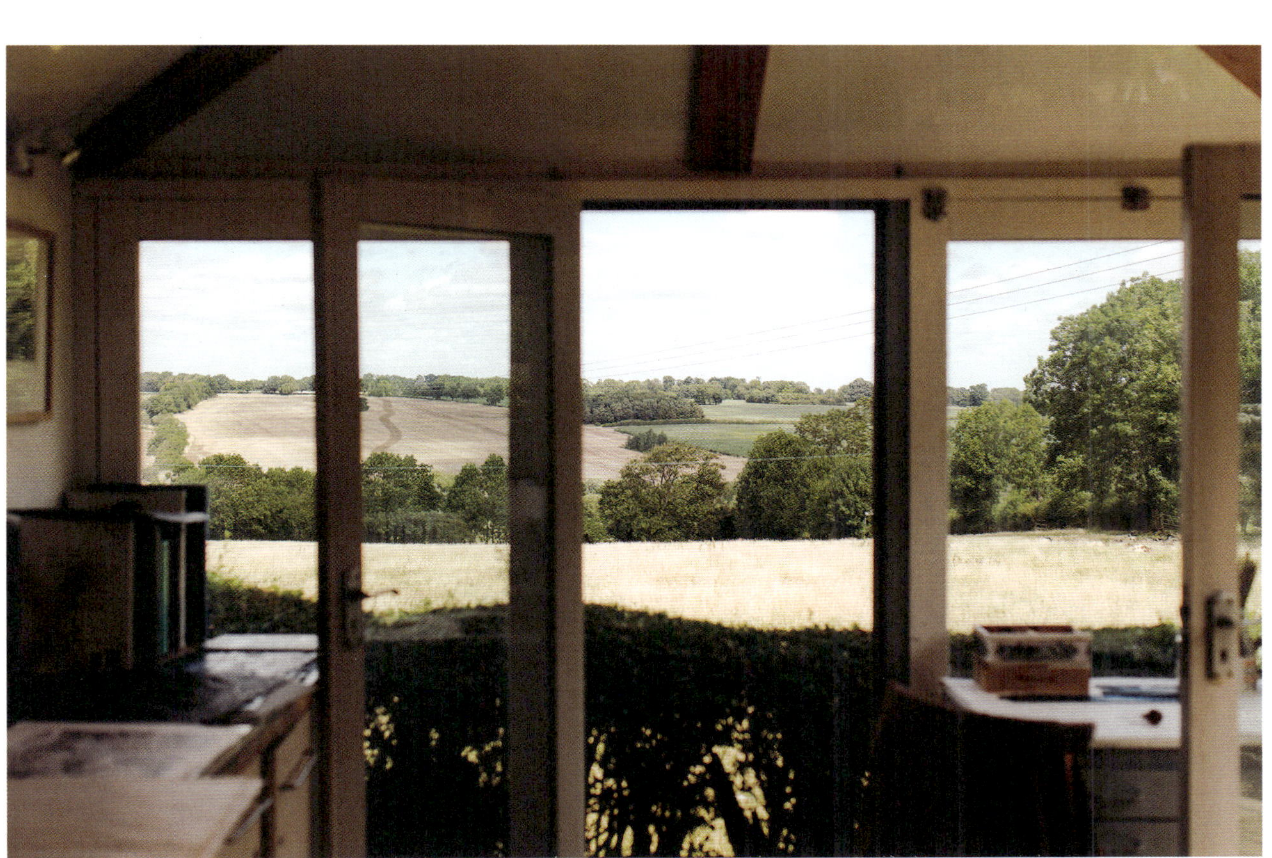

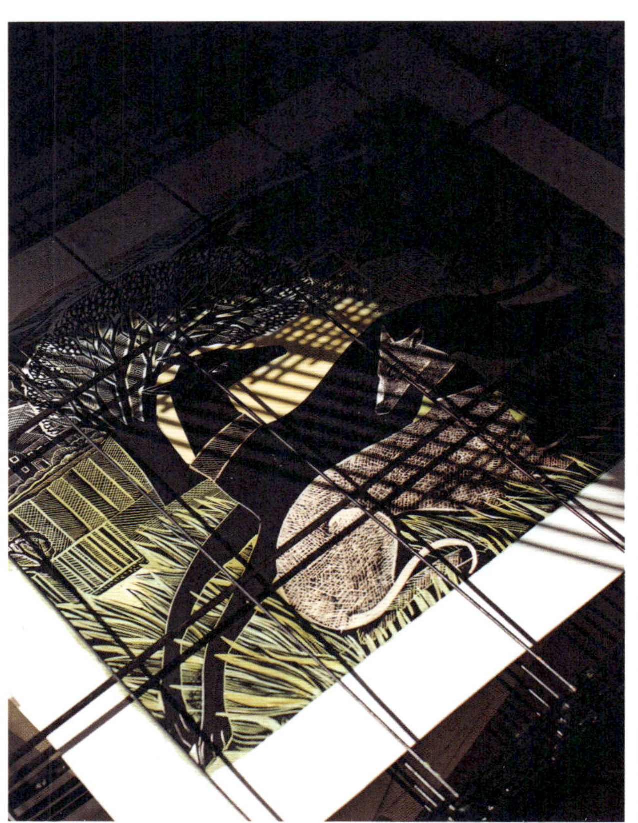

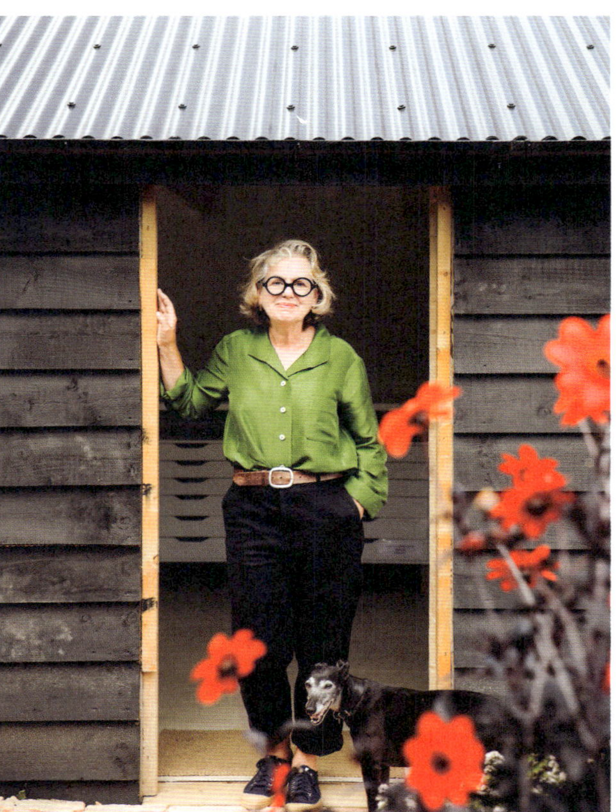

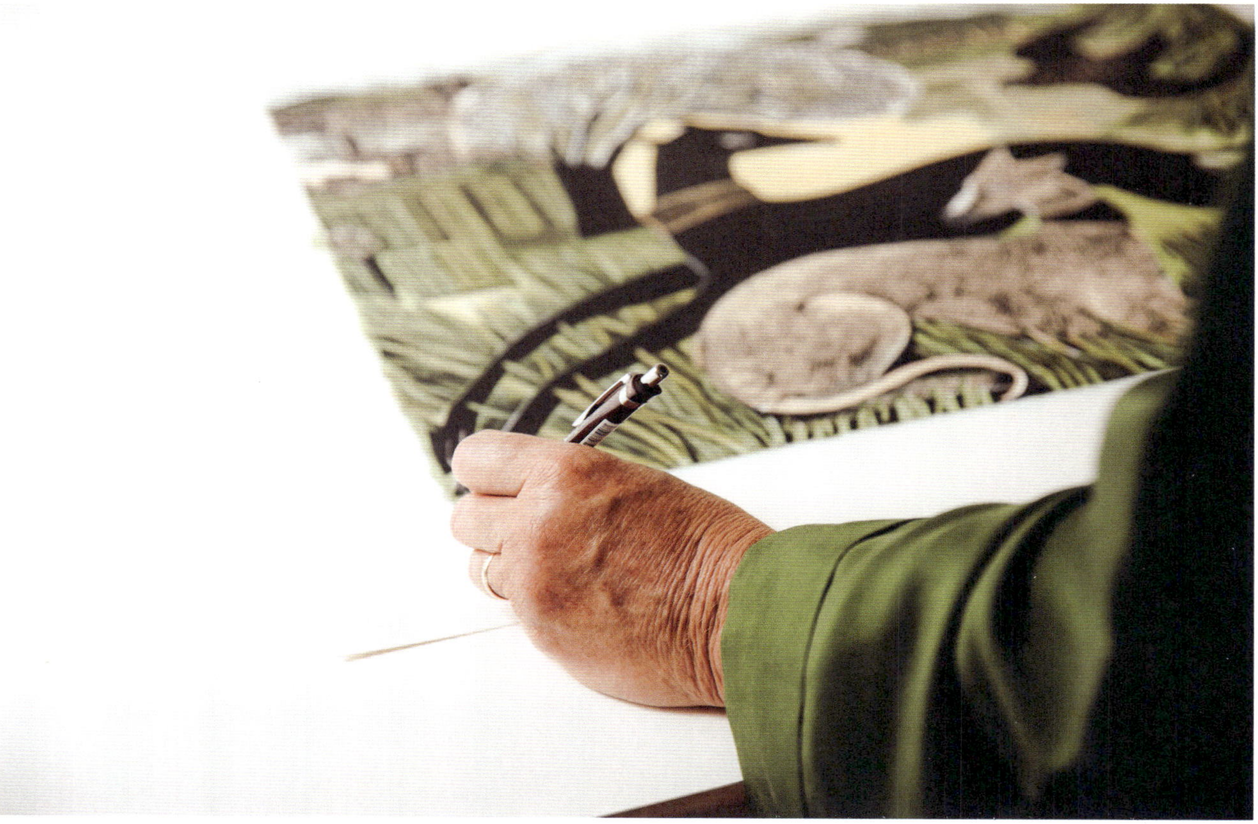

Background

I live in a 1930s railway worker's cottage with my husband Mark and our two ageing whippets. We have four grown-up children who now have homes of their own. Our house is part of a terrace of four; it is not the archetypal pretty Rutland home you might expect an artist to live in, it is very workaday. Two up, two down with a long garden that backs on to farmland. The terrace has a shared tunnel to access the back and it is only when you walk through the tunnel you see the view. Visitors are always surprised by the contrast of the front of the house with the back and it is this element of surprise that I love about our home. It is our own personal Narnia and even before lockdown it meant I was very happy not to move beyond the garden and studio for weeks on end. Outside my studio window is a small flock of Jacob sheep – currently ladies in waiting for their spring lambs. Behind the sheep is a patchwork of arable land that changes colour and pattern with the seasons. The fields are ploughed with ridged lines and furrows – crops sown, harvested, the land ploughed again.

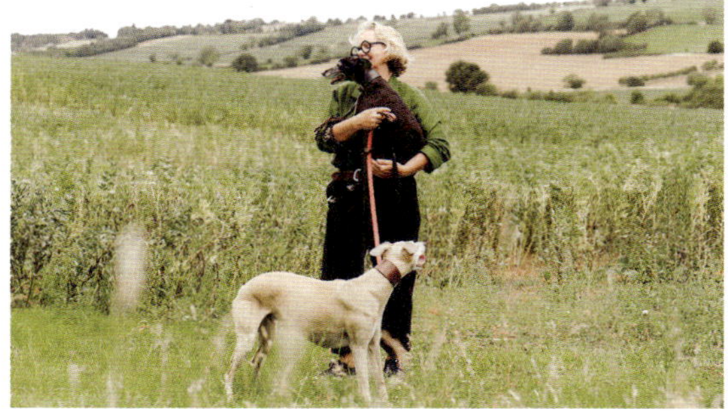

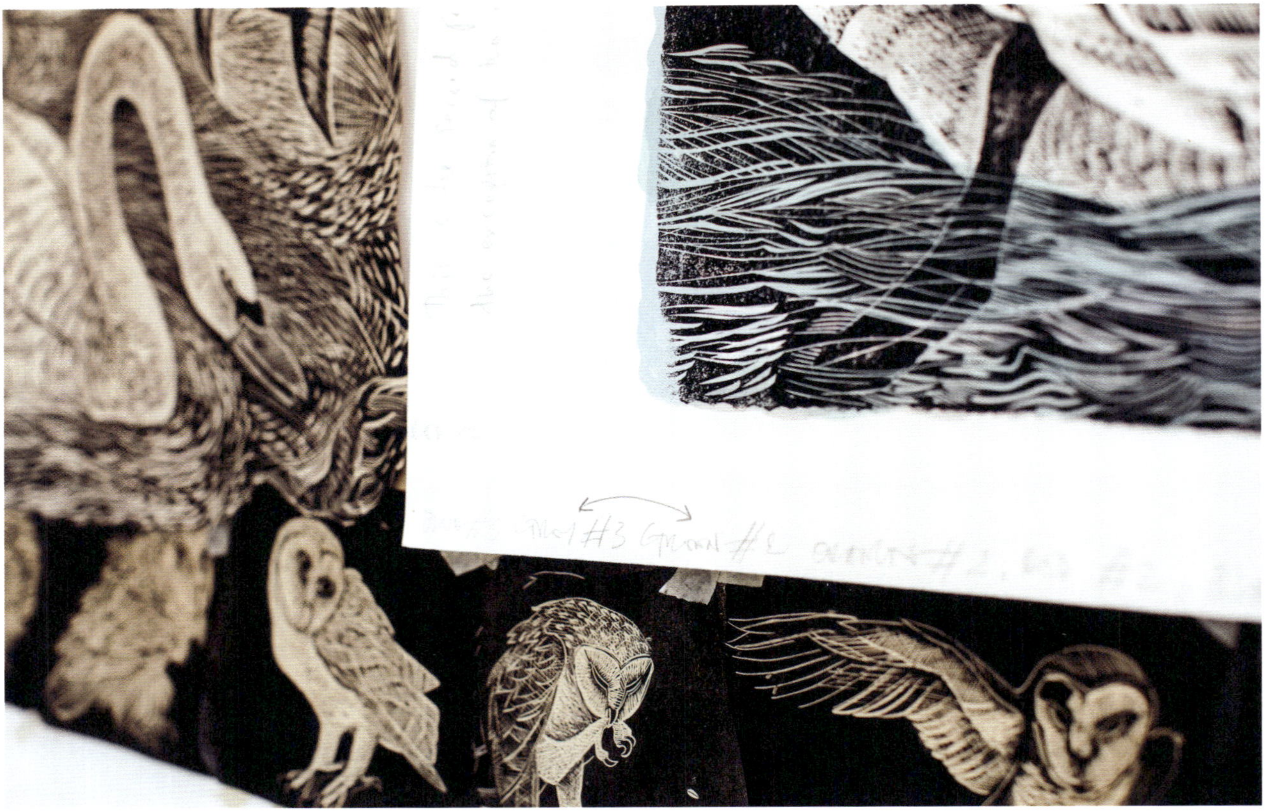

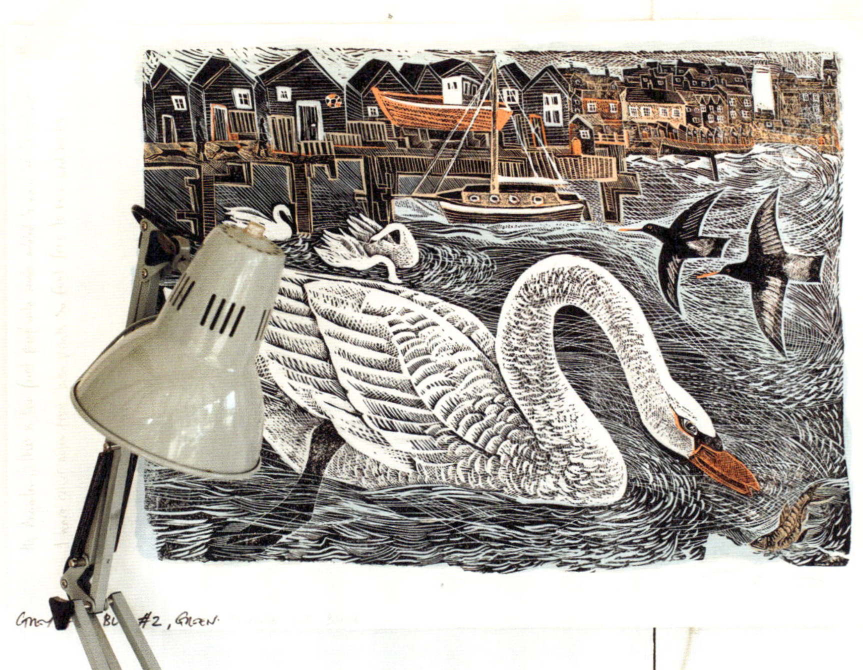

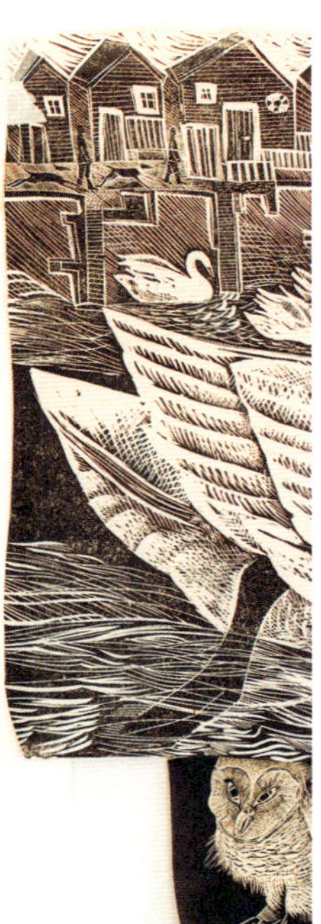

Bikes, Birds and Boats

Our lifestyle provides much of the imagery I use in my work, so my prints are influenced not only by the landscape of Rutland but also by the places we visit during the year. My husband Mark has a small wooden sailing boat, *Windsong* – a Finesse 24 – and during the summer months we spend many weeks sailing the east coast of England. In previous years we have ventured to Shetland and other parts of the British coastline. Many of the summer and sea images I make come from drawings done on board *Windsong*. There is no better way to observe birds and other wildlife than from the back of a sailing boat. We sleep on board, so the end of the day and early mornings are the perfect time to sit and watch with my sketch book in hand. I have to admit I am not a great sailor, too prone to sea sickness, and as the boat is very small I always seem to be in the way of my husband Mark who is the real sailor!

This allows me to cycle to our next mooring. I have always loved cycling, but I'm not the Lycra-clad speedy type, I like to take my time.

Time alone on my bike is a great pleasure and over the years I have completed a number of long-distance rides. Just me, a tent, a small bag and a pair of binoculars. The longest ride I did was in 1984, cycling 3,000 miles of the British coastline. All done in four weeks – I was then twenty-four and fit as a flea! That trip was sponsored in aid of Voluntary Service Overseas in the summer before I became a volunteer myself in Bangladesh at The Rehabilitation Center for the Paralysed in Dhaka.

The most recent solo long ride was in 2018: I cycled from home in Wing to Treen at the western tip of Cornwall, then back to Rutland via Guernsey where I met Mark who had sailed there on *Windsong*.

Now I am over sixty, I do take the help of the train in parts of the journey. But the principle is the same as when I was young; that is to see and experience things in a way you don't when you're in a car or with other people or when you're just too comfortable. It is these experiences that I draw upon to make my artwork.

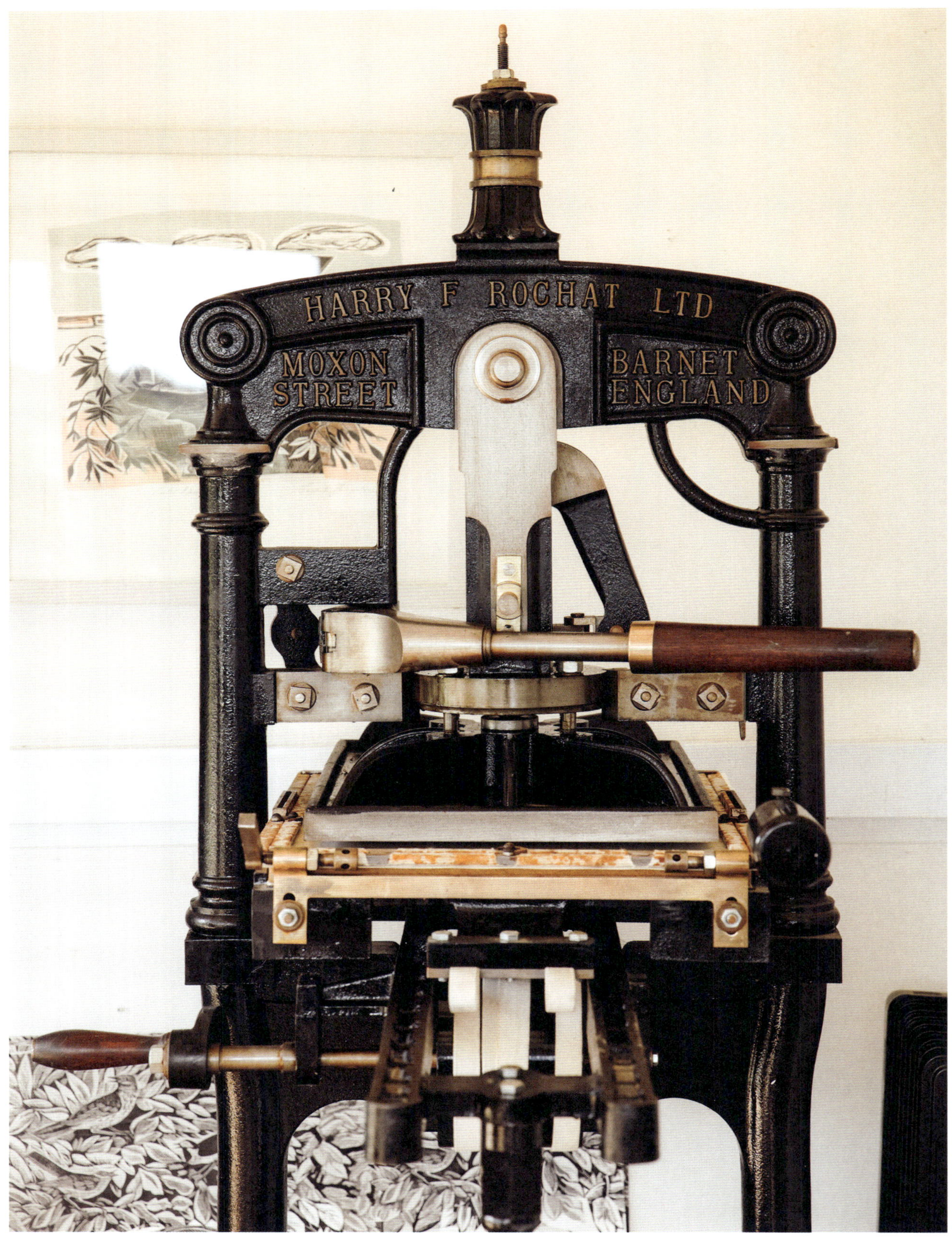
HARRY F ROCHAT LTD
MOXON STREET
BARNET ENGLAND

Studio and Techniques

Printmaking has been my great love for many years. I was introduced to making prints as an art student at Leicester Polytechnic in the late seventies. During my student years I was mainly an etcher, but over the years I have used a wide variety of printmaking techniques. Since 2008 I have worked in a combination of lino and vinyl cutting and silk screen. Bringing these two techniques together gives my work a distinctive look. I always start with the block work, cutting the main image directly on to the lino or vinyl. The design work done on the block acts as the guide for the areas of colour.

What is a lino/vinyl cut?

Lino/vinyl cut is a printmaking technique: a sheet of linoleum or vinyl is used for the relief surface. A design is cut into the surface with a V-shaped chisel or gouge, with the raised (uncarved) areas representing a reversal (mirror image) of the parts that will show when printed. The resulting block is inked with a roller and then impressed onto paper. The actual printing process can be done by hand or with a press – I use a Rochate Albion Press.

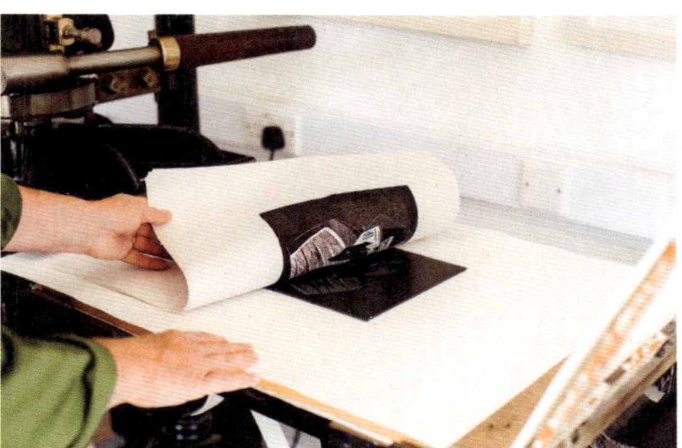

What is silkscreen printing?

Silkscreen printing is a printing technique that uses a woven mesh of very fine holes. I then use a paper-cut stencil to block areas of the mesh – the open areas of the stencil allow ink to be pushed through the mesh on to the paper using a squeegee. A different stencil is required for each colour and each stencil is cut from paper using a sharp knife. This means the hand-cut mark of the stencil and the hand-cut blocks work well together when one is printed over the other.

Rochate Albion Press

The most dominant piece of equipment in my studio is a Victorian-style Rochate Albion Press – although it looks like an antique it is a modern replica and prints beautifully. This press is still made today in Barnet, near London, by the Rochate family.

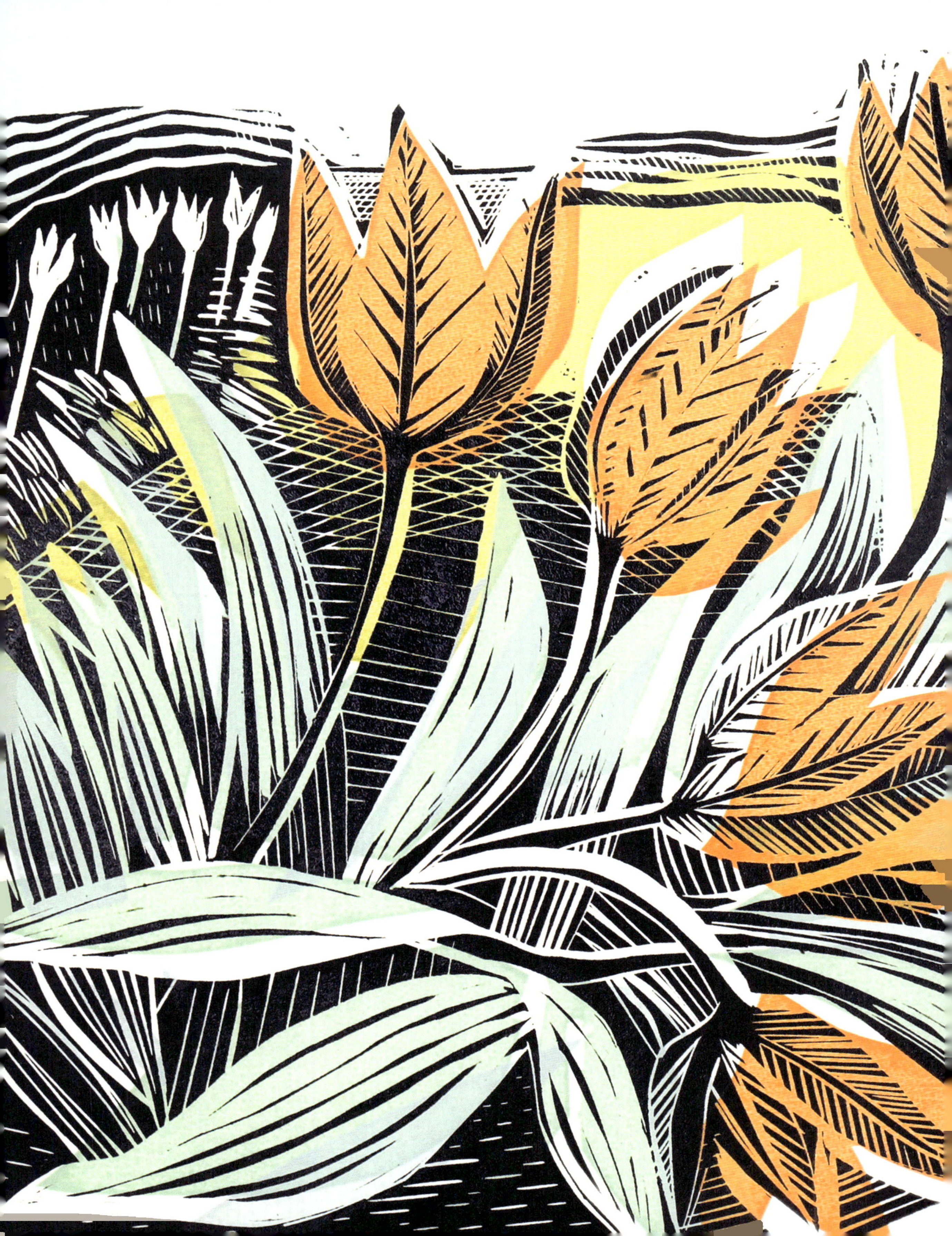

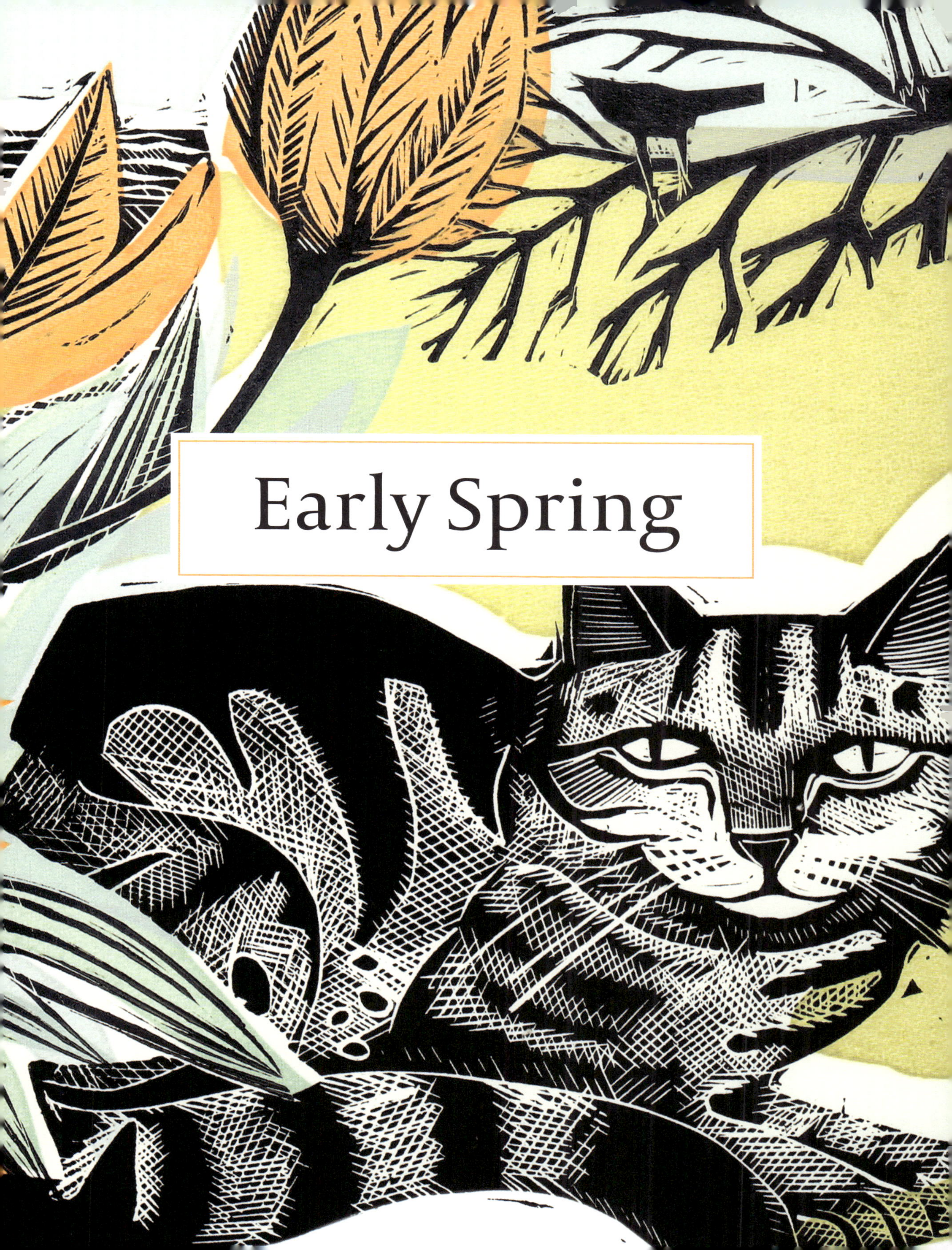

Early Spring

Over the land freckled with snow half-thawed
The speculating rooks at their nests cawed
And saw from elm-tops, delicate as flowers of grass,
What we below could not see, Winter pass.

Thaw
Edward Thomas, 1878–1917

Early Spring

Bird Song and Nests

It is hard to say when one season stops and the other begins; the changes are not necessarily gradual but come in fits and starts. Seasons have no regard for the official times written down in a calendar. Spring more than any other of the seasons is like this. Perhaps this is because in the darkness of the winter months, we long for it to begin before nature is really ready. It cannot be called spring when the rooks start to gather sticks for their high tree-top nests or the first glimmers of aconite and crocus leaves push through the frozen ground, but it feels like a little bit of spring is starting.

Early spring is very different to the full-force frothy green of spring proper; it is understated, it is bare branches, it is the blue-green leaves of white glowing snowdrops and hellebores that manage to flower through the harshest of weathers.

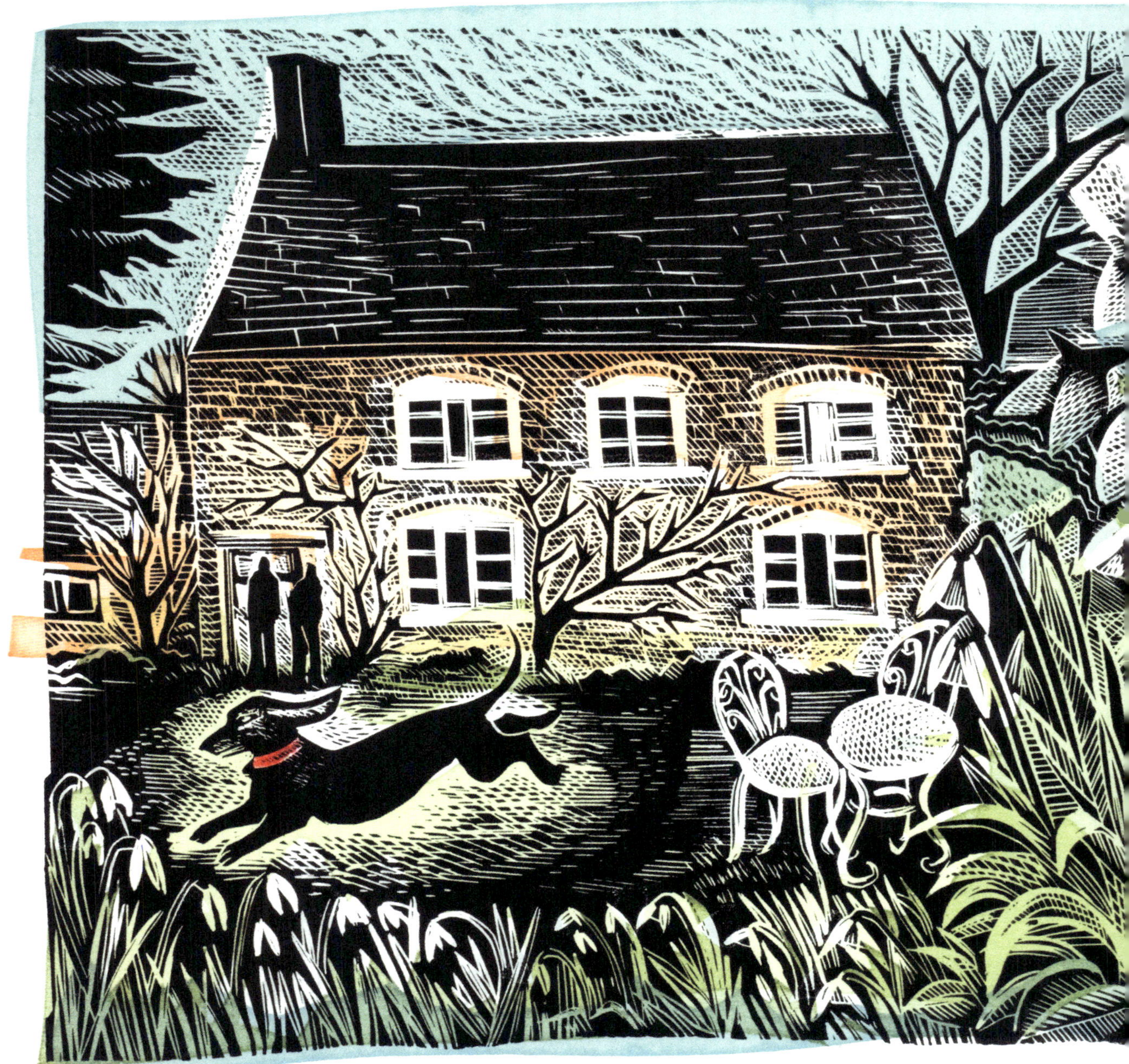

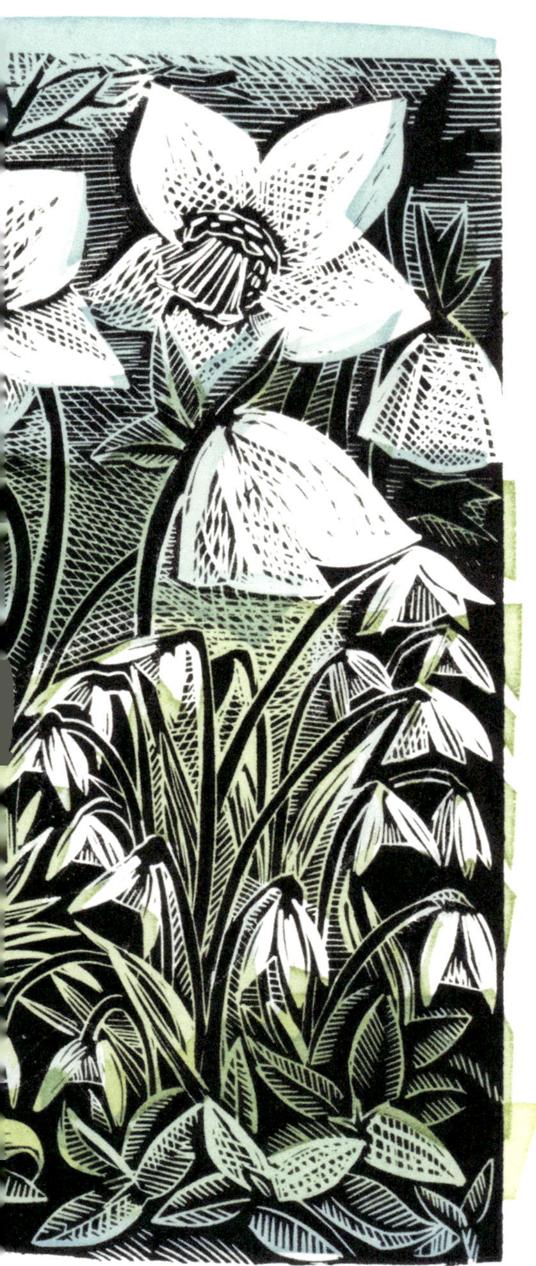

Gardener's Cottage

In Gardener's Cottage I have tried to capture that feeling of early spring, of the joy of the first flowers appearing in the garden. This print was a commission from a friend of mine, Andrew Jones, who is Head Gardener at Deene Park in Northamptonshire. He has dedicated a large amount of his career to snowdrops and the development of the snowdrop collection at Deene Park. Andrew lives in this beautiful cottage with his partner and Mildred, a very exuberant miniature dachshund. Along with the crowd of snowdrops the tall larger white flowers are my interpretation of hellebores – also known as the Christmas rose. It is one of my all-time garden favourites and I have a large patch of them in my own garden. They are not only white but soft pinks with spotted centres, lilacs, and some wine-dark purple ones with yellow centres. Their nodding heads shimmer in the cold winds of this season and their leathery, glossy green leaves can withstand the winter frosts, giving the garden colour when it is most needed.

Hellebores and Hound

Hellebores and Hound is an illustration of hellebore flowers with the silhouette of our little black whippet, Amy, in the background. It was commissioned by *Gardens Illustrated* magazine. For many years I produced a monthly editorial illustration for one of their regular features. I would always try to find something from my own garden to illustrate the brief, which I hope gave the work a personal voice. It seemed apt to incorporate Amy in the background of the image, with purple spotted hellebores in the foreground. These flowers do not usually tip their heads to the sky, so I have used a bit of artistic licence to highlight their speckled pattern that I love so much. They are a promiscuous flower, so when the seedlings mature they will often have cross-bred, mixing the whites, pinks, purples and spots of their parent plants. You never know what you might get!

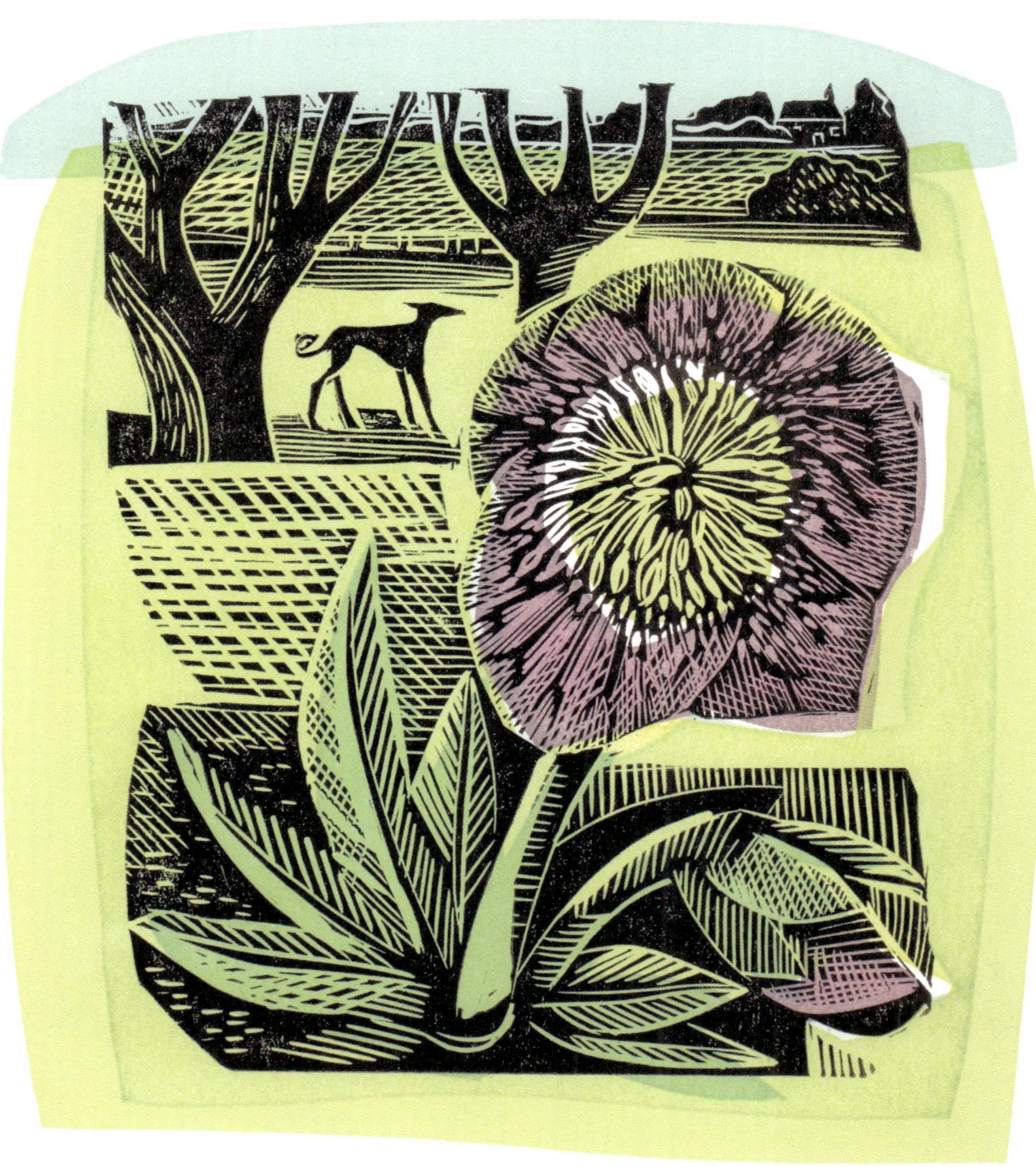

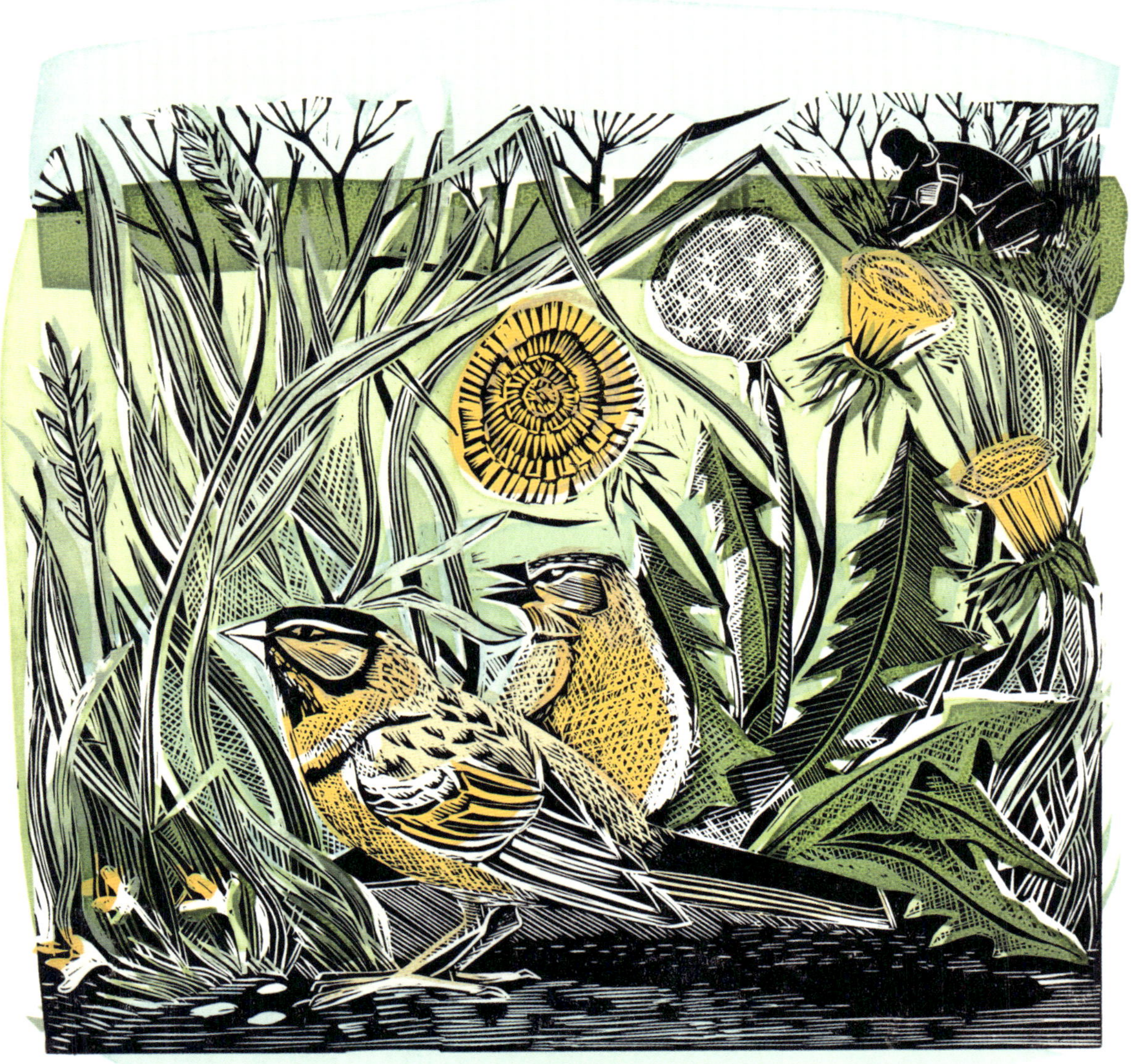

Wonders of Weeding

My garden is not that big, but large enough to hold different varieties of the seasonal plants I love the best. The garden is my great joy and something I see as a pleasure, not a chore. If you work for yourself it is difficult to take a day off, but when I do there is no greater pleasure than spending all day in my garden. Naming the plants I grow is not my area of expertise; I am very much an intuitive gardener and regard the plants I grow as a box of paints. I choose them for their colour and shape in the same way I chose a colour palette for my prints. I do have friends in the village who are much better gardeners than me and I think it is a universal fact that gardeners are the nicest of people – always willing to share their knowledge as well as their extra seedlings!

Wonders of Weeding is an illustration that represents the start of my gardening year. I always start the year with the thought that this is the year I will have a weed-free garden! But of course, it never happens – I have too many artwork deadlines and trips away to ever have the garden looking as I would truly like. I expect all gardeners feel the same. However, the untidiness of my garden does bring the benefit of hiding places for hedgehogs. I have included two yellowhammers in the image. We are very lucky that they still tumble down the local lane in a bright flash of yellow as while they were once very common in the UK they are sadly no longer as prevalent.

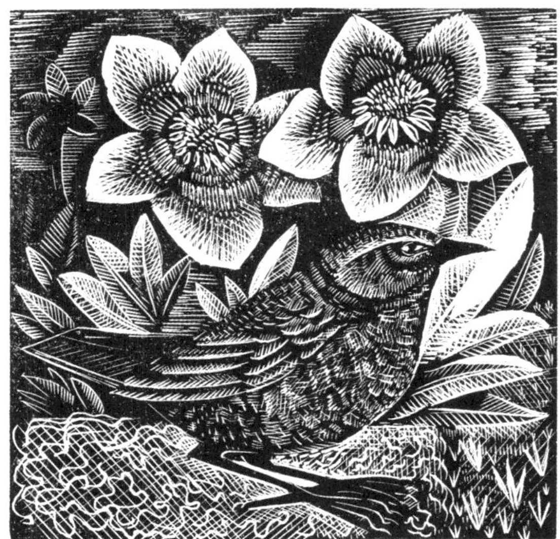

Dunnock

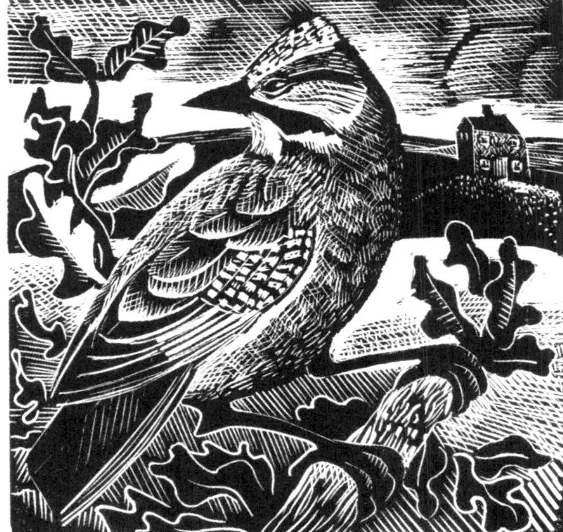

Jay

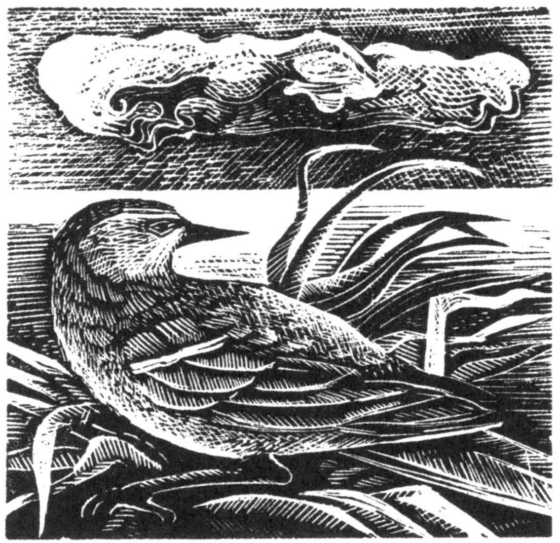

Warbler

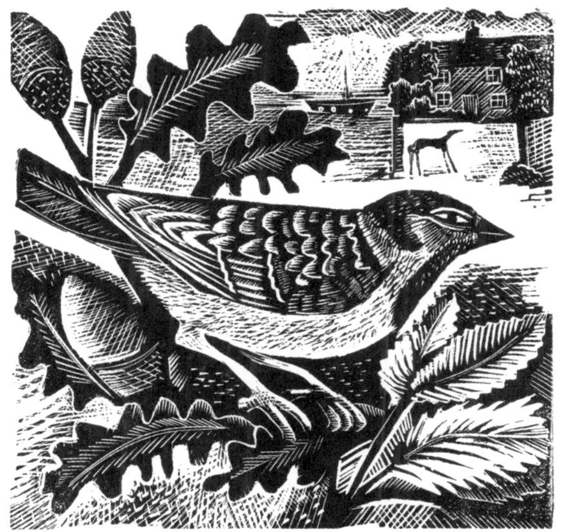

House Sparrow

Dunnock, Blackbird, Jay and House Sparrow

There is nothing that announces spring more strongly than the dawn chorus led by the beautiful song of the blackbird. By the time of the official spring equinox the volume of bird song is loud enough to wake you up – you know that spring has arrived. The dawn chorus is multi-layered: an undercurrent of the dull soothing rhythm of wood pigeons; layer two is the sharp shrill unbelievably loud wrens, with dunnocks, chaffinch, great tits and blue tits adding their song on top; and finally the best layer of all, just below our bedroom window – the clatter chatter of the house sparrows.

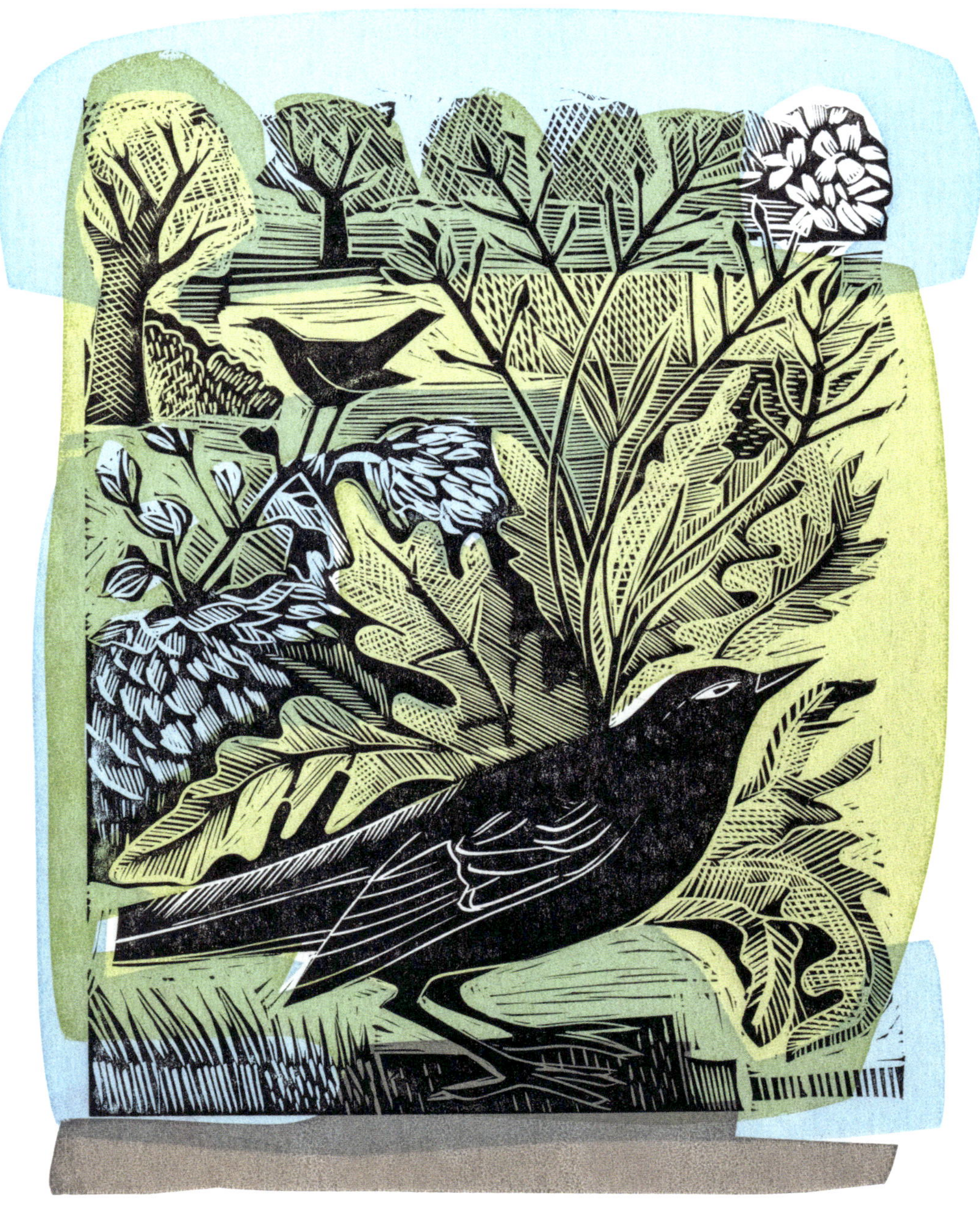

Spring Blackbird

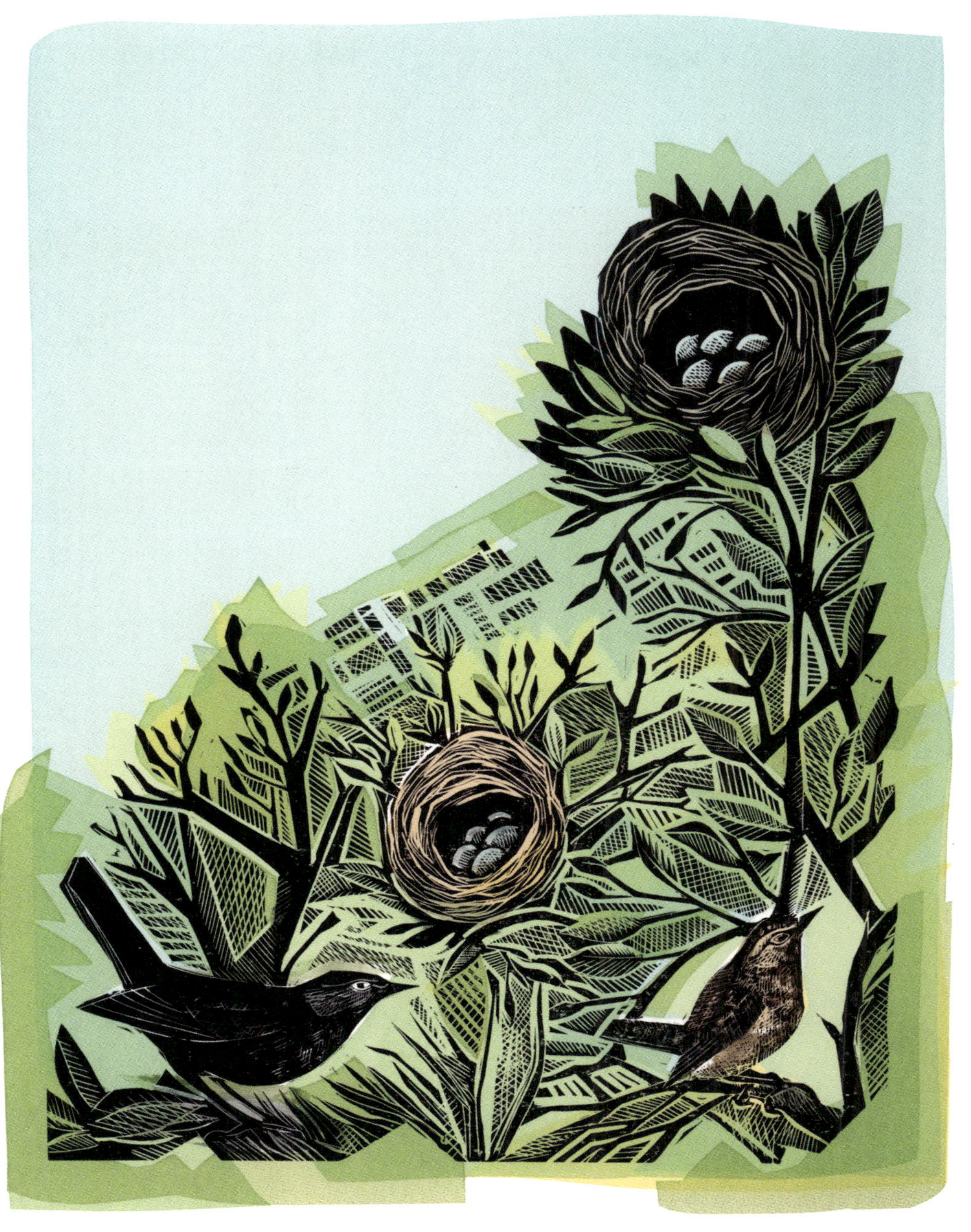

Spring Nests

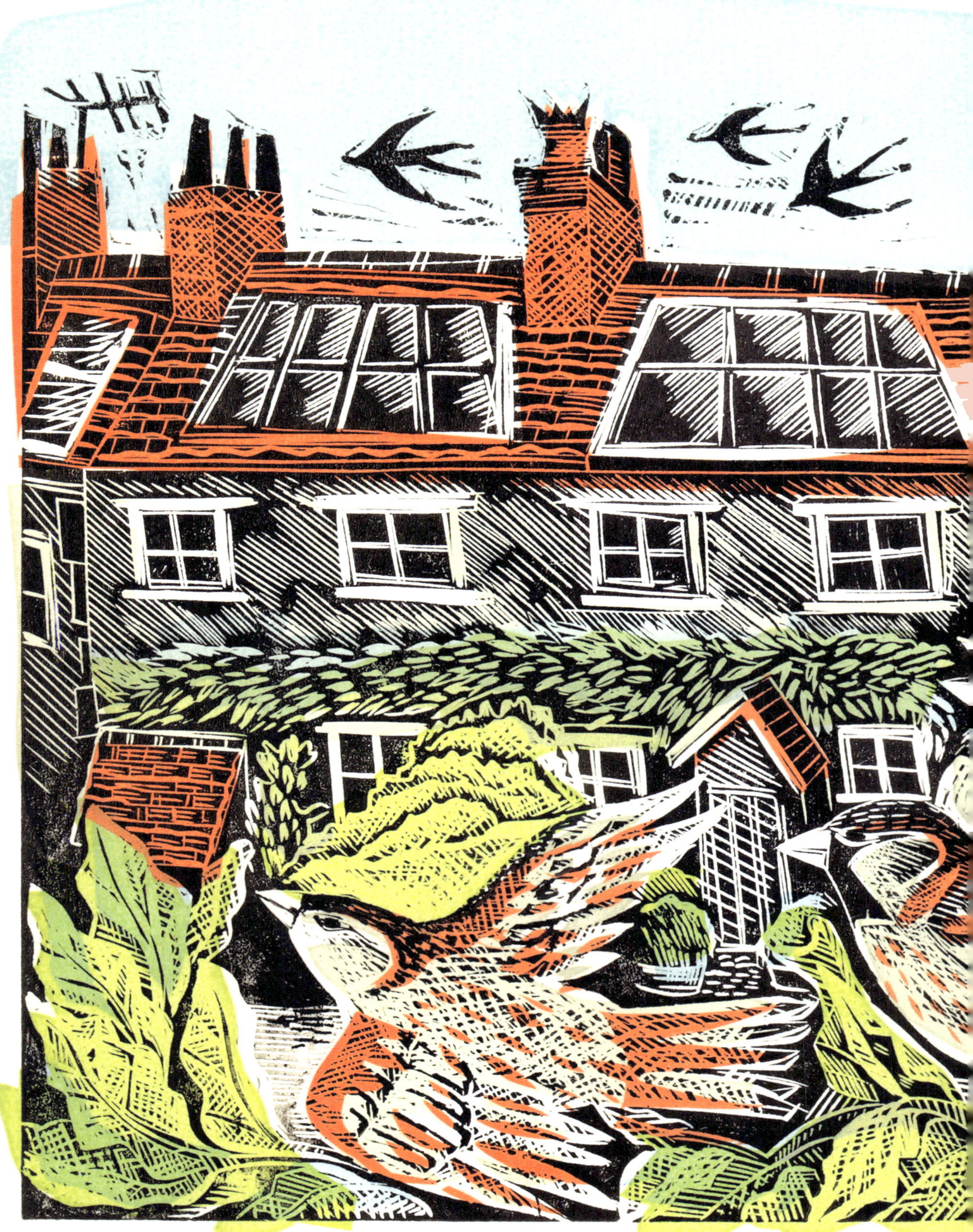

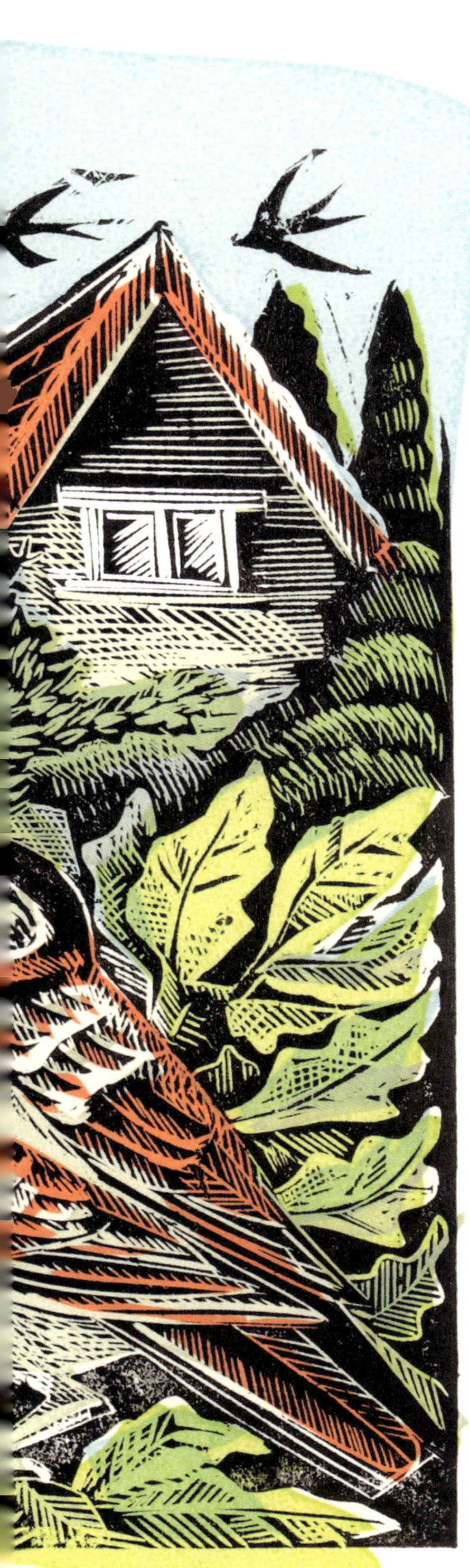

House Sparrows

The house sparrows live in the thick ivy that climbs up the front of the house and keep us entertained throughout the year with the lively discussions they hold amongst themselves of the pecking order in their group and their great love of dust baths. I love them dearly and they are very much part of our home.

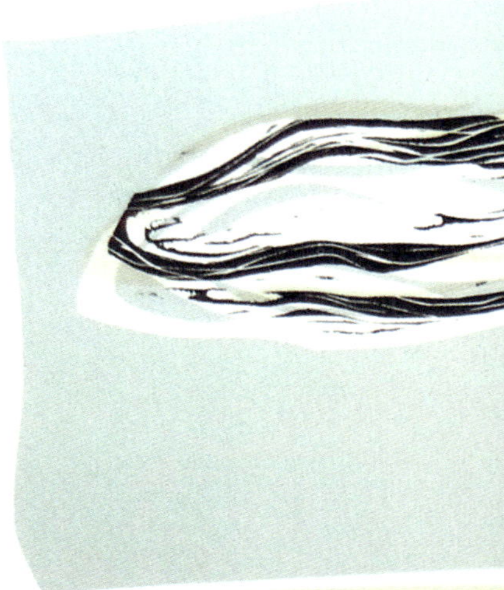

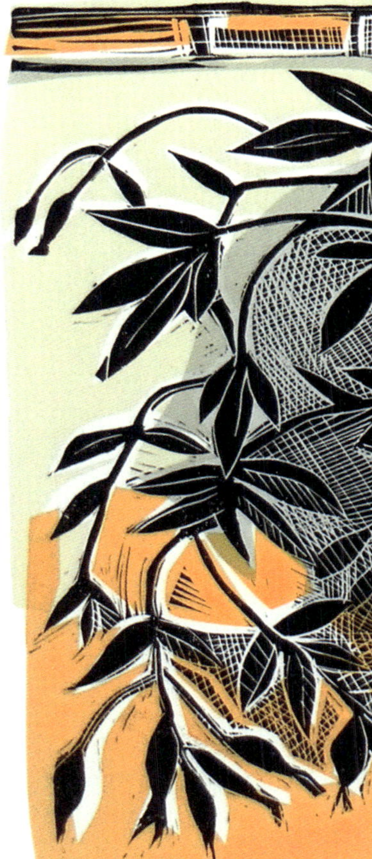

Early Nesters

I can't remember where I heard it, but I was once told that Valentine's Day – 14 February – is the official day for birds getting together. So, I think Valentine's Day should be called Nesting Day. I am not sure this is true, but it is certainly very noticeable that blackbirds start to pair up around this time. The males start to defend their territory, their beaks seem to become a brighter orange and there is generally a lot of showing off. In our garden we have a very tame male blackbird, named Bert. He is my gardening companion and comes closer to me than any of the robins. When I am digging he will come so close you could almost touch him – he cocks his head to one side then, quick as a flash, darts in at my feet to collect worms and any other tasty thing he has spied in the soil. Bert has the remarkable ability to sing while still having a mouth full of food for his young. Male blackbirds look after their young for longer than the females – Bert is a great single dad.

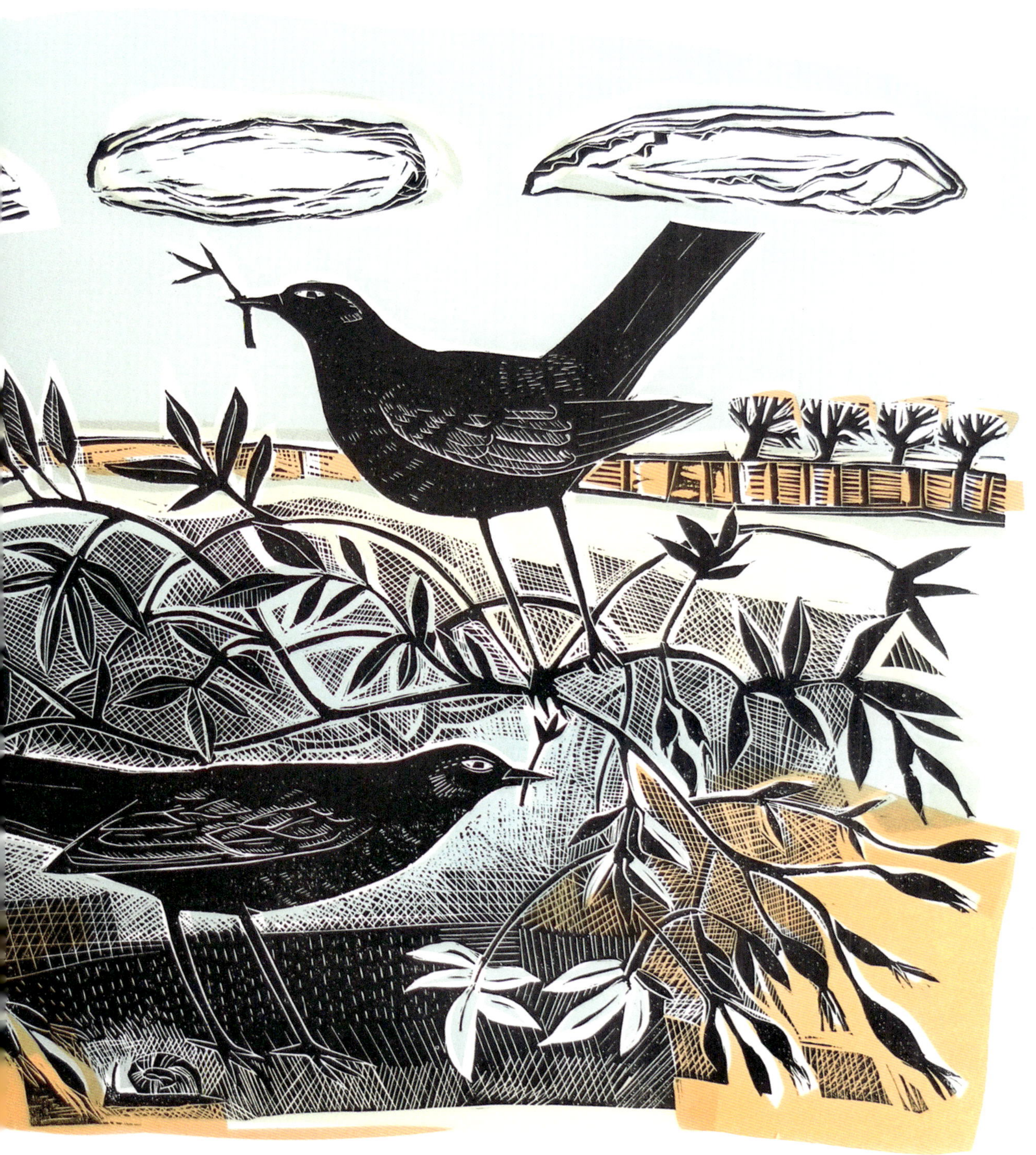

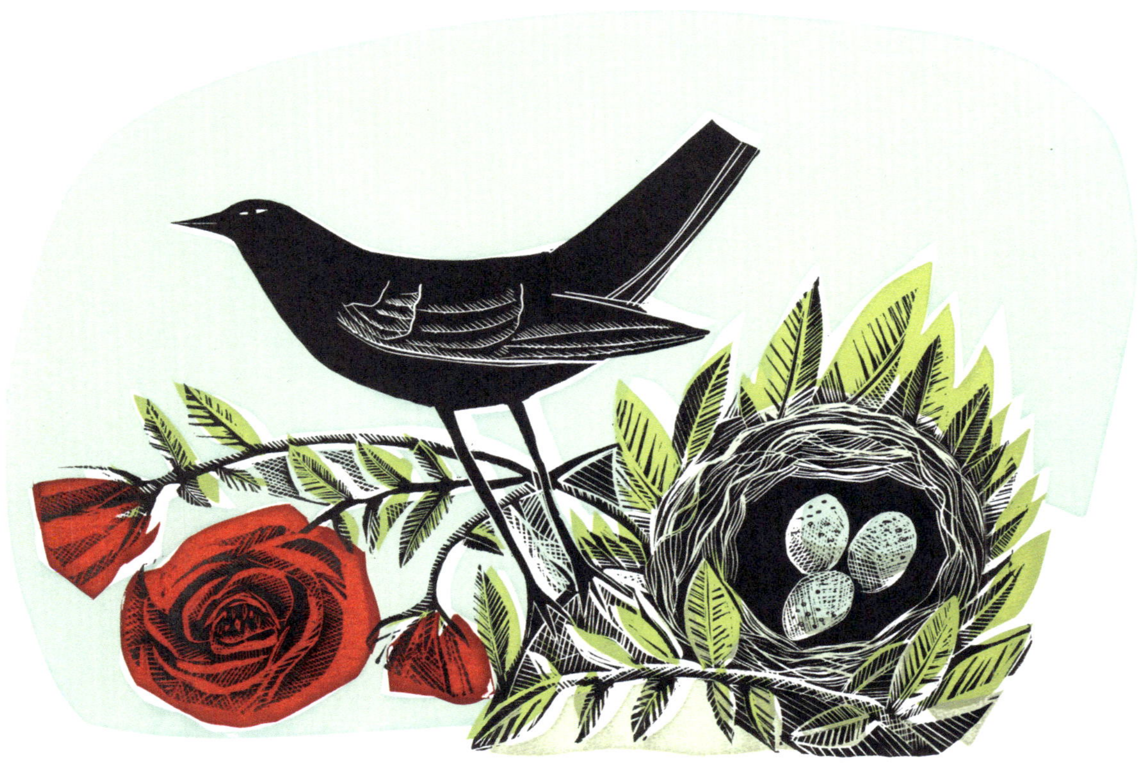

Blackbird and Rose Nest

At the front of our house there is no porch, the front door opens straight into the sitting room and there is always someone coming or going so the door is constantly banging shut. It was therefore very surprising when one of our resident blackbirds decided to nest in the climbing rose which trails over the front door. She seemed very happy and not disturbed by the banging of the door or the fact that our faces were often peering through the branches to see how she was doing. I am pleased to say she raised her brood successfully and has returned a number of times.

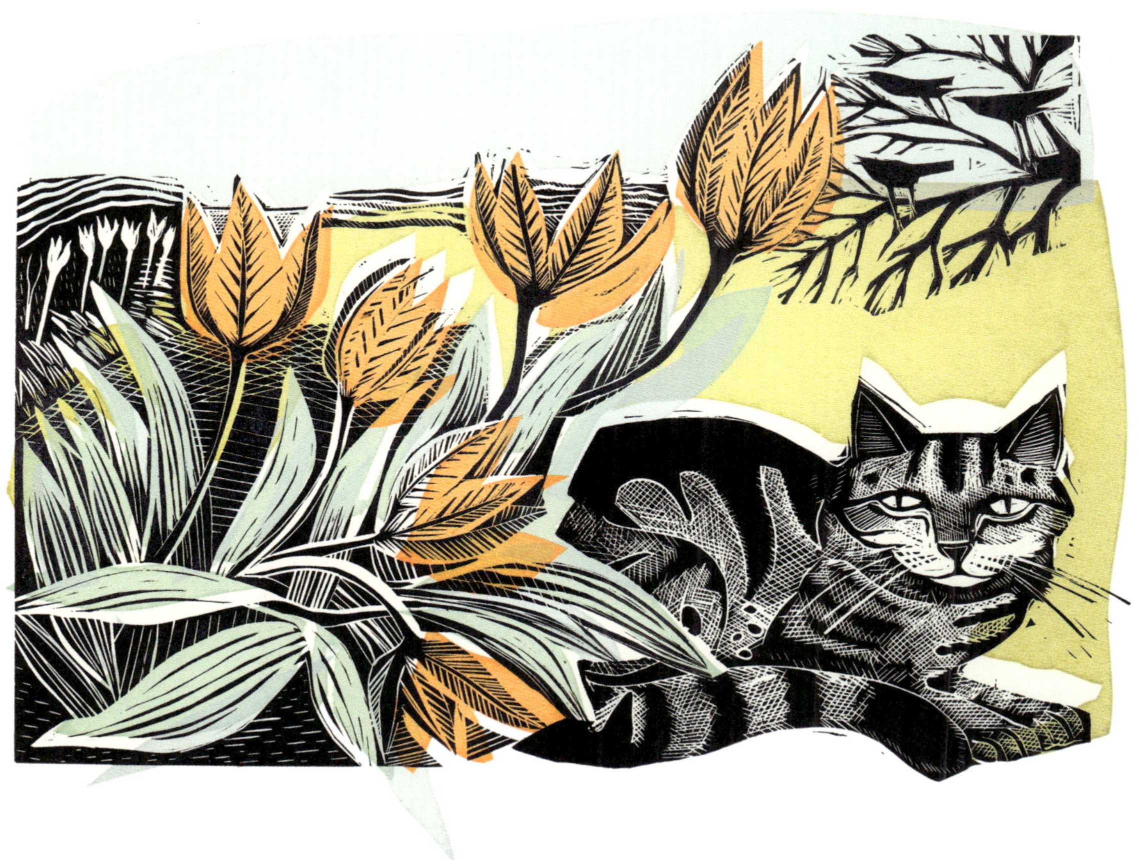

Cat Amongst the Tulips

We do not have a cat but there are plenty in our neighbours' houses and they are often to be found hiding in the flower bed on the prowl. This is a worry, but only happens at the front of the house, as, thanks to the whippets, the cats are kept away. Though it doesn't sound like it, I am a cat lover and if it wasn't for the sighthounds and my husband's allergy to their fur, I might have one again. But I am not sure that the comfort of a cat is not outweighed by the death toll to the bird population.

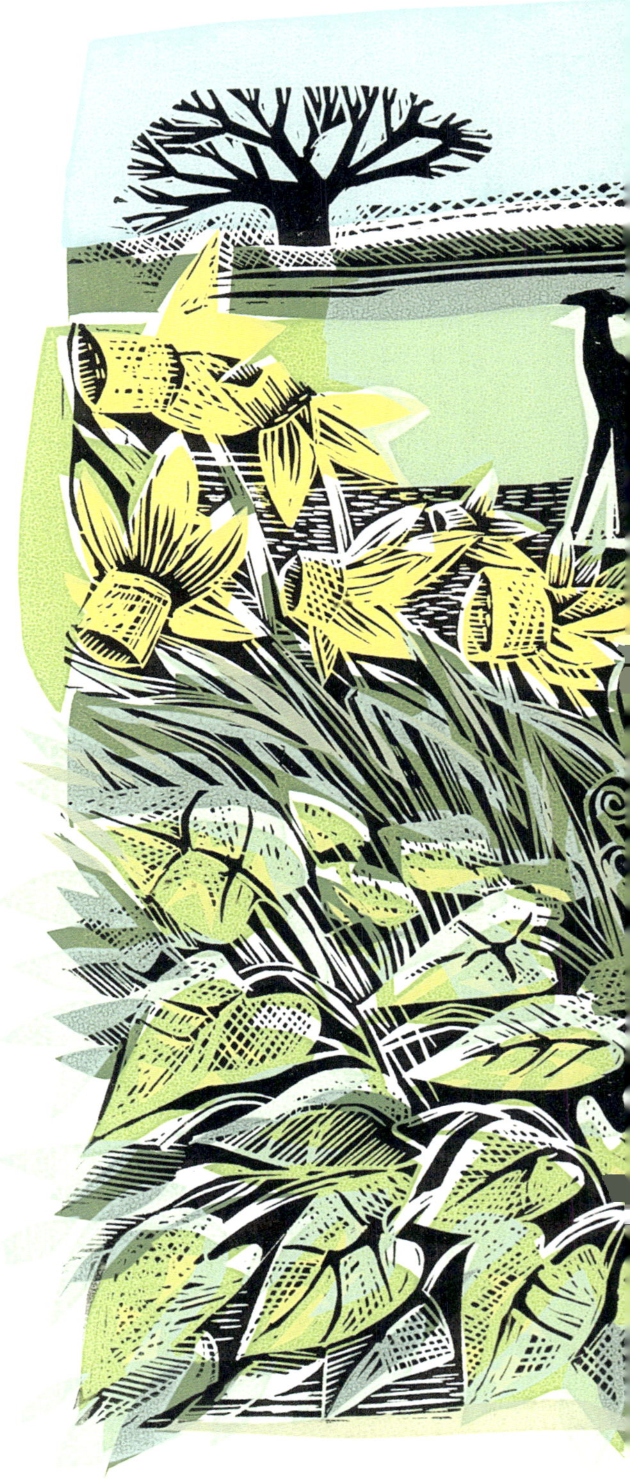

Look Out

Over the years we have owned a number of sighthounds – part of our daily routine is walking the dogs. As our whippets are getting older, walks are not as long as they used to be, generally around the village or down muddy lanes and across the fields to home.

Look Out shows the daffodils that are planted at the entrance to our village with our black whippet in the background. I am very pleased to say that all our sighthounds have been particularly bad at catching things. Amy is seen here looking the wrong way as two rabbits continue their breakfast. Definitely a hound with bad eyesight!

In the twelfth century our village of Wing was known as Wenge, which is thought to be the old Norse word for field. There is a beautiful church, St Peters & St Pauls, which dates back to Norman times and where my husband and I got married. Behind the church is the playing field and at the back of that is Wing Maze – a medieval turf maze. The maze attracts a lot of visitors, but I have to say they often look disappointed as although the maze is about 40 feet in diameter it is only a few inches tall!

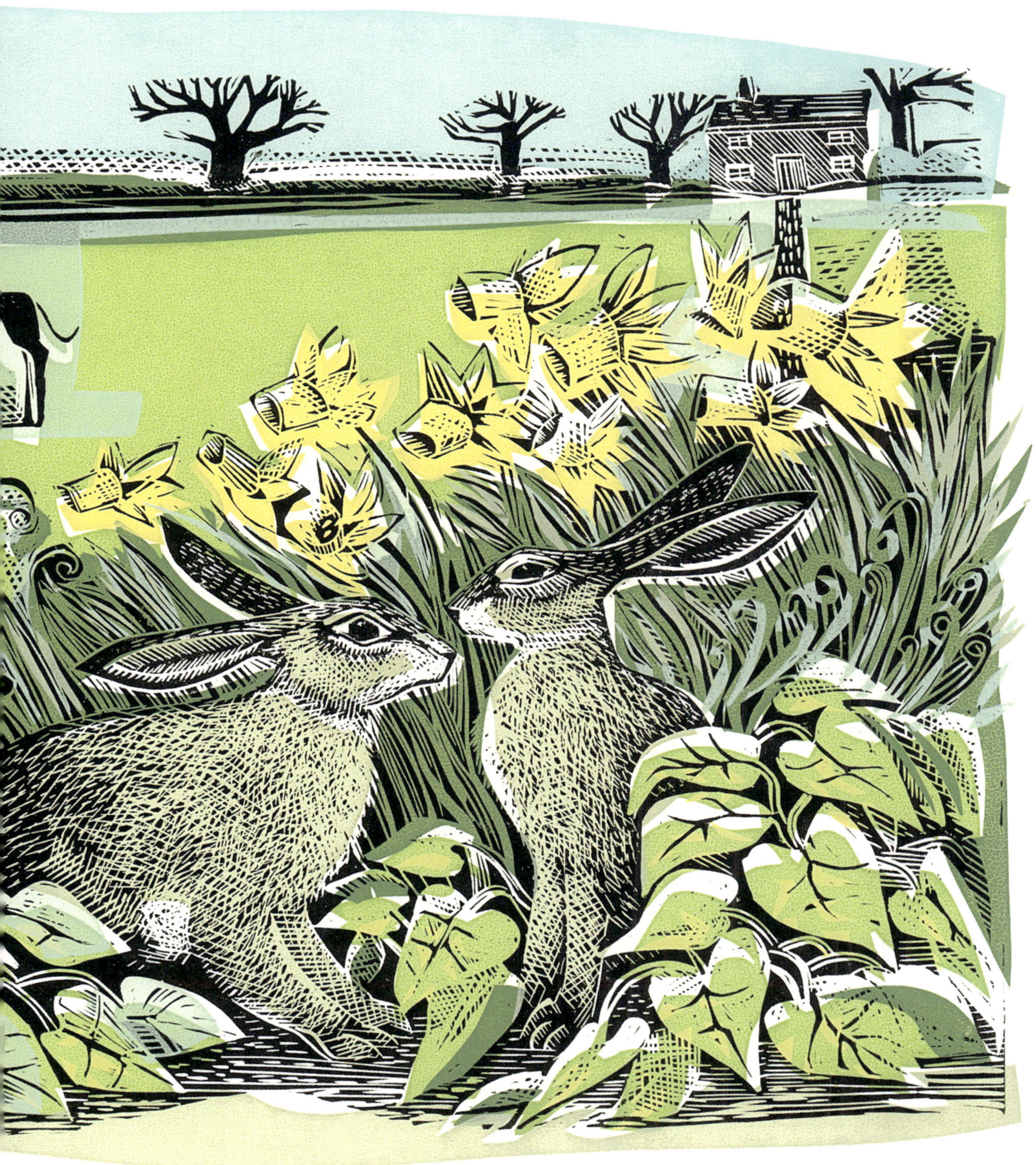

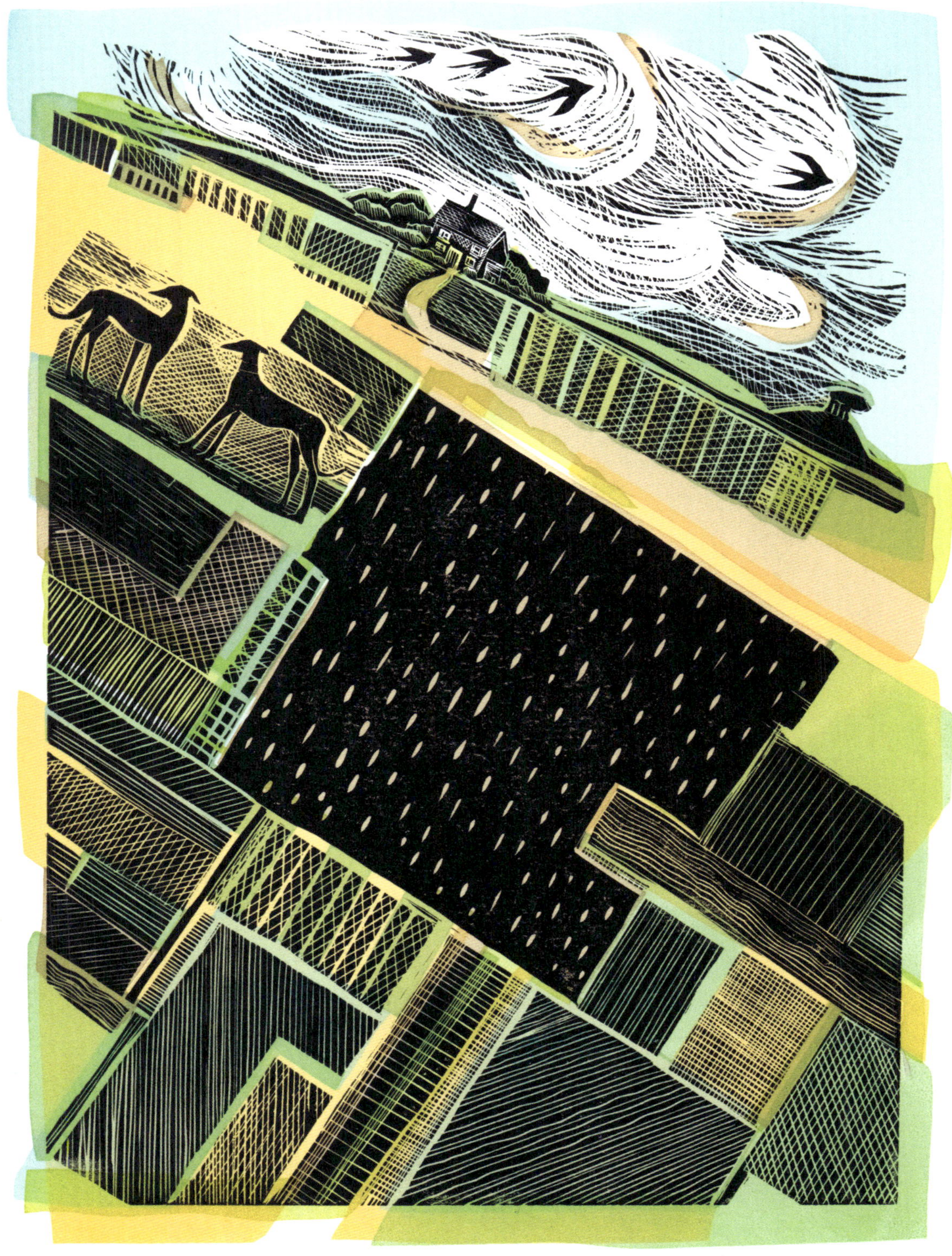

Spring Fields

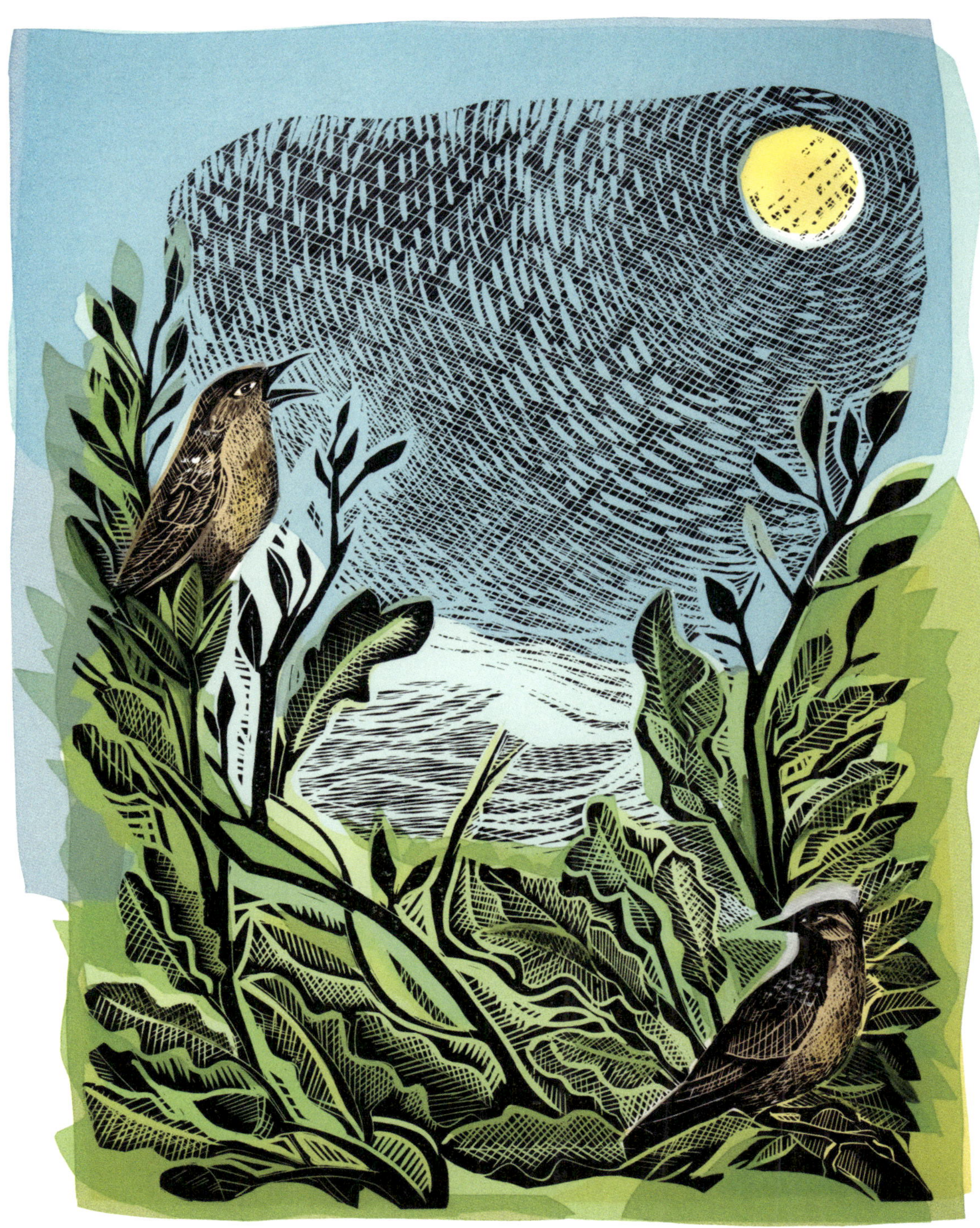

Spring Song

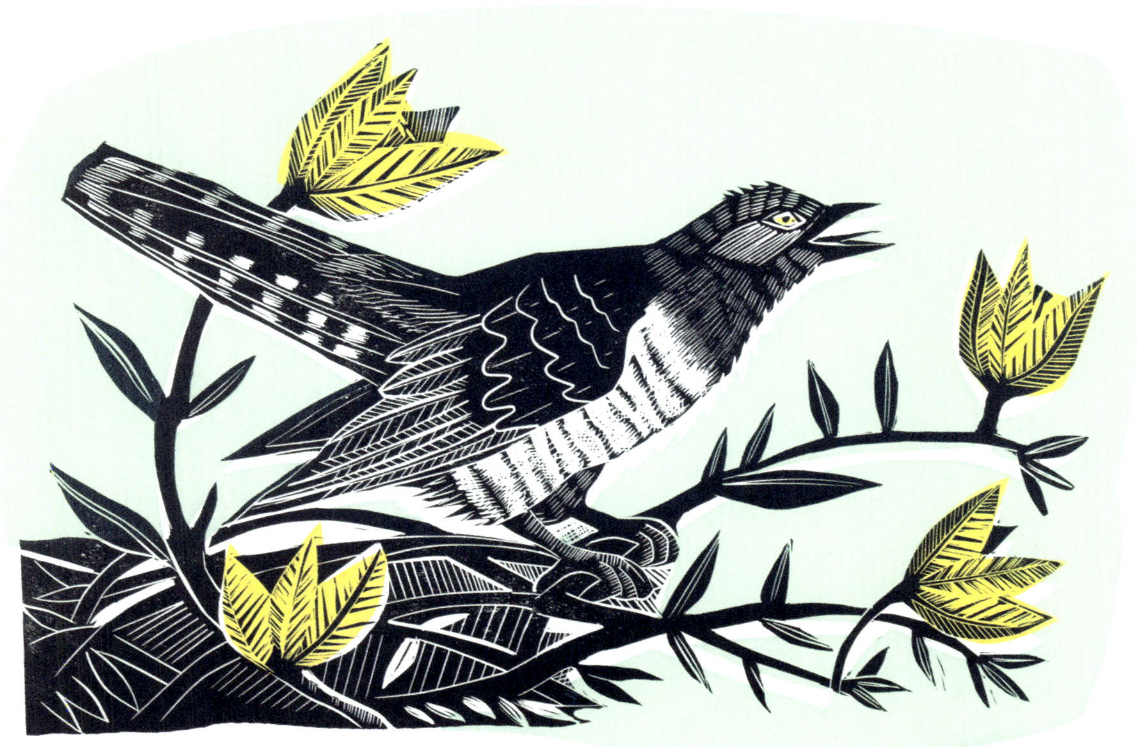

Cuckoo

We have one pub in the village, The King's Arms; the other pub, the Cuckoo Inn, sadly closed in 2004 but its name is interesting as it comes from a local legend. It is said that long ago the villagers of Wing tried to keep spring and stop winter from reappearing. They thought if they caged a cuckoo winter would be kept at bay. But the cuckoo escaped and winter returned. The villagers then became known in Rutland as Wing Fools for attempting such a silly thing.

The cuckoo is a summer migrant; its distinctive call can be heard in Wing from April and it is a definite sign that spring is here. I have to say I do not hear them as often as I did when we first came to the village sixteen years ago. But it is a wonderful sound and though you may hear it the cuckoo is remarkably hard to spot. You usually just see a long-tailed blur flying across the sky.

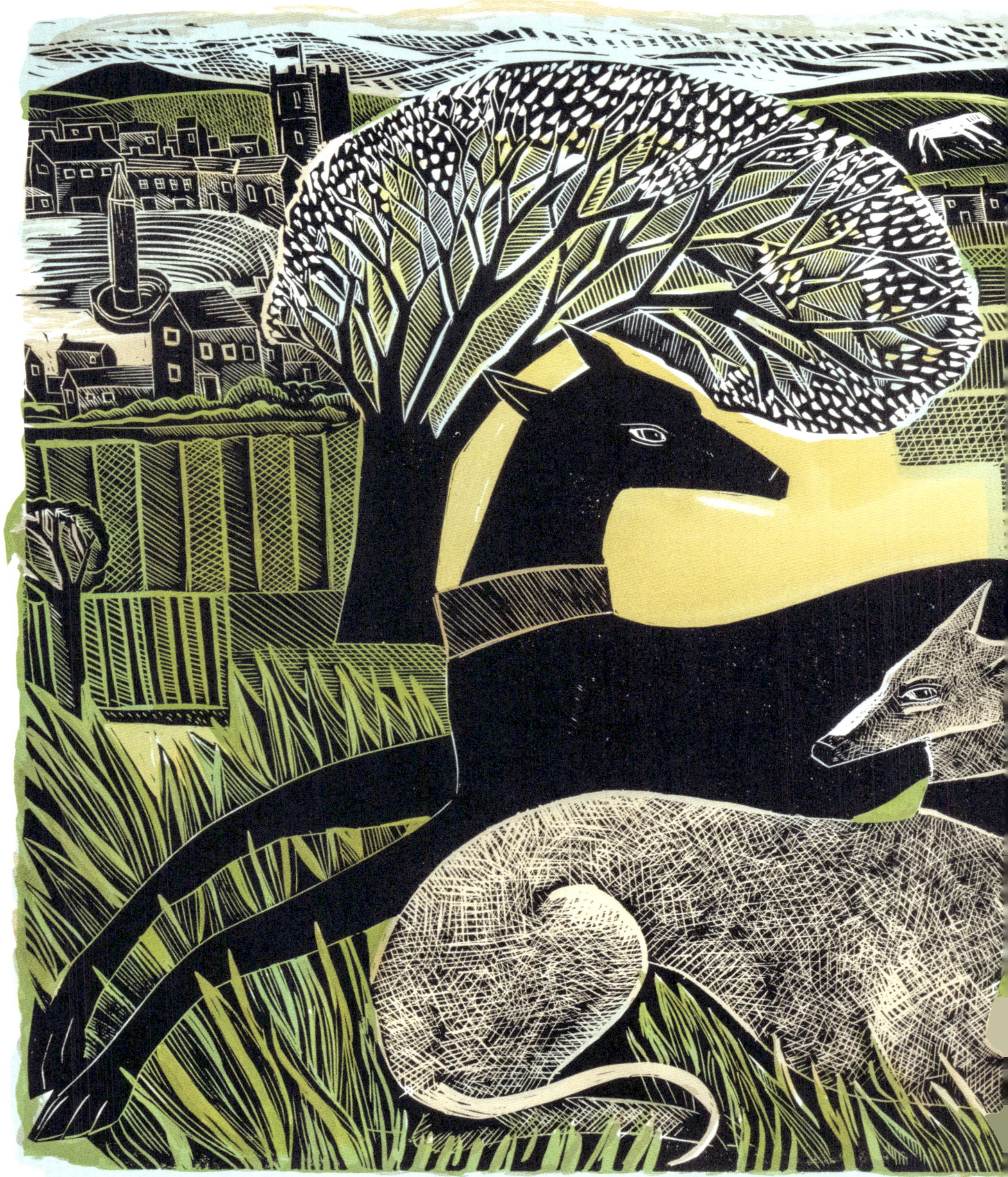

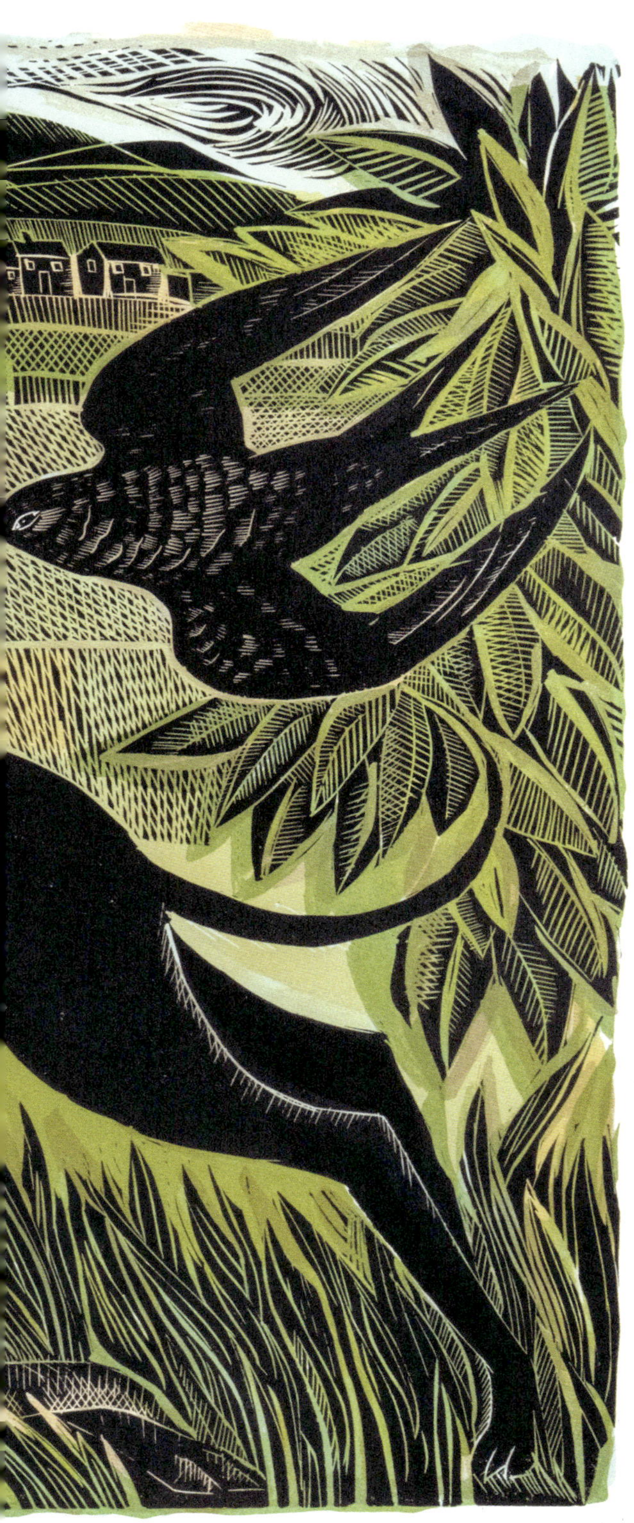

Two Yorkshire Whippets

A swift features in Two Yorkshire Whippets. This print is about living in Richmond as a small child. Two Yorkshire Whippets is part of a series of three prints I made in collaboration with Penfold Press and the Yorkshire Sculpture Park. The other prints in the series are Newby Hare and Summer Foxes at Marske Hall (the latter can be seen in the summer section). Penfold Press is an editioning studio established by Dan Bugg in 2005. I feel very honoured to be one of a small group of artists who work with them. Dan acts as both publisher and printer – this is a is a very collaborative process and a way of working I very much enjoy. Dan has great expertise in his technical skills, but almost more importantly his methods of working allow the artist to strengthen their voice and produce work of very high quality.

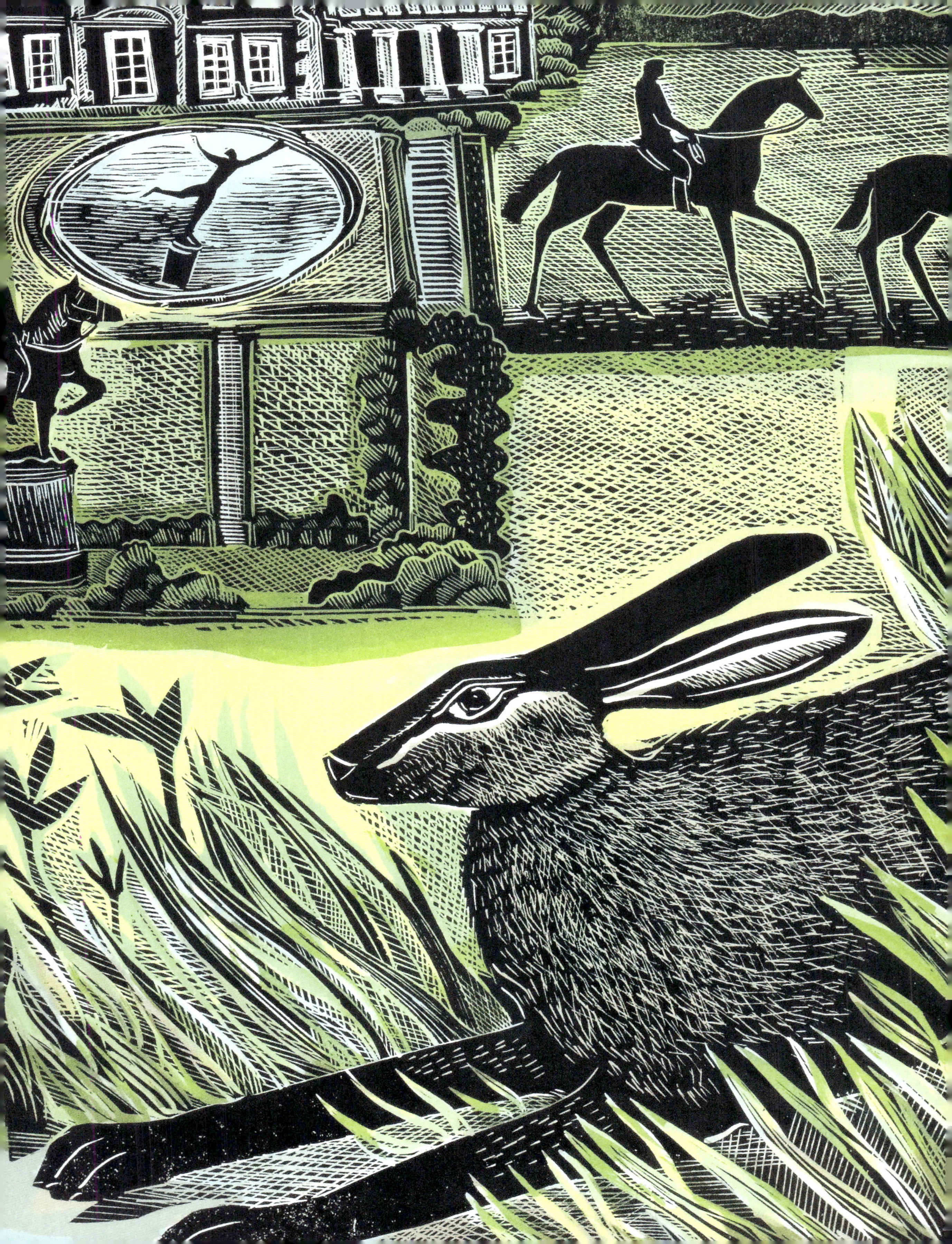

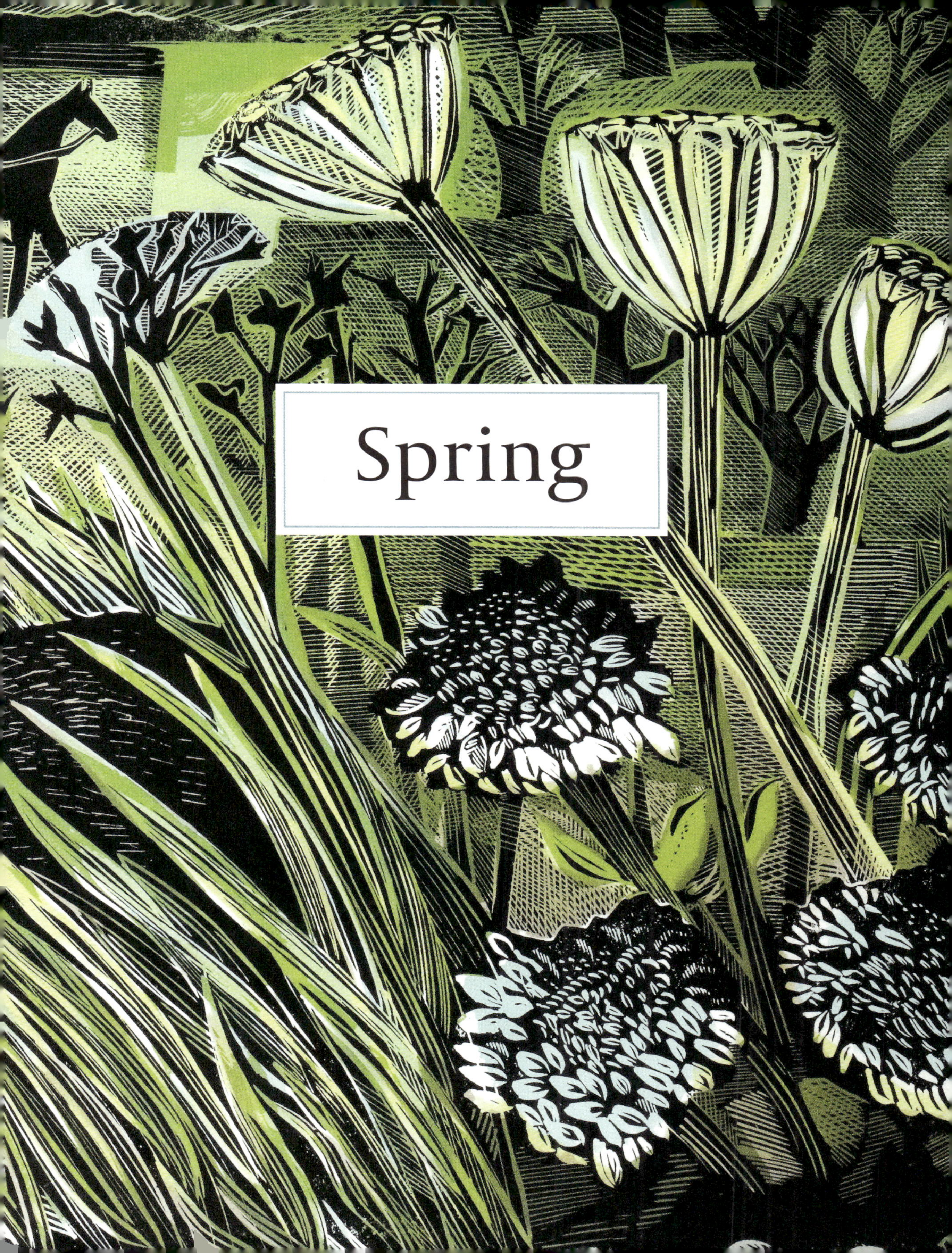

Spring

Loveliest of trees, the cherry now
Is hung with bloom along the bough,
And stands about the woodland ride
Wearing white for Eastertide.

Now, of my threescore years and ten,
Twenty will not come again,
And take from seventy springs a score,
It only leaves me fifty more.

And since to look at things in bloom
Fifty springs are little room,
About the woodlands I will go
To see the cherry hung with snow.

A Shropshire Lad 2:
Loveliest of trees, the cherry now.
A. E. Housman, 1859–1936

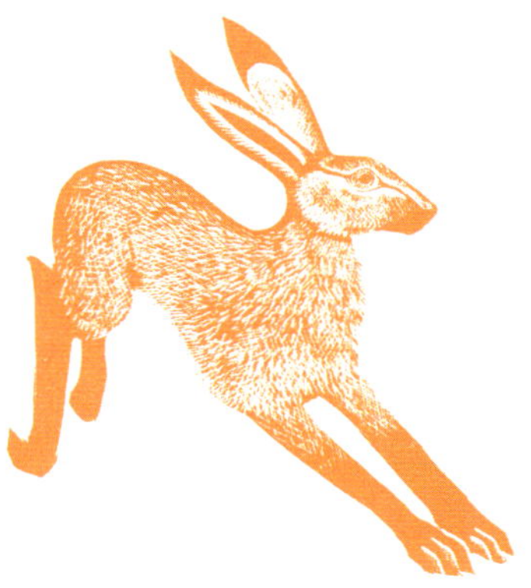

Spring

Frothy Greens and Swallows

Spring in full swing is noisy, the bird song at dawn intensifying each morning until it is this chorus that wakes us. As the days grow longer and the light stronger, the bare branches of early spring turn into bursting buds of green unfurling leaves. The garden becomes a place of energy and life, a vibrant yellow-green that glows against the dark soil. Every day the garden changes and every day the wildflowers that line our dog walks become more interesting. There is a patch of violets that always pop up in the same place every year. Bright jewels of purple beauty. When spring has advanced to April it means the arrival of the swallows is imminent. Spotting the first one in the field behind my studio is always marked with a whoop of joy, usually from both me and my husband. It is true that one swallow, or even two does not make a summer. The first pair of swallows always seem to be on their own for some time. But then before you know it, instead of two swallows skimming the sheep field there is a squadron. The swallows have been joined by house martins and swifts. The high screeching swifts mean that the season has definitely turned.

Spring Hedgerow

April brings in blackcaps and the chiffchaffs return; this is another sign of spring. High in the branches is the chiffchaff chirping out its name in a short staccato rhythm. Its song is rather flat and dull when compared to the tumbling melody of the blackcaps. The blackcap's song is so beautiful it is worth just stopping and listening to; it has been compared to the sound of tumbling water. Perhaps the most beautiful song of our local birds is that of the skylark. Skylarks, along with many of our other native birds, have been under threat from modern farming methods, but we still seem to have a good population in Rutland. It is rather wonderful that on a sunny spring day you can hear the skylark's song from my garden.

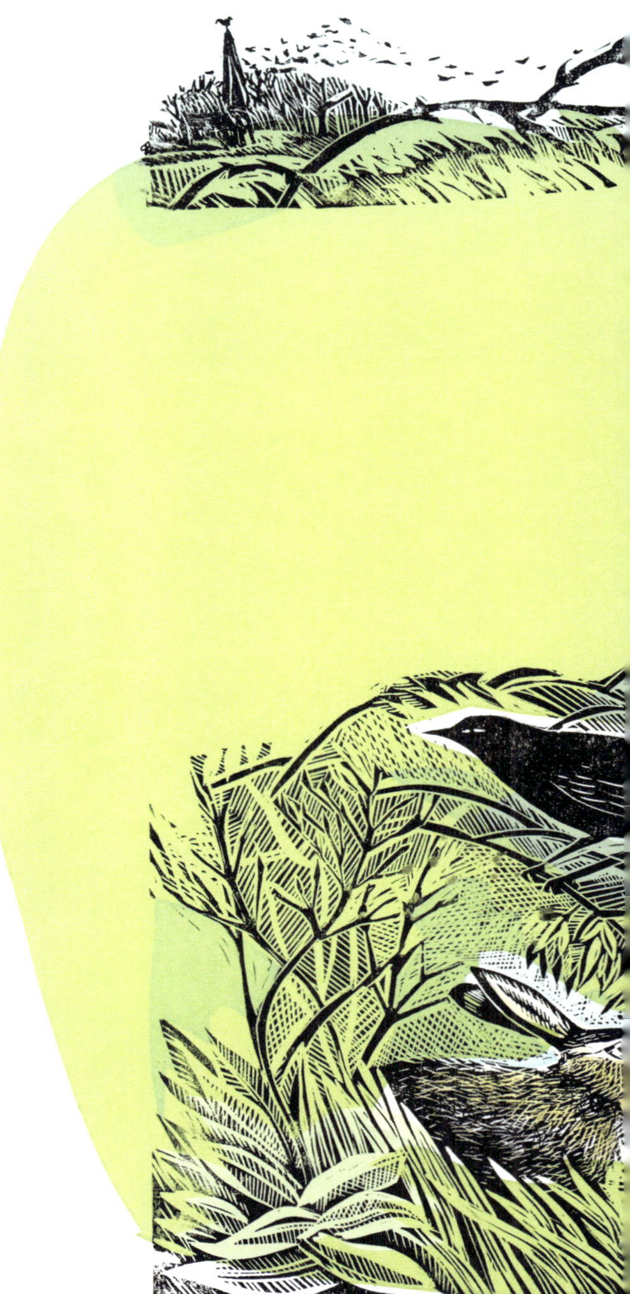

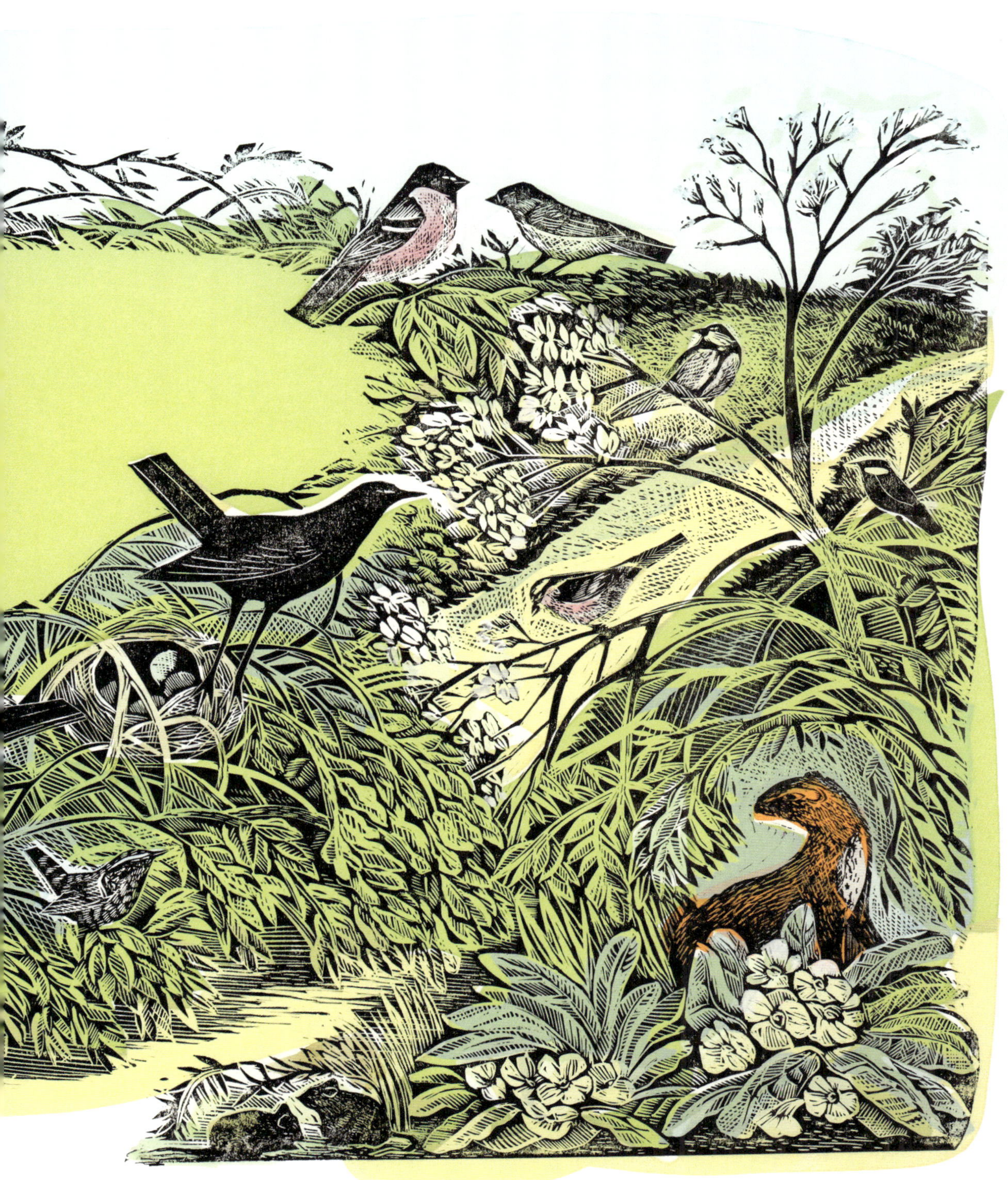

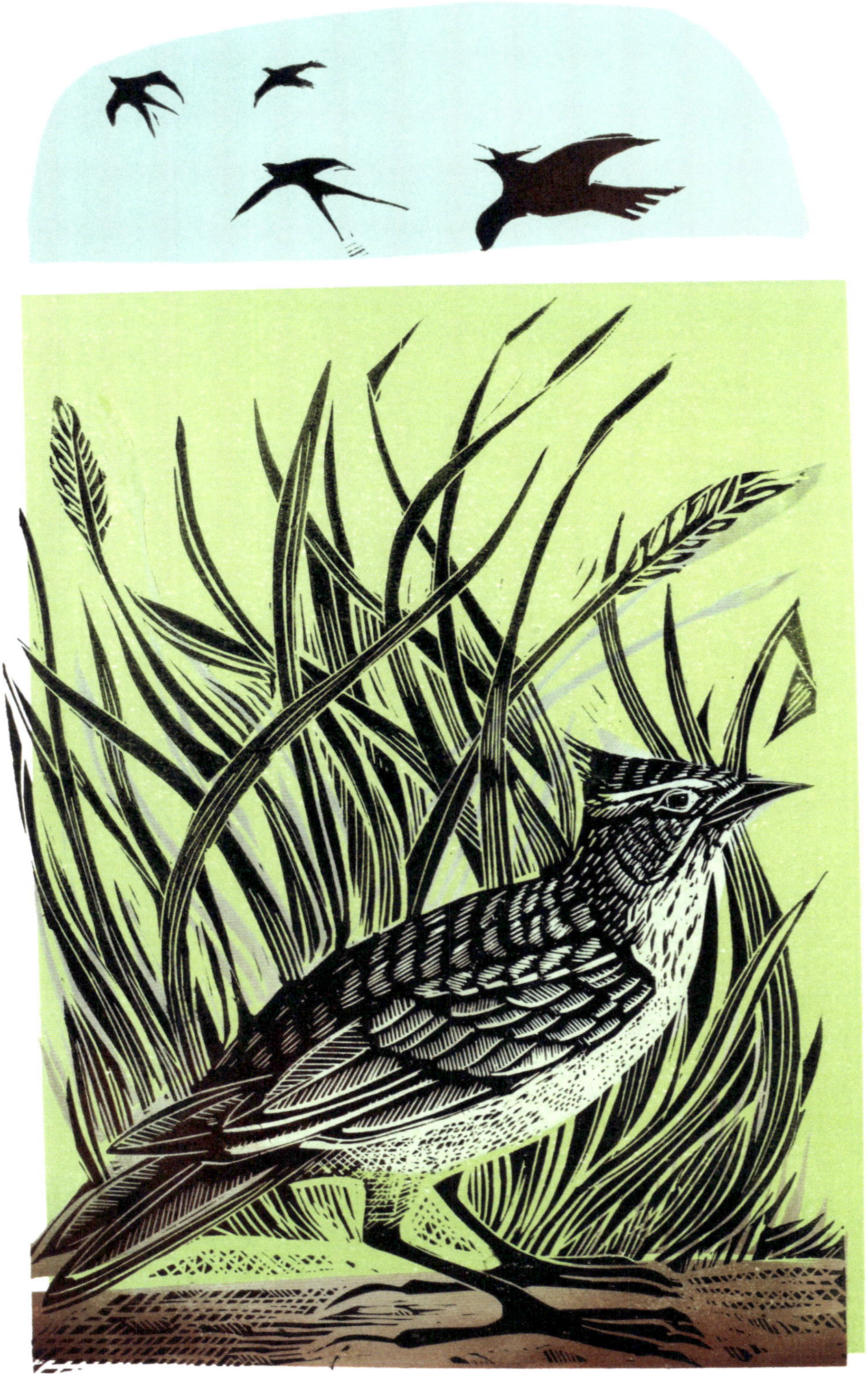

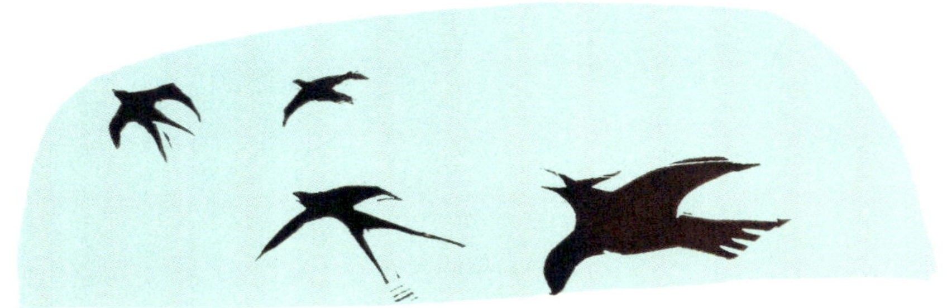

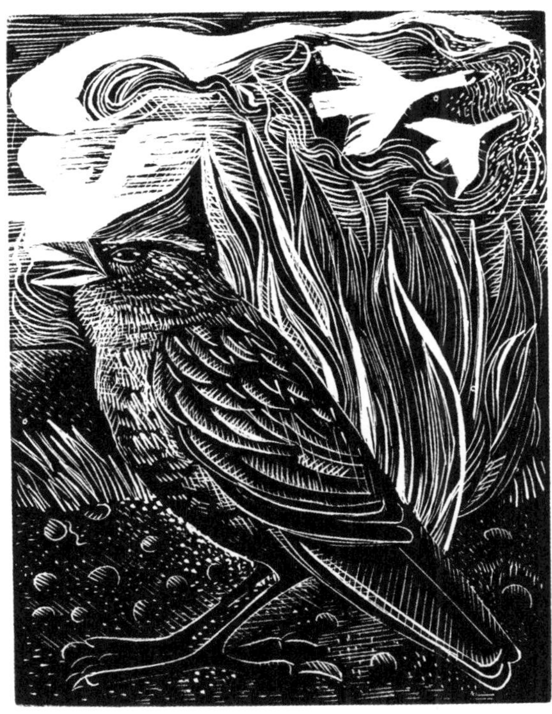

Skylark

As an art student I would spend a lot of time drawing stuffed birds at Leicester New Walk Museum. I was once told a story by one of the attendants there about the skylark that I always think of when I hear them. The museum attendant was Russian – his story was thus:

> *Do you know how the skylark came to have such a beautiful song? I will tell you. God created the earth, and God created Man and that man was Russian. God gave the man all he could want – a family, a horse, a plough and food. One day the Russian said to God, 'I do have all I need to feed my family and work the land, but there is no joy in my world.' So, God bent down and picked up a clod of earth. He then threw the earth into the sky. As the clod rose in the sky it turned into a skylark and began to sing – and created joy. So that is why the skylark sings as it rises higher and higher in the sky and that is why the skylark nests in the soil as it returns to be a clod of earth.*

Growing up in Shropshire on the border of Wales, the sound of the skylarks in the hills was a common one, as was the sound of curlews calling. The curlew is without doubt one of my favourite birds. The song of the curlew hits you to the core with its beauty. It is not a joyous song; it is haunting, melancholic and always moving. I have made many prints that feature curlews – it is not only their song but their exquisite shape that inspires me.

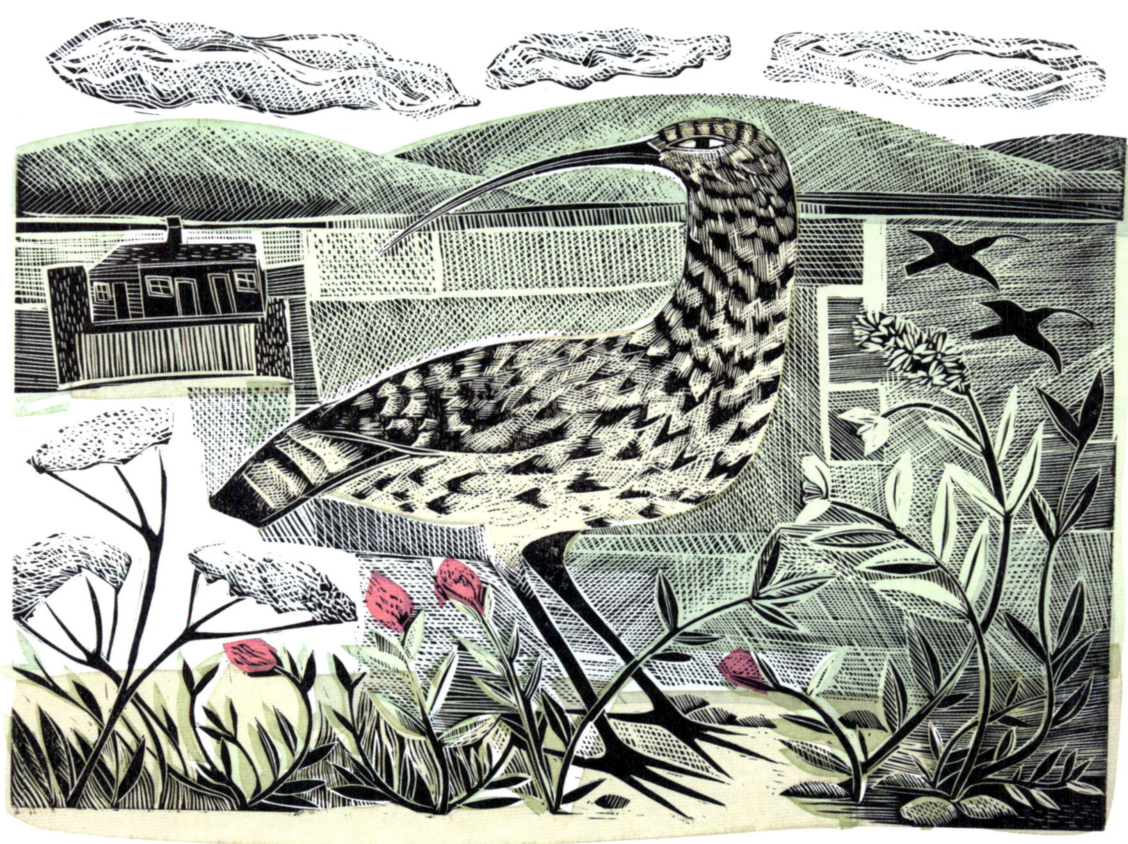

Shippen Curlew

The Curlew

Bent billed, mottled feathers and a song that goes straight to your core: the curlew is a bird that has long fascinated me. In the early 1980s as a student many of the images I made contained curlews and over the years their presence in my work has not diminished. I find them utterly inspiring. The Shippen Curlew came from a drawing I did in Shropshire while I was staying with my friends Mary and Hugh Elliot who run the Twenty Twenty Gallery in Ludlow. They are long-standing friends; as well as exhibiting my work they have lovely accommodation that I have stayed in many times. I use these stays as an opportunity to do some drawing. The Shippen is a converted barn, shippen being the Shropshire name for a sheep barn. The barn sits in beautiful Shropshire countryside and I have seen one or two curlews. But it is not like the days when I lived in Shropshire in my youth and there was the constant sound of the curlew's song. It is sad that today the curlews in Shropshire are very much diminished. I see far more of them when I visit the Suffolk coast than I do in Shropshire, but thanks to the charity Curlew Country they are starting slowly to make a comeback.

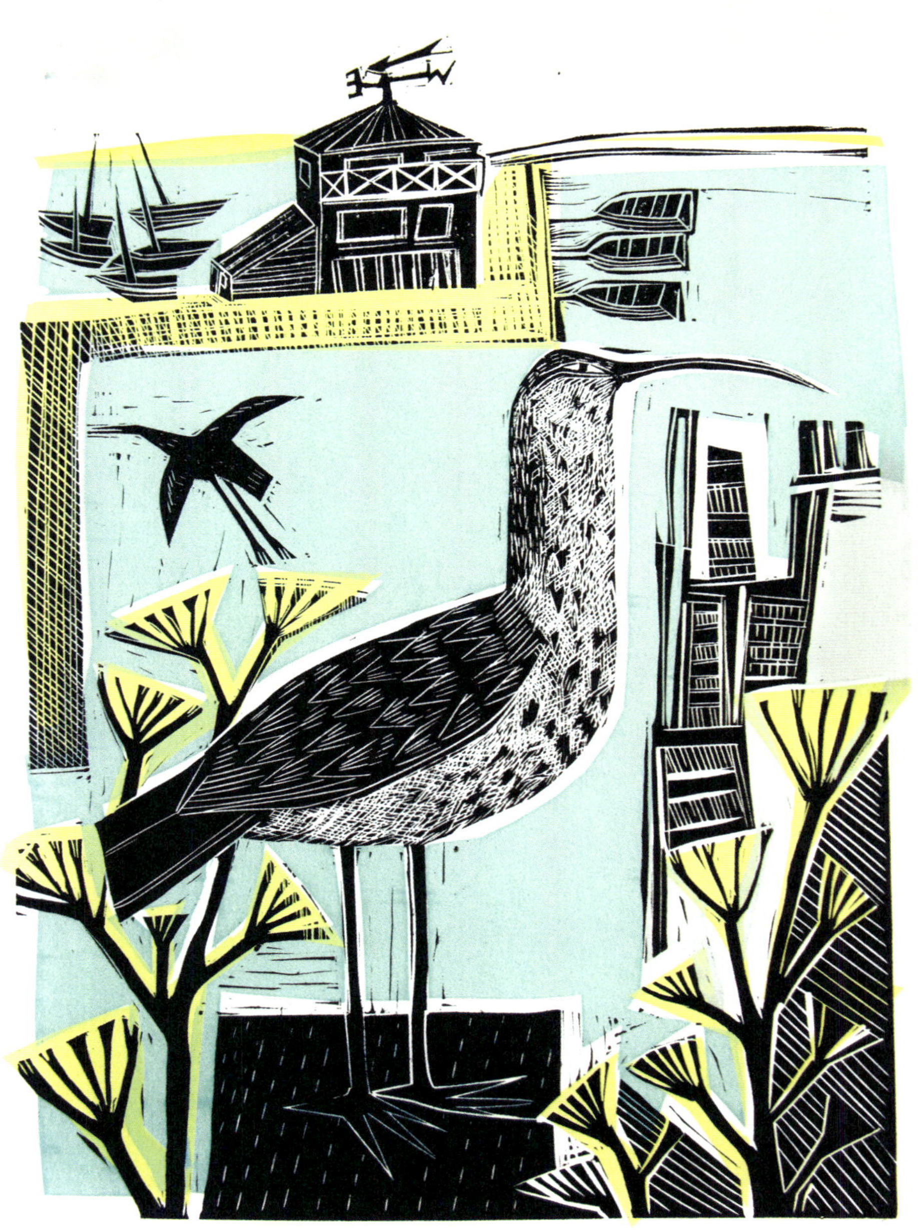

Curlew at Morston

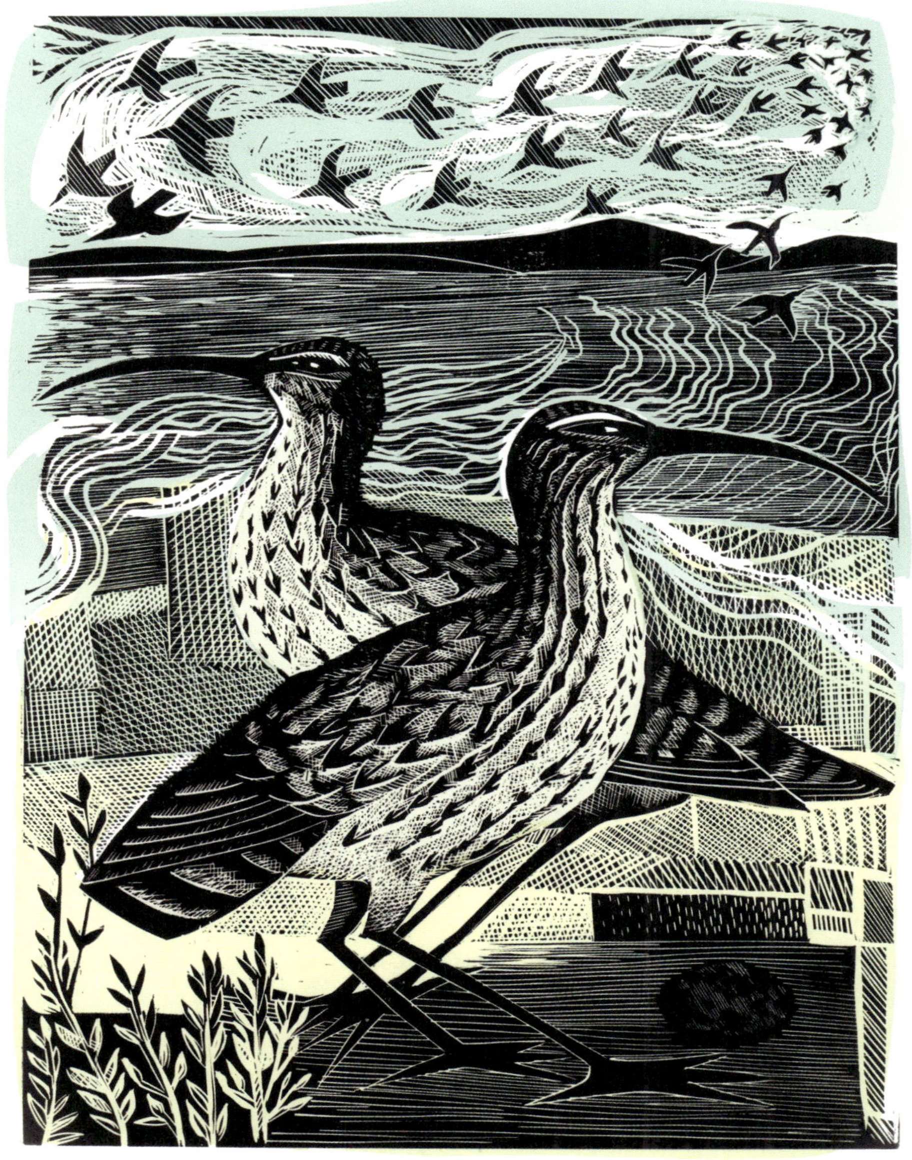

Two Curlews

Orford Hares

In spring the Rutland hares are more visible; in the fields of seedling crops you can easily spot them. If you're lucky you can watch them box and chase. It is an amazing performance, a spring dance of strength and agility. Hares are another key theme in my work and we see lots locally – the open countryside seems to suit them. We also see them on our summer trips to the Suffolk and Norfolk coast. Perhaps the most common place to spot hares is Orford Ness in Suffolk.

Orford Ness is a small shingle island that can only be reached by boat. It is now a National Trust nature reserve but from 1913 it was owned by the War Department, which spent seventy years using it for military experiments. The remnants of the military are still very evident in strange mushroom-shaped concrete bunkers and other abandoned buildings. These buildings have become shelters for the wildlife that has now populated the island. It is greatly reassuring to see how quickly nature can reclaim a place when left alone. Orford Ness now has a thriving population of hares, water deer and many birds – including barn owls who often make their homes in the abandoned buildings.

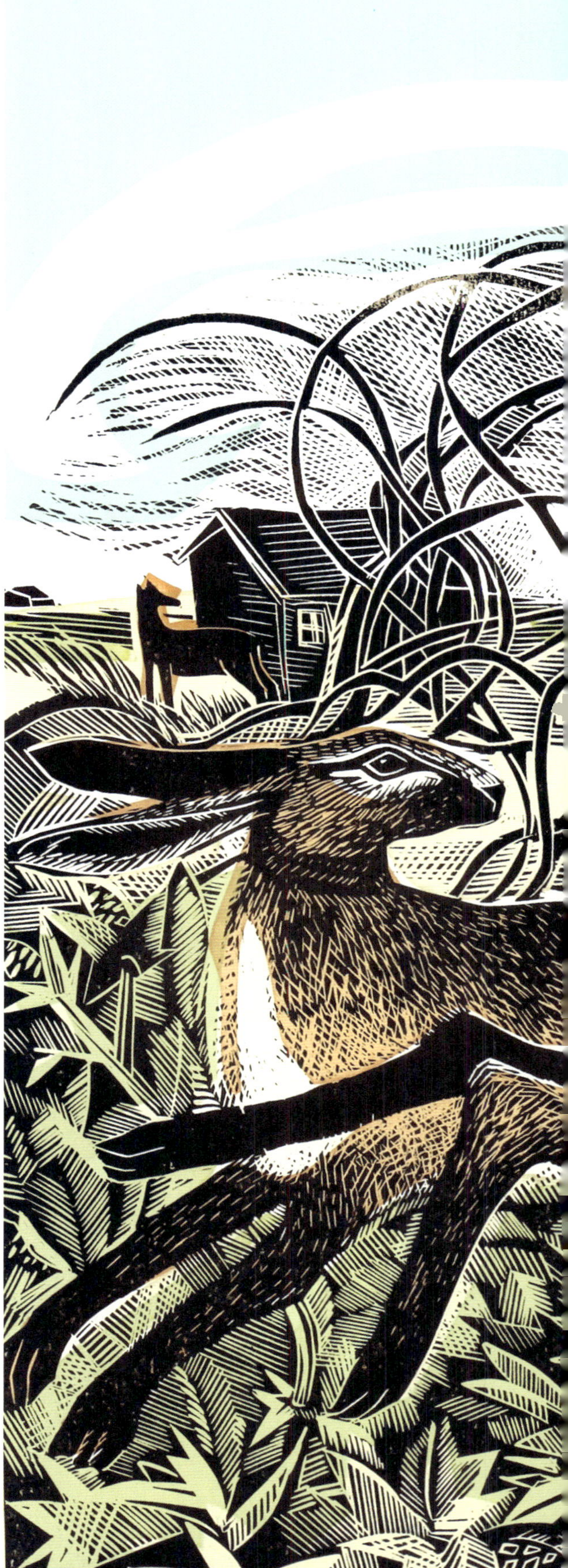

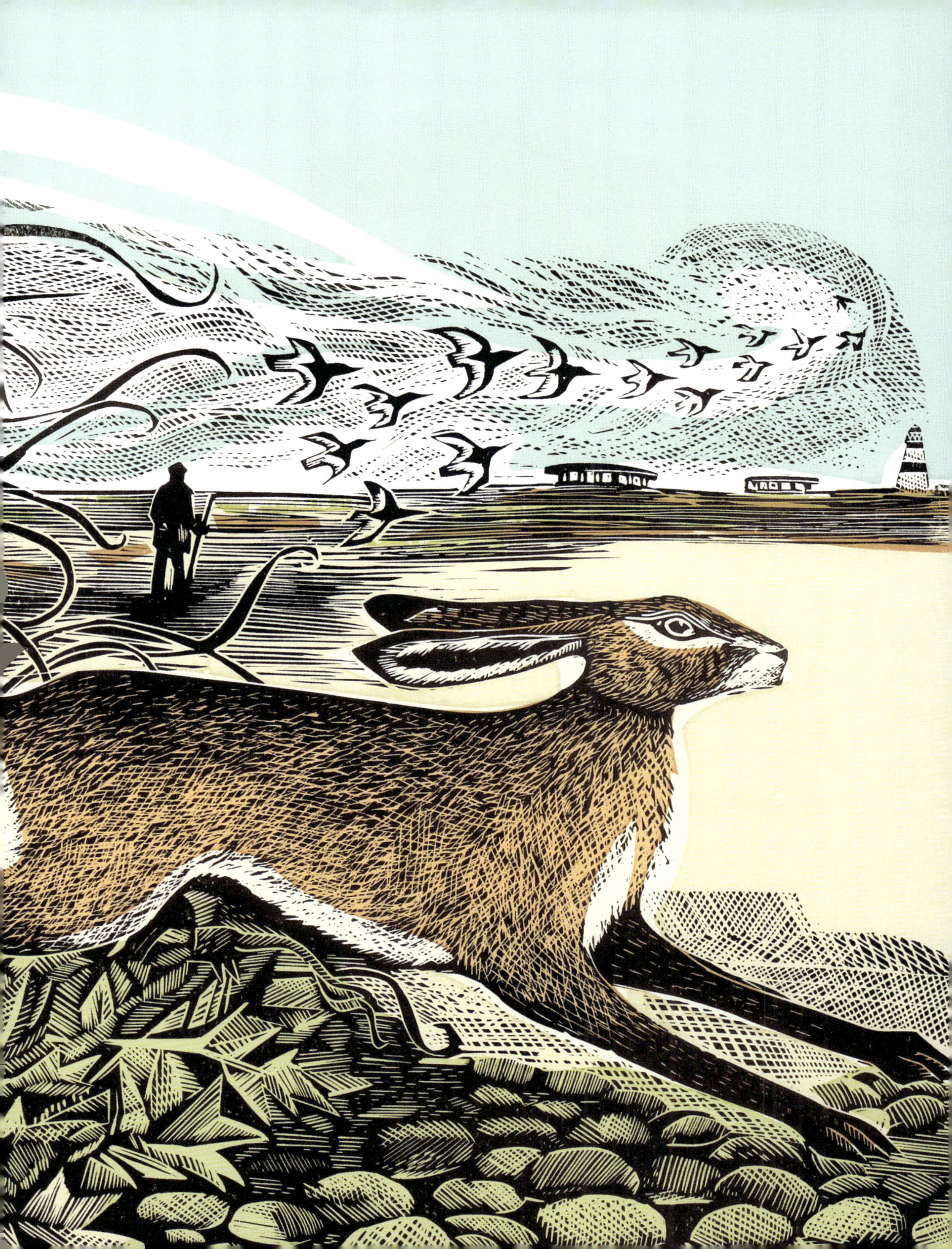

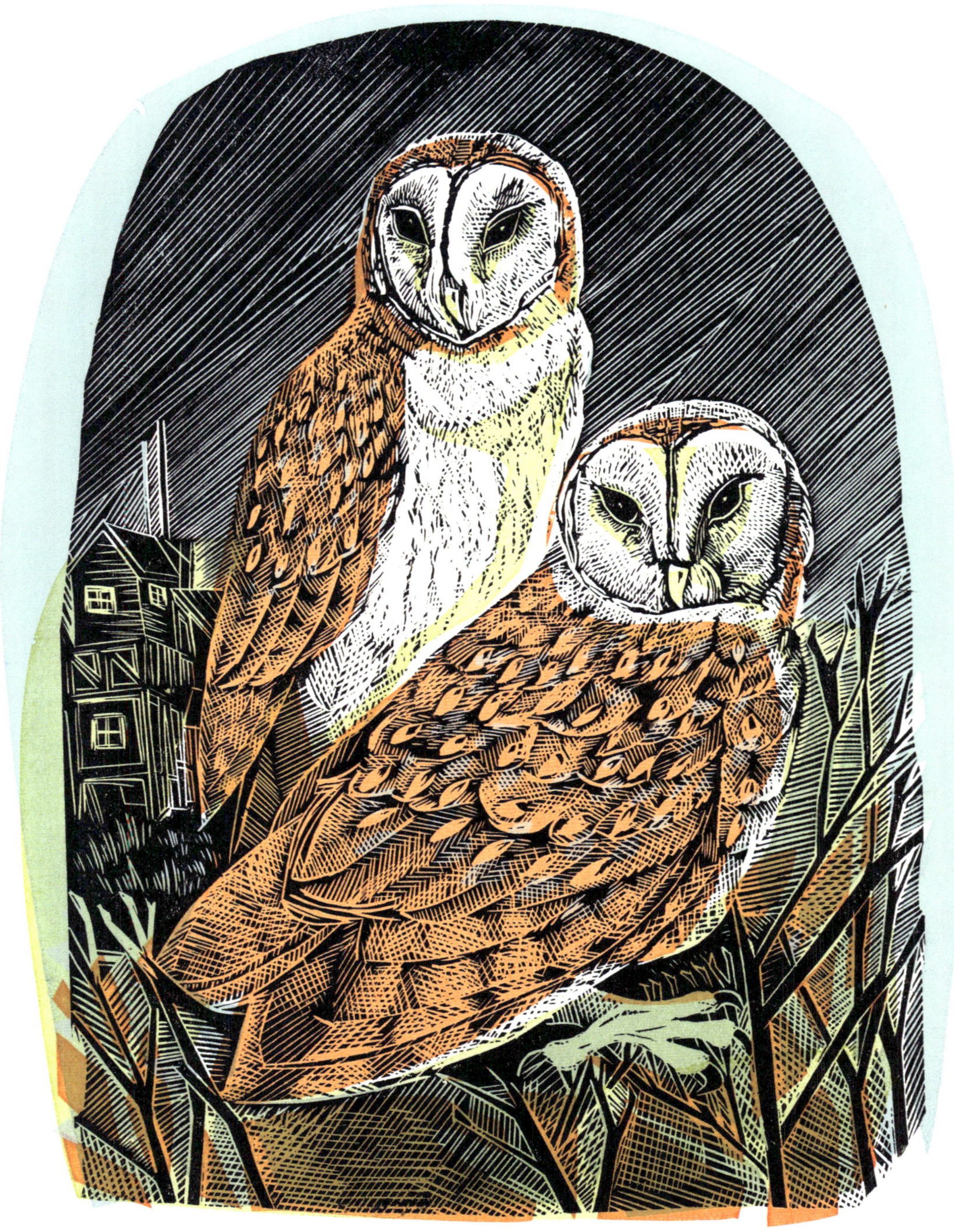

Barn Owls at Orford

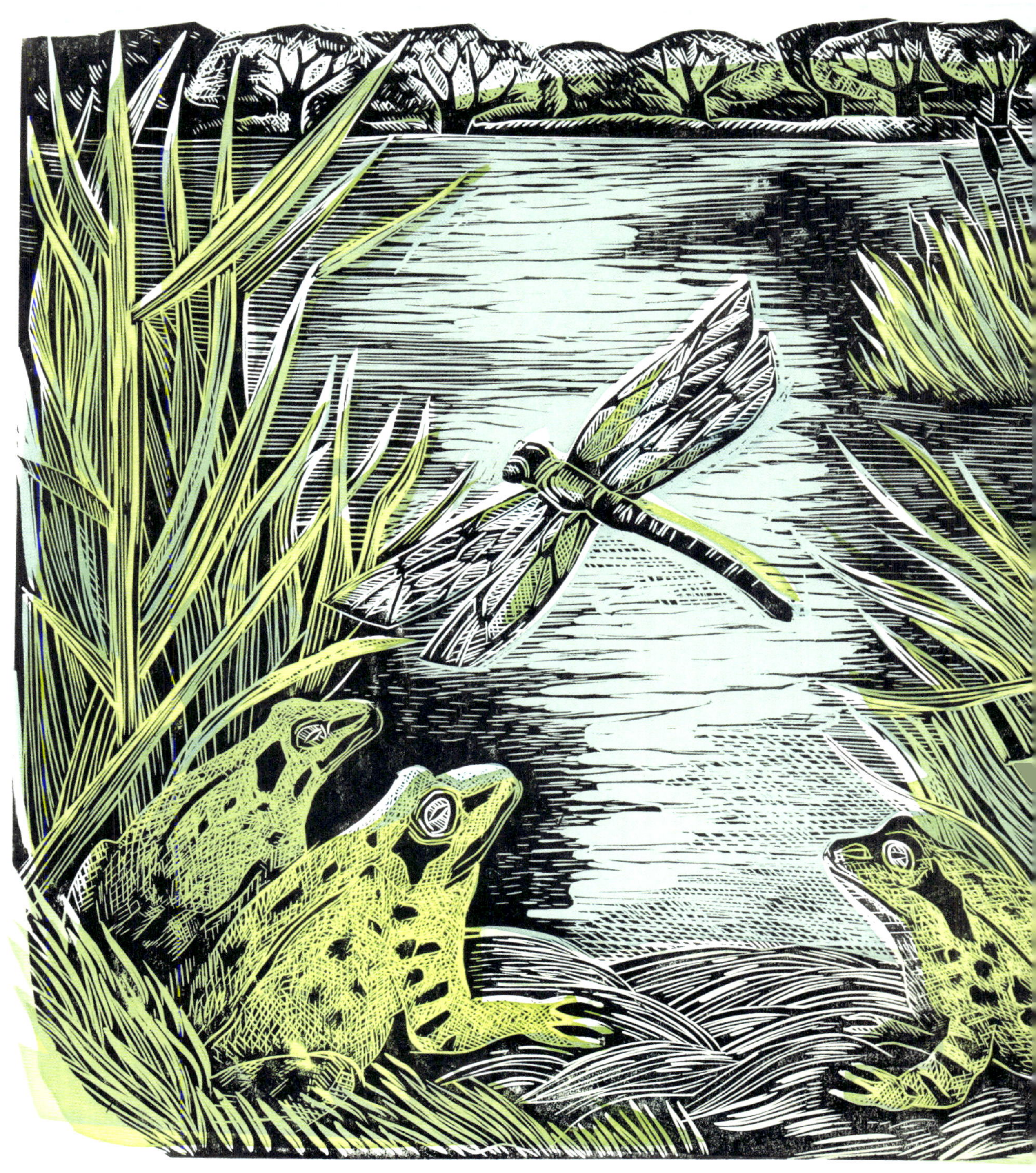

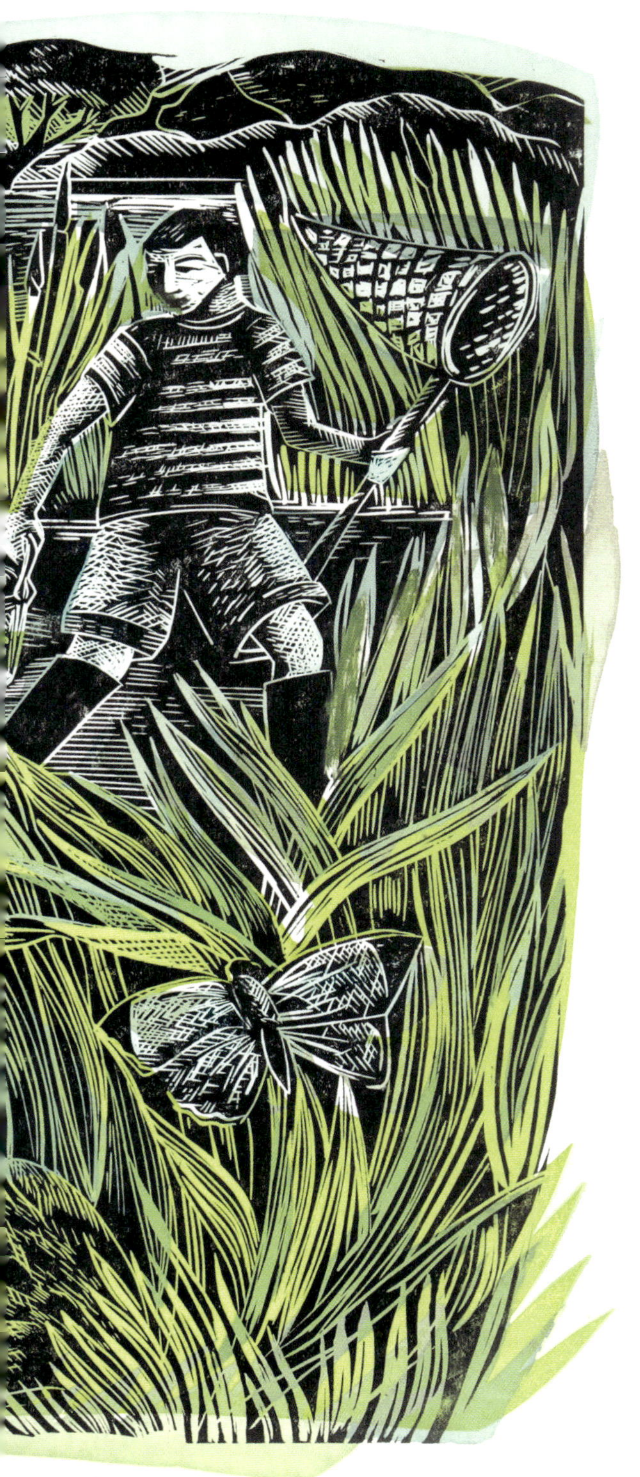

Frogs and Flax Dam

For many of us frog spawn is synonymous with spring and with childhood memories of fishing for it. The print Frogs and Flax Dam is an illustration commissioned by BBC *Countryfile* magazine to accompany a feature by Candida Lycett Green (the daughter of John Betjeman). The article was about Seamus Heaney's poem 'Death of a Naturalist', and I hope I have managed to capture the feeling of unease that the poem portrays – that nature can put us in our place even if it is frogs surrounding a pond.

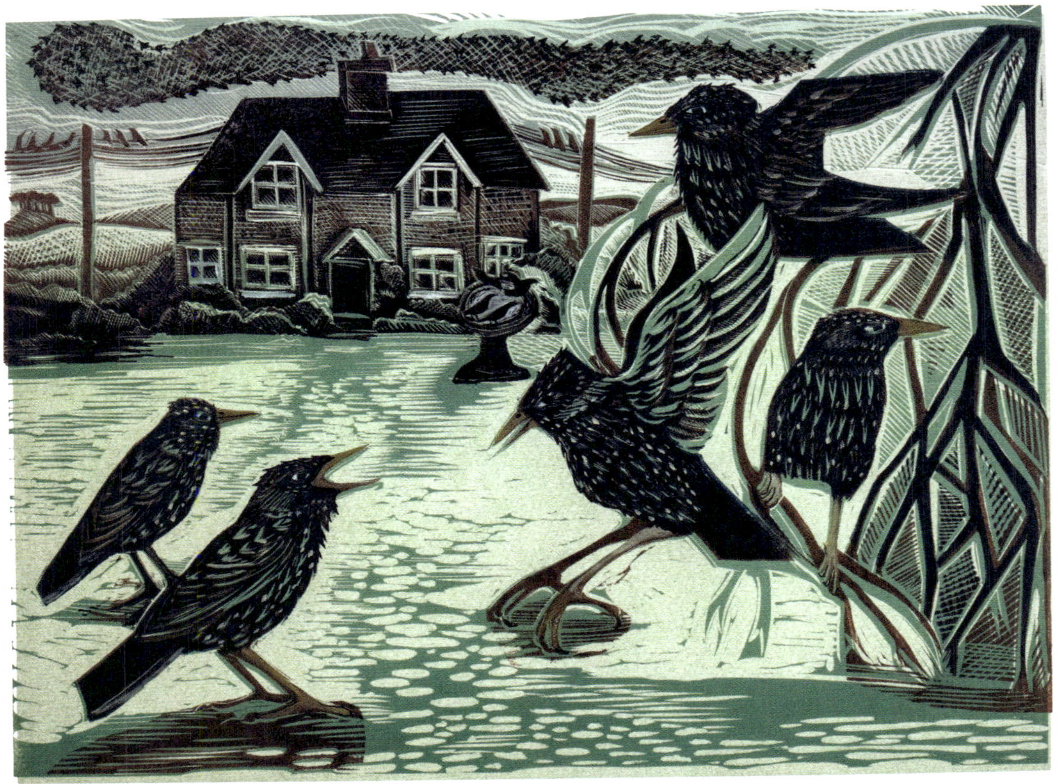

Spring Starlings

Visitors for Tea

Poetry has always inspired my work. It was introduced to me, not by school, but by my father, Stephen Harding. He studied English literature at Cambridge under Professor Leavis in the late 1940s. I am very far from having great literary knowledge but the poems he read to me have always stayed close to my heart. The extracts that begin the chapters in this book are from the library I carry in my head and I hope they set the tone and mood of each season. In many of my prints you can see my father in the background – usually as a silhouette. He was a great walker, so he is often the small figure with his walking stick in hand. You can see him in Visitors for Tea; he too was a whippet lover as well as a great tea drinker.

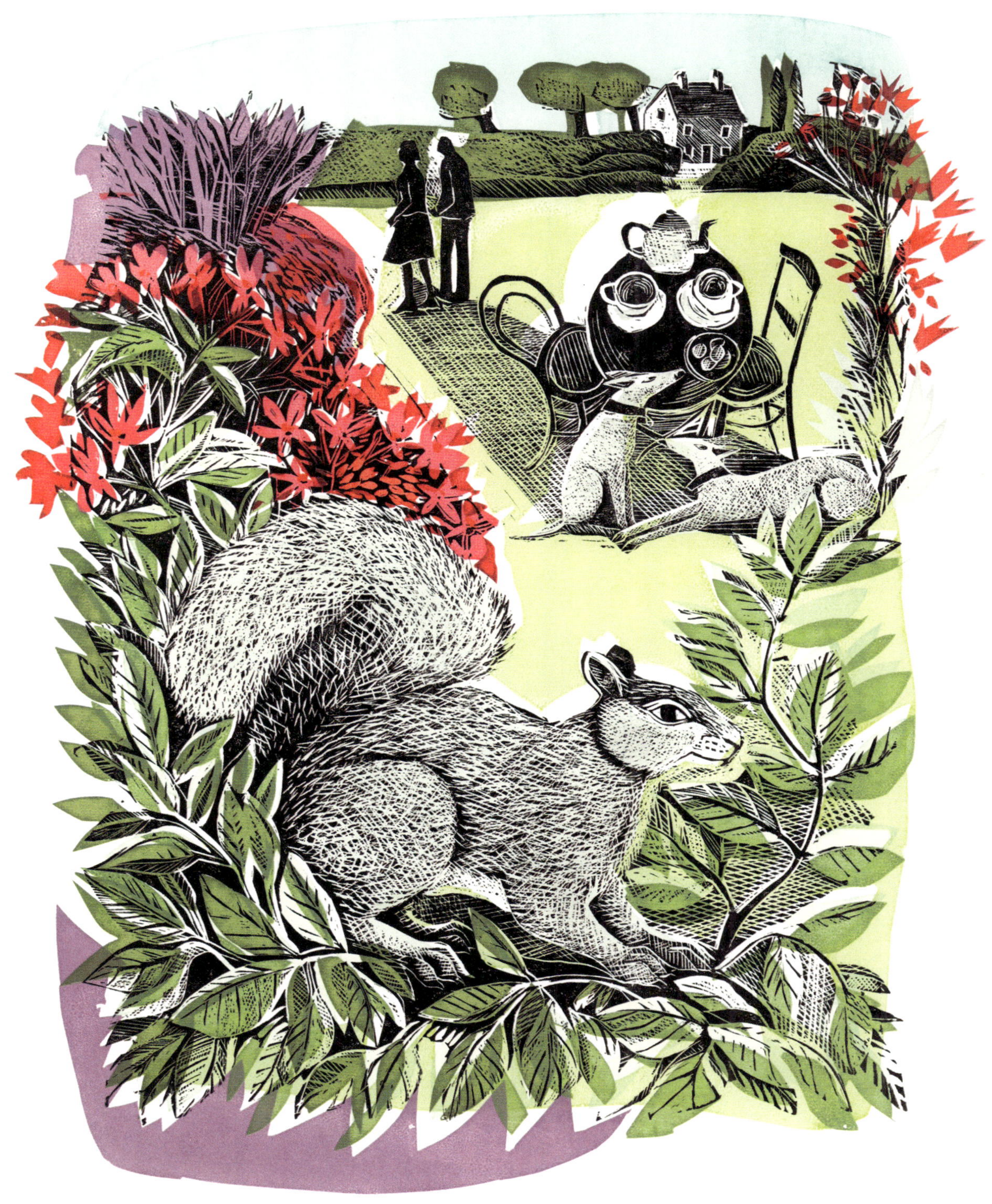

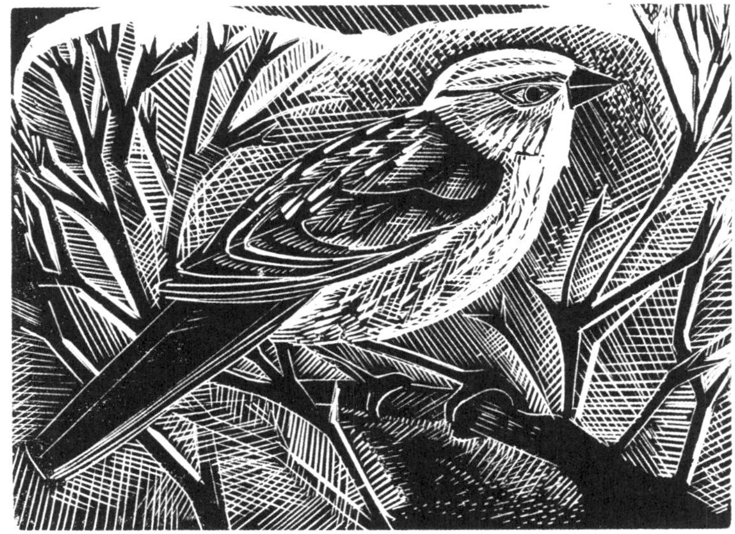

Yellowhammer

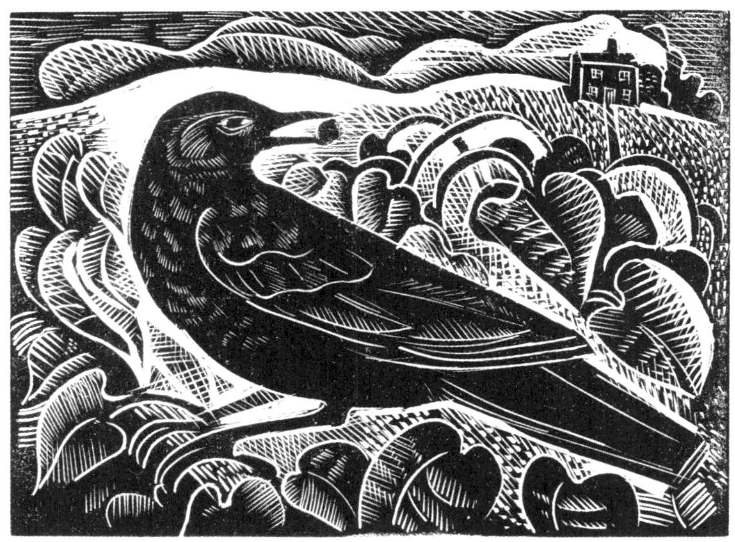

Blackbird

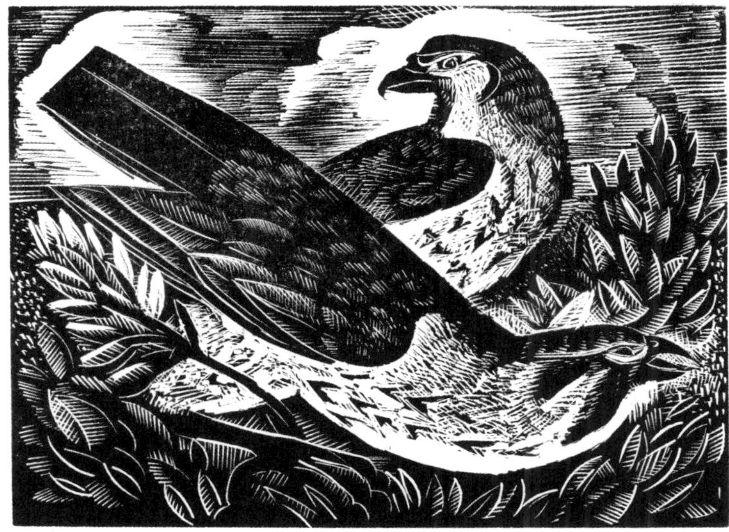

Two Falcons

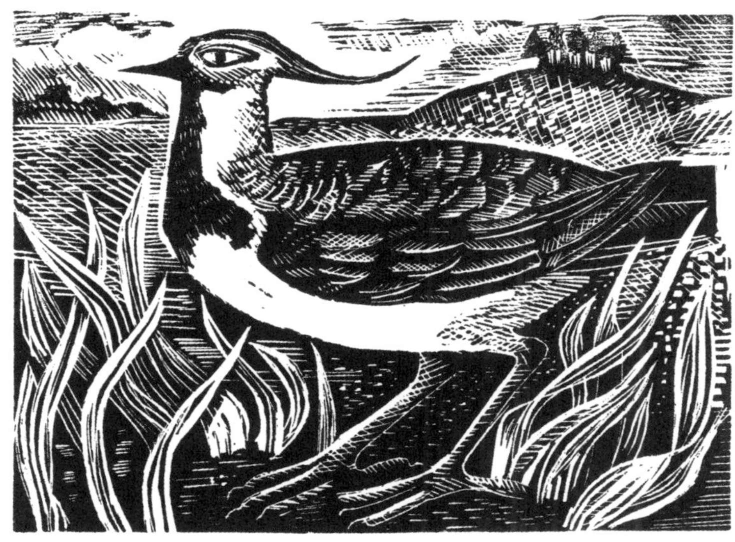

Lapwing

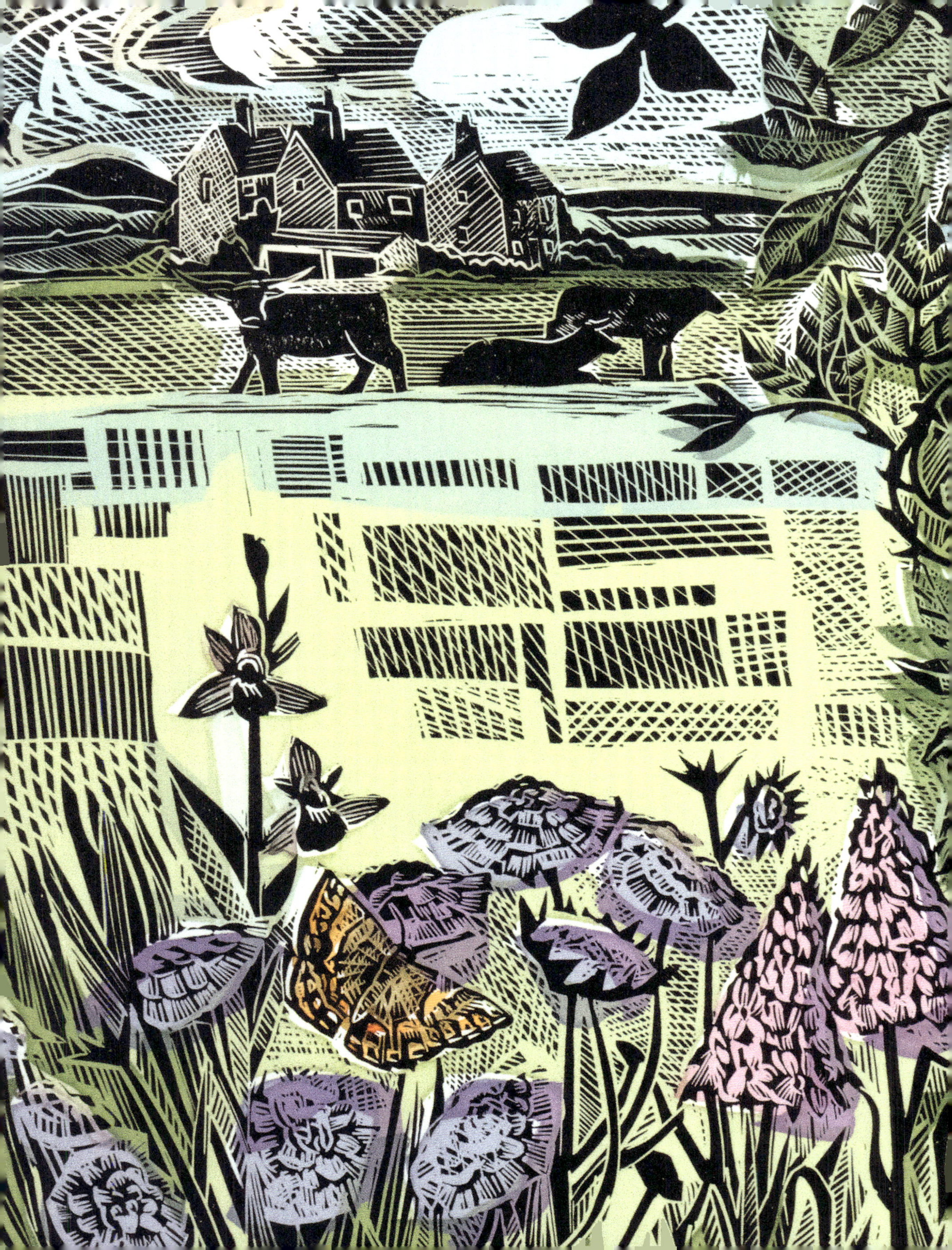

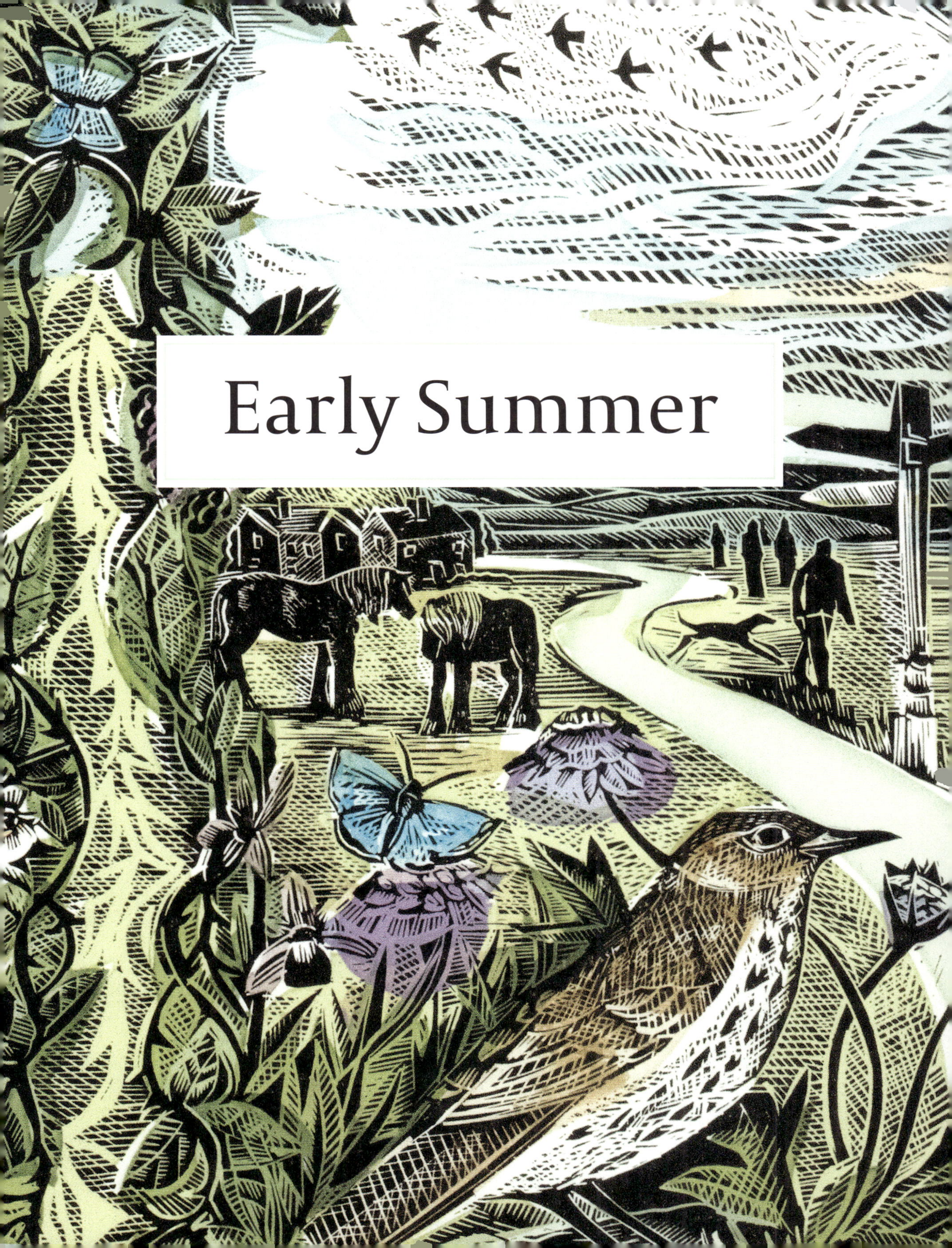

Early Summer

Yes. I remember Adlestrop—
The name, because one afternoon
Of heat the express-train drew up there
Unwontedly. It was late June.

The steam hissed. Someone cleared his throat.
No one left, and no one came
On the bare platform. What I saw
Was Adlestrop—only the name

And willows, willow-herb, and grass,
And meadowsweet, and haycocks dry,
No whit less still and lonely fair
Than the high cloudlets in the sky.

And for that minute a blackbird sang
Close by, and round him, mistier,
Farther and farther, all the birds
Of Oxfordshire and Gloucestershire.

Adlestrop
Edward Thomas

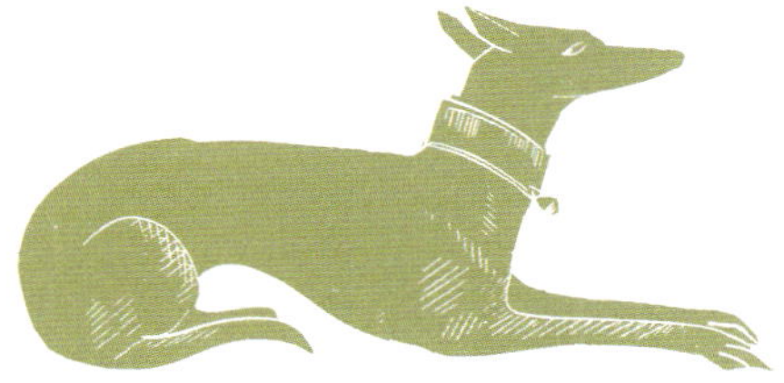

Early Summer

River Swans and Nightingales

Early summer is the start of our slightly nomadic lifestyle – that is a bit of an exaggeration but during the summer months Mark and I take full advantage of owning a small wooden boat, *Windsong*. She was built in the 1980s on the Essex rivers and has a lifting keel which allows us to visit both rivers and coast. Many of the coastal and river images I make are inspired by our trips away. Where we live is about as far away from the sea as you can be in the UK, so our boat is over-wintered near Woodbridge on the Deben River.

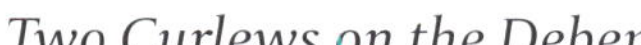

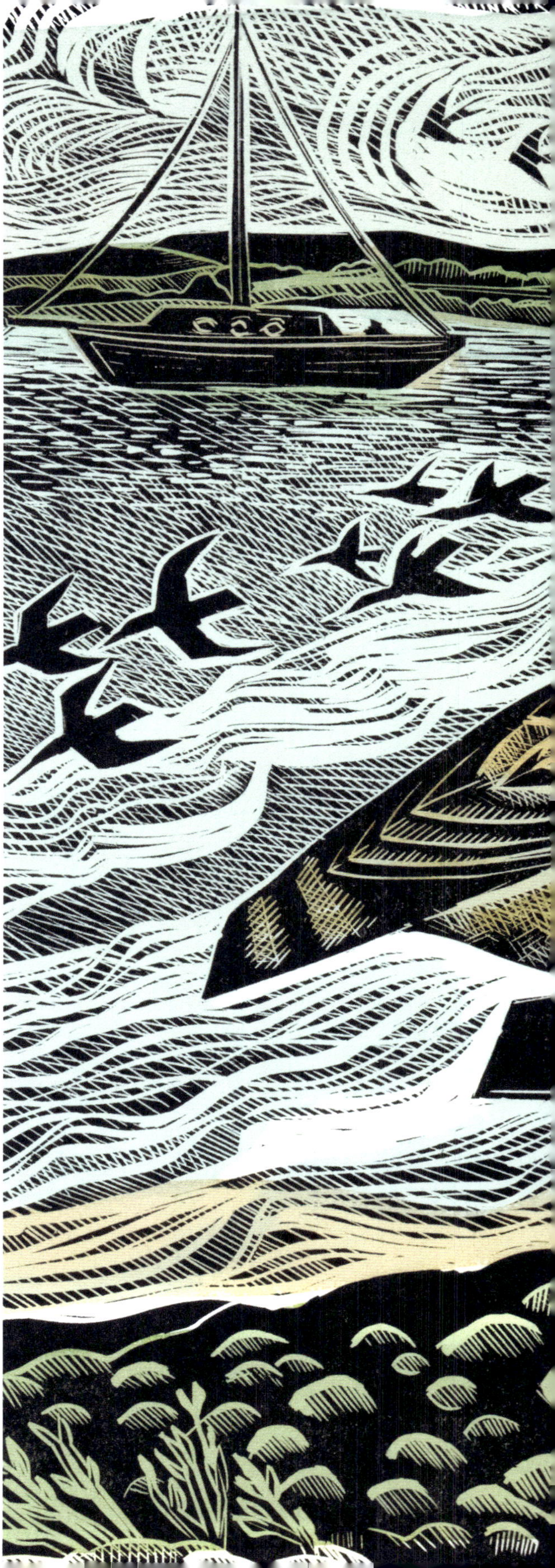

Two Curlews on the Deben

Woodbridge has a beautiful old white tide mill, that is ghost white and seems to glow as you approach the town by river. The mill contrasts with the scrambling mess of the boat yards and the lines of characterful life aboard barges. Birds line the shore, most notably the black-tailed godwits, oystercatchers and curlews. As you move away from the town up river the banks are thickly wooded with British native trees. Branches from these trees lean out across the water and are the perfect place for kingfishers to fish from, while in the tree-tops the noisy nests of grey herons and white egrets are a common sight.

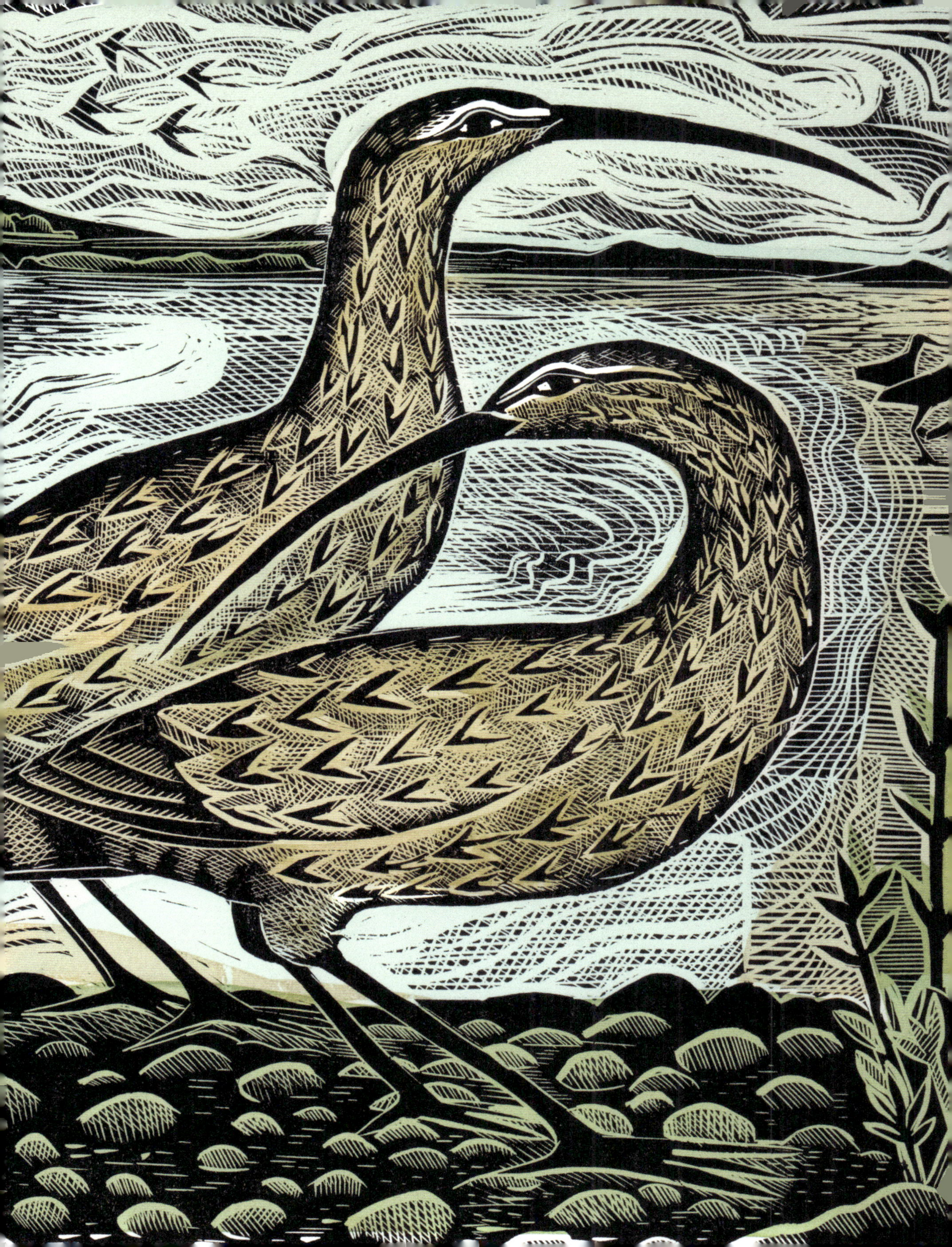

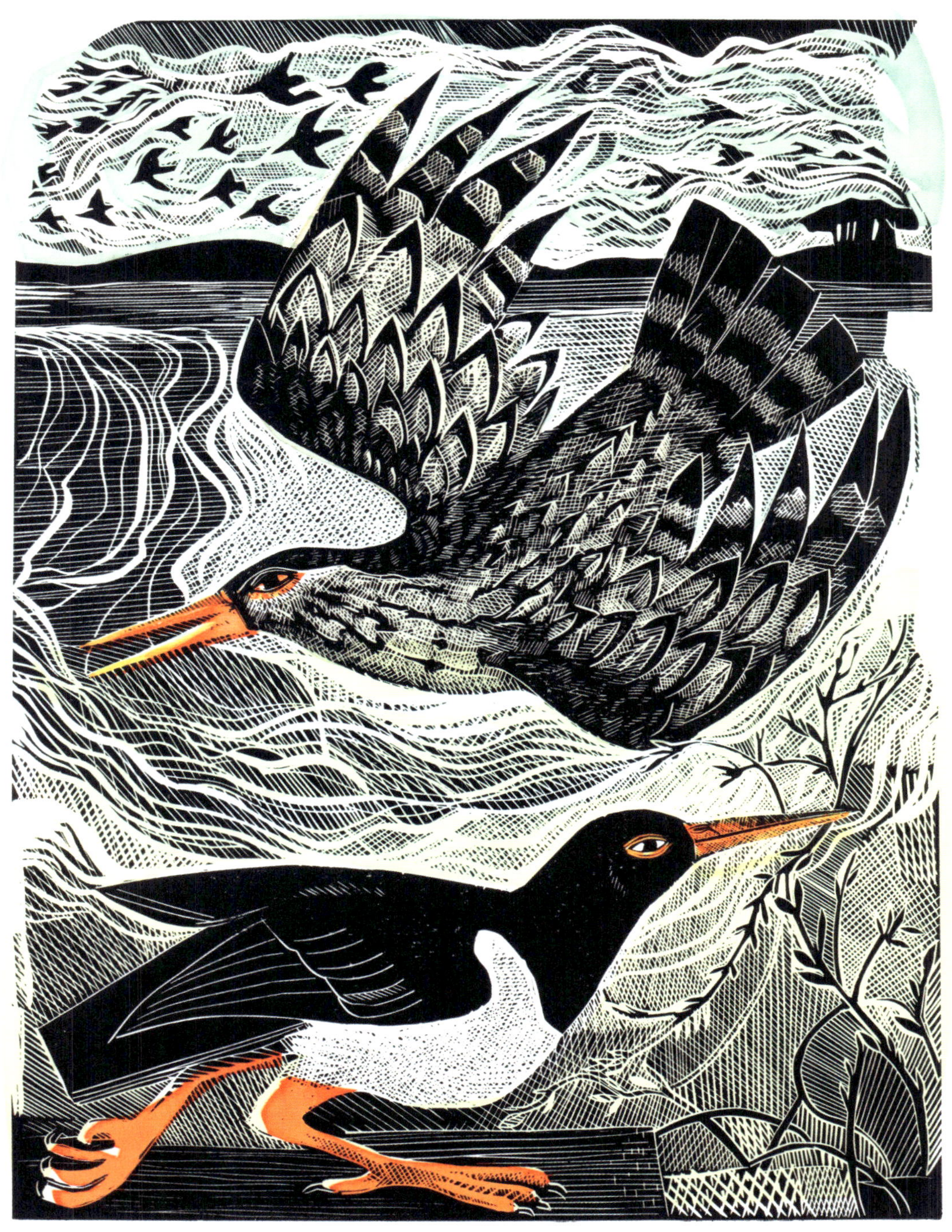

Redshank and Oystercatcher

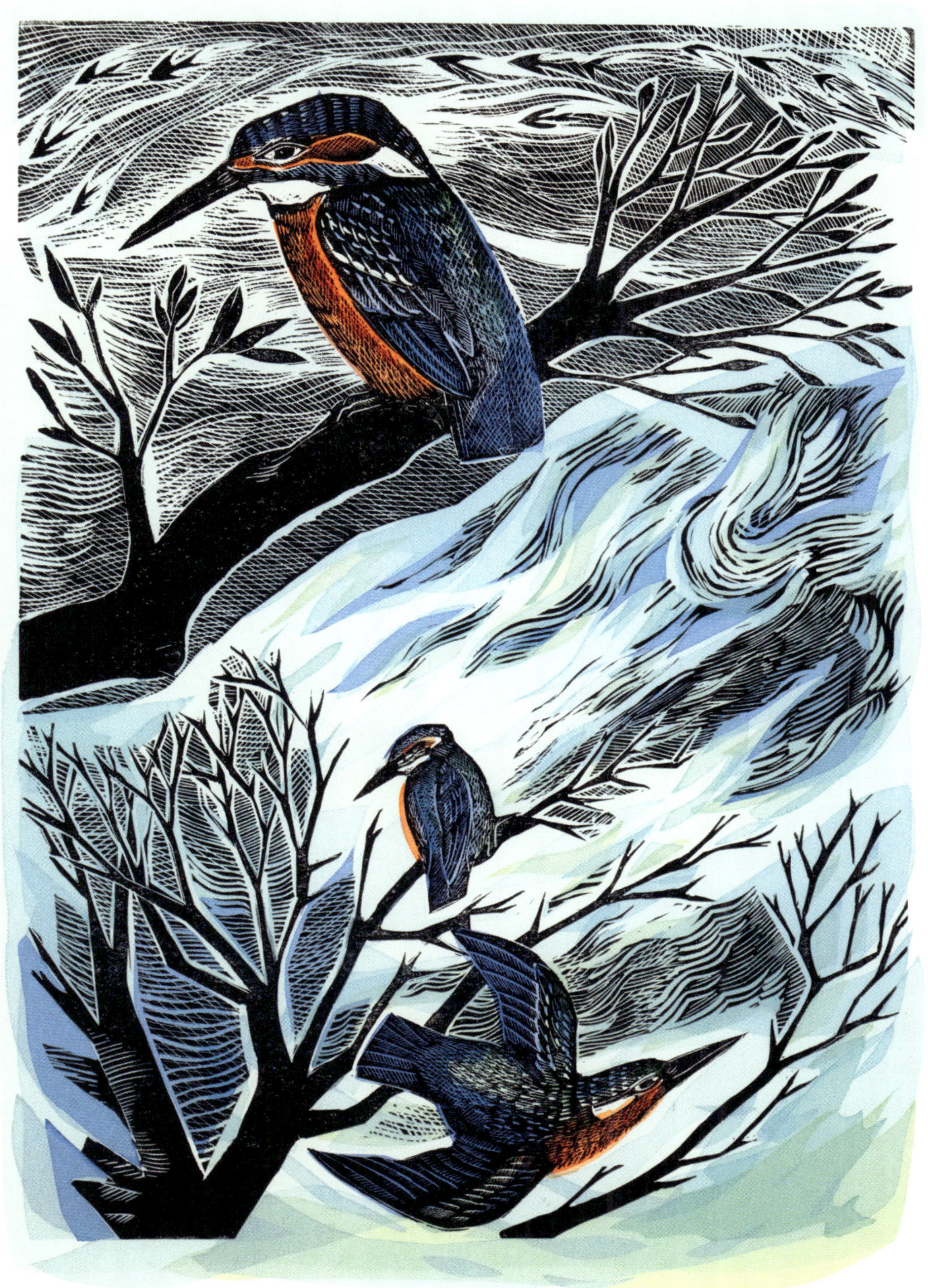

Suffolk Kingfishers

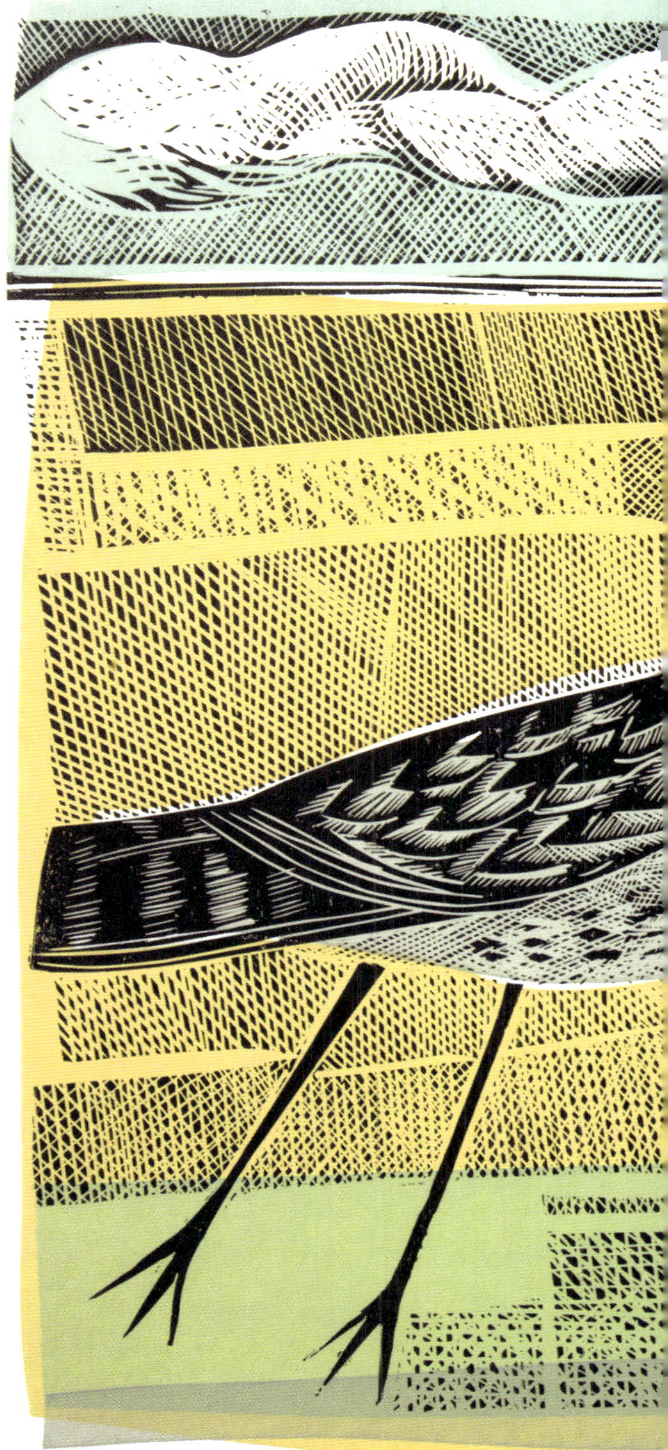

Norfolk Birds

Much more than some of my other prints, Norfolk Birds demonstrates my great love of line and pattern to create form. The birds guarding the egg are based on godwits and the background is Stiffkey beach, a vast area of sand on the North Norfolk coast. We have walked this beach many times and the changing colour and light on the sand is something I have endeavoured to portray in this print.

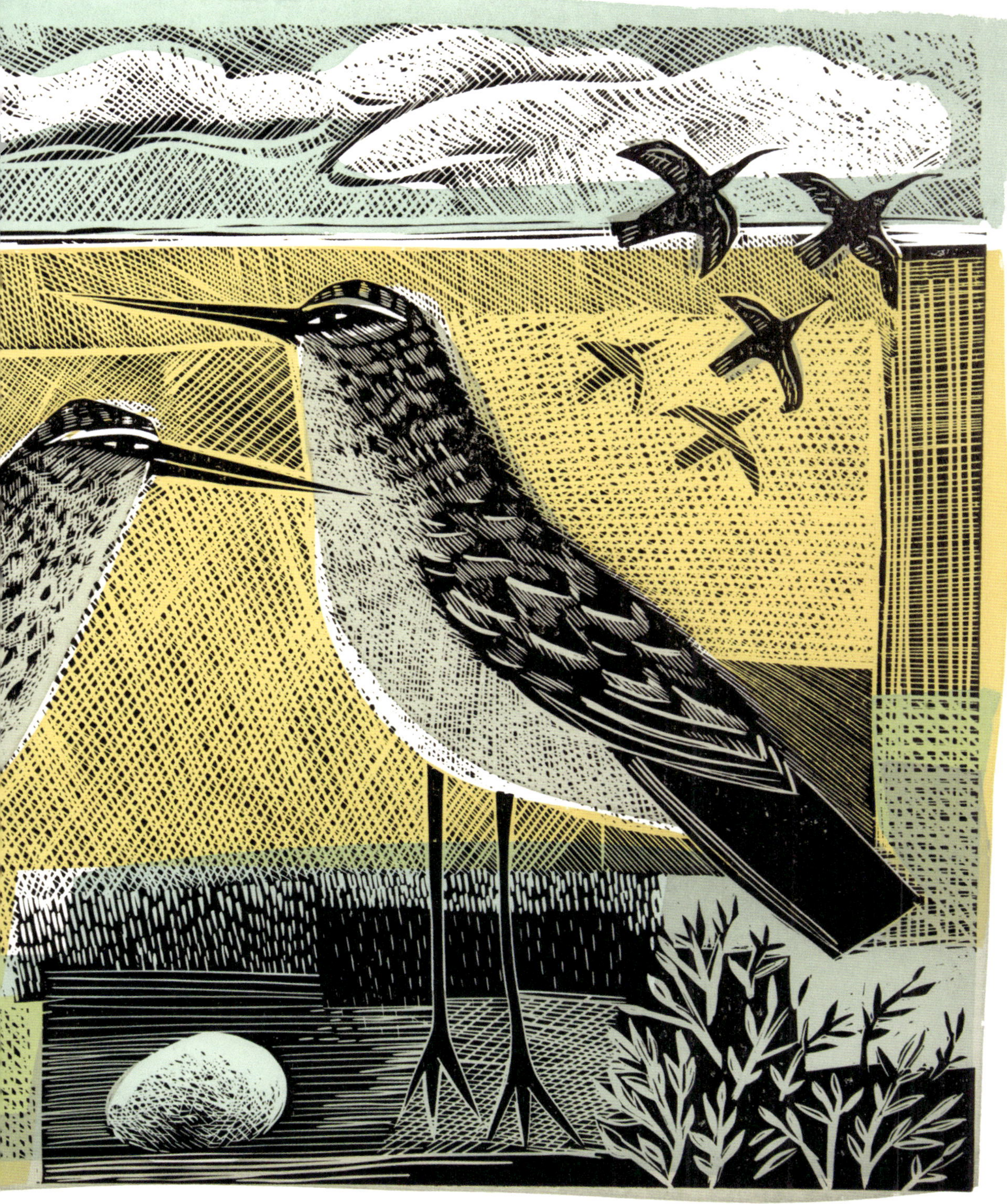

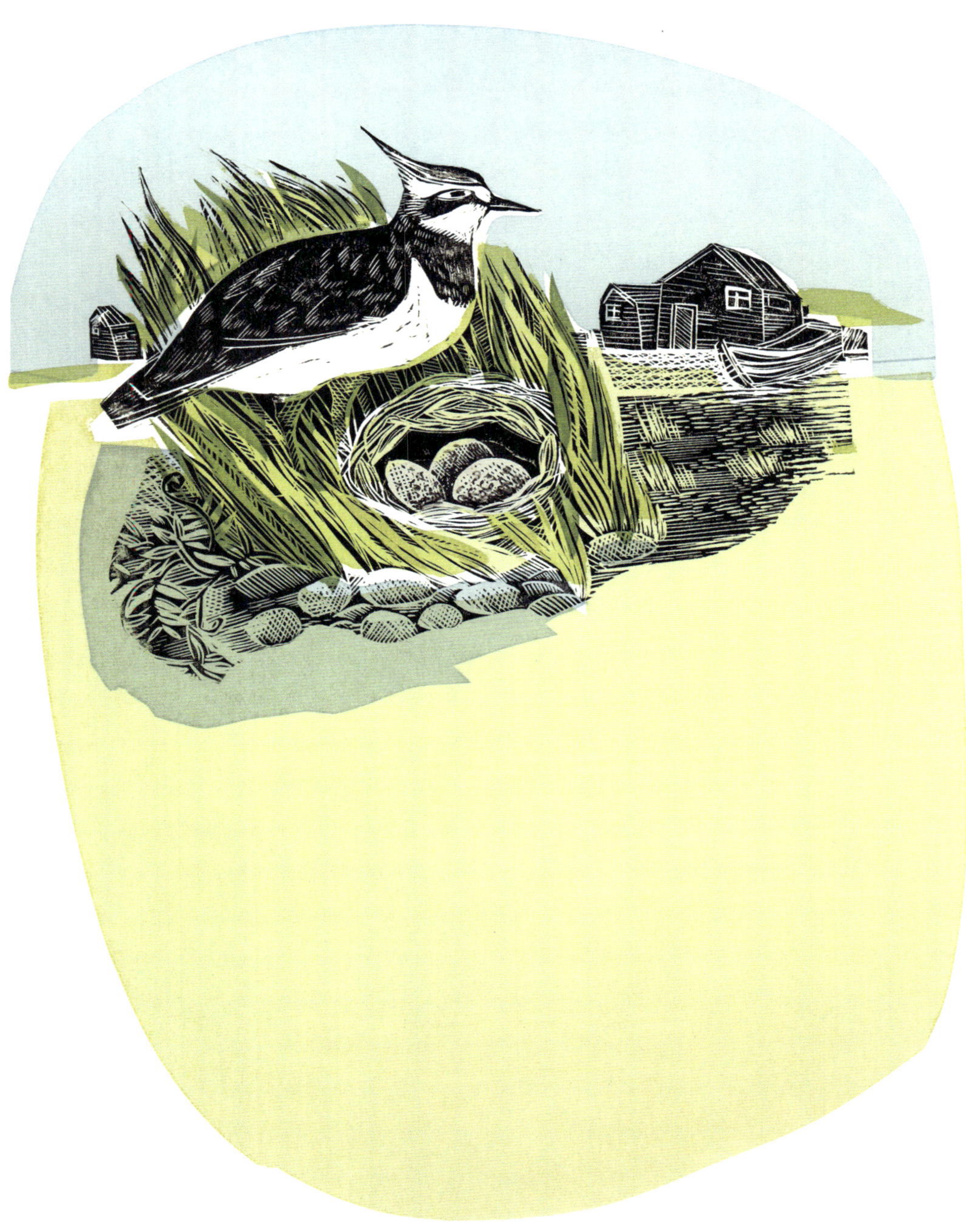

Lapwings Nesting

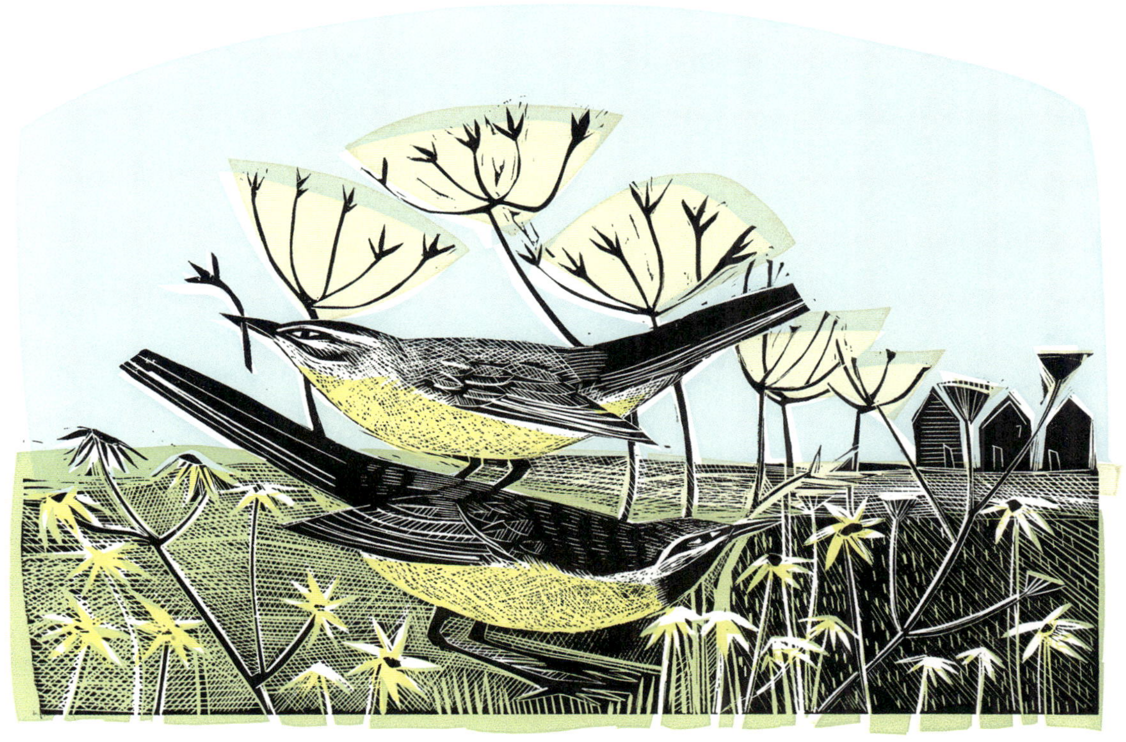

Wagtails and Daisy Fields

The Nightingale

Hearing a nightingale in full song just outside the Minsmere RSPB bird reserve remains a cherished memory. I was on my bike at the time and I had been heading to the reserve but was stopped in my tracks by the nightingale's song. It was in a thicket close to the road. I kept very still and to my amazement the bird came nearer and nearer. Though the song of the nightingale is unmistakable it is quite rare to see one. It looks very much like a drab robin without the red breast, but the song is very far from drab and once heard you can see how that sound has inspired artists and poets throughout the ages.

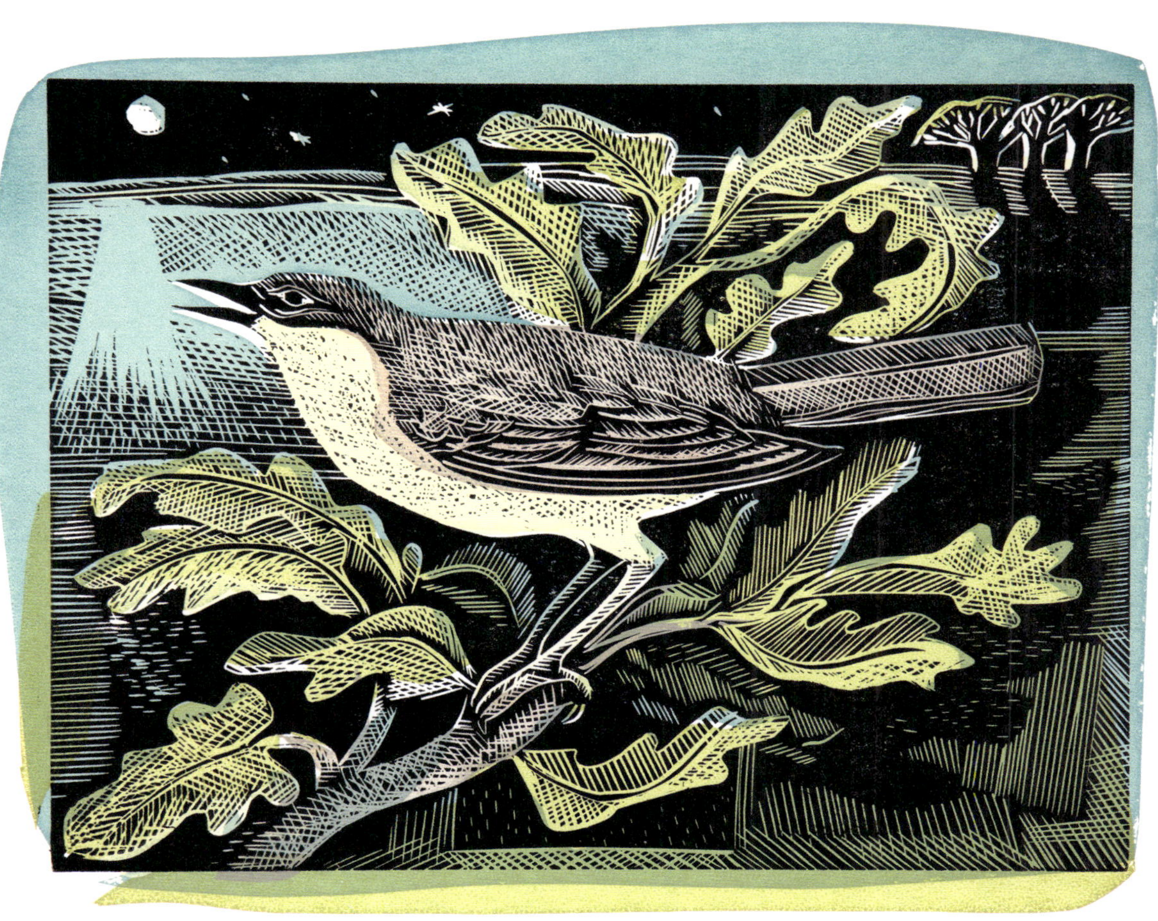

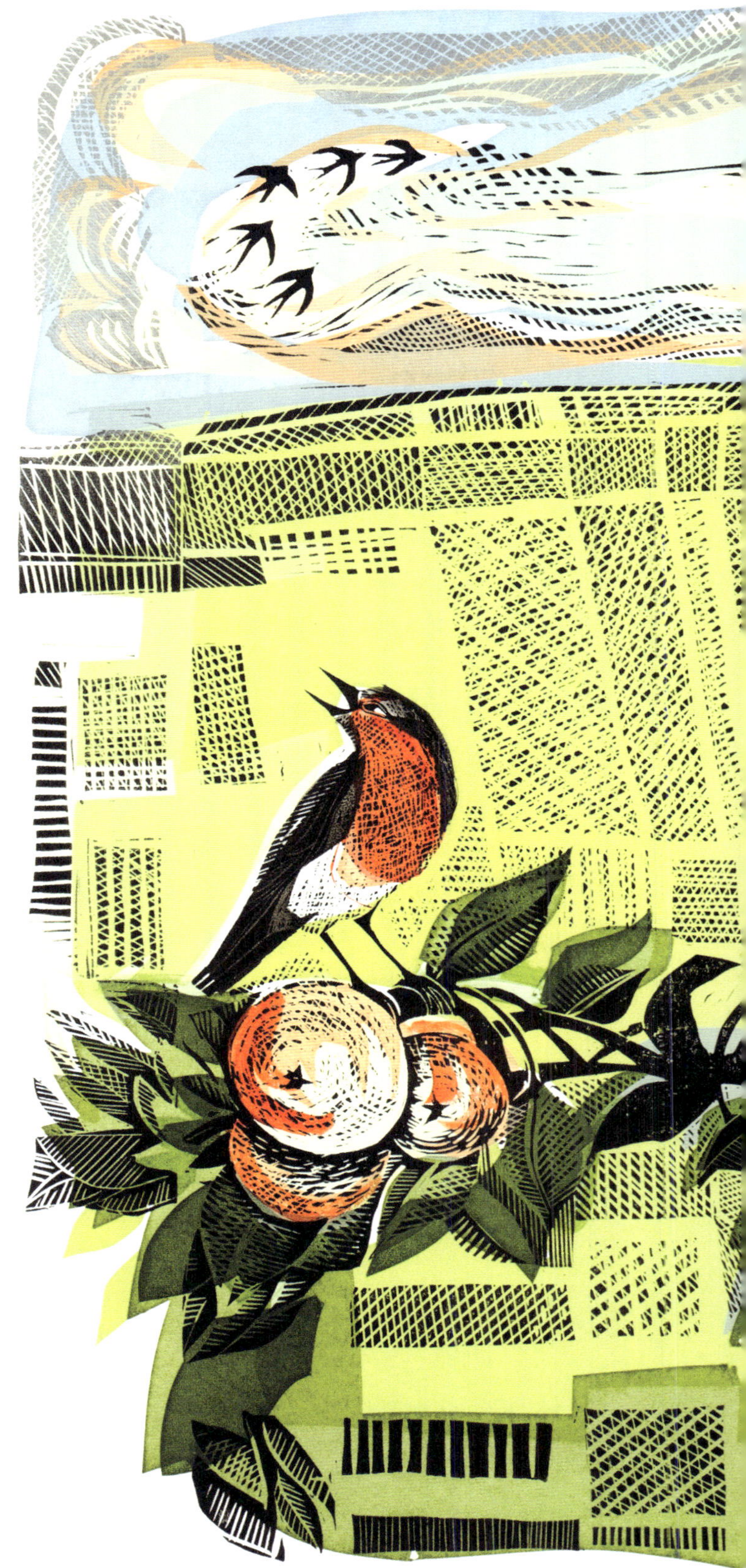

Keats's Nightingale

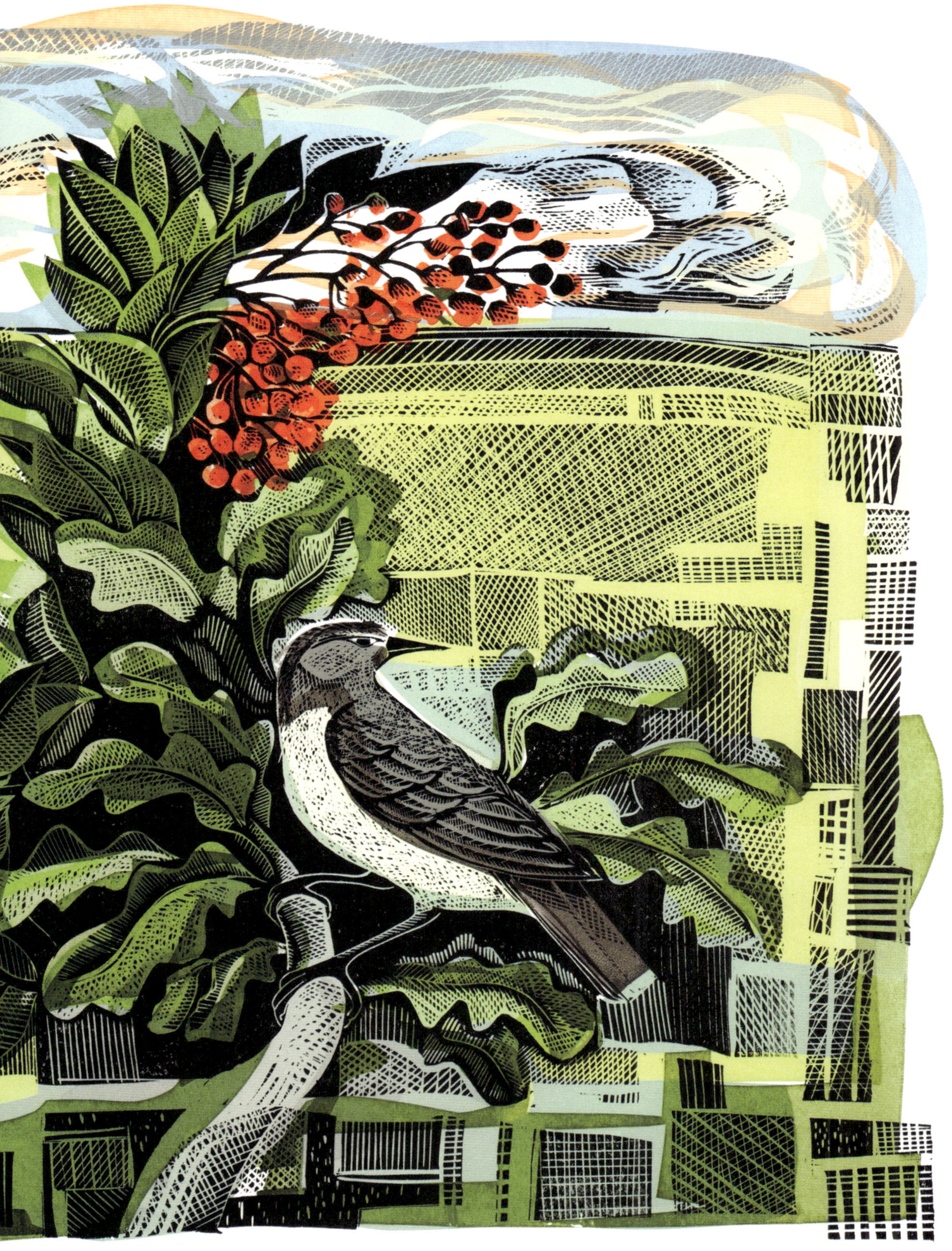

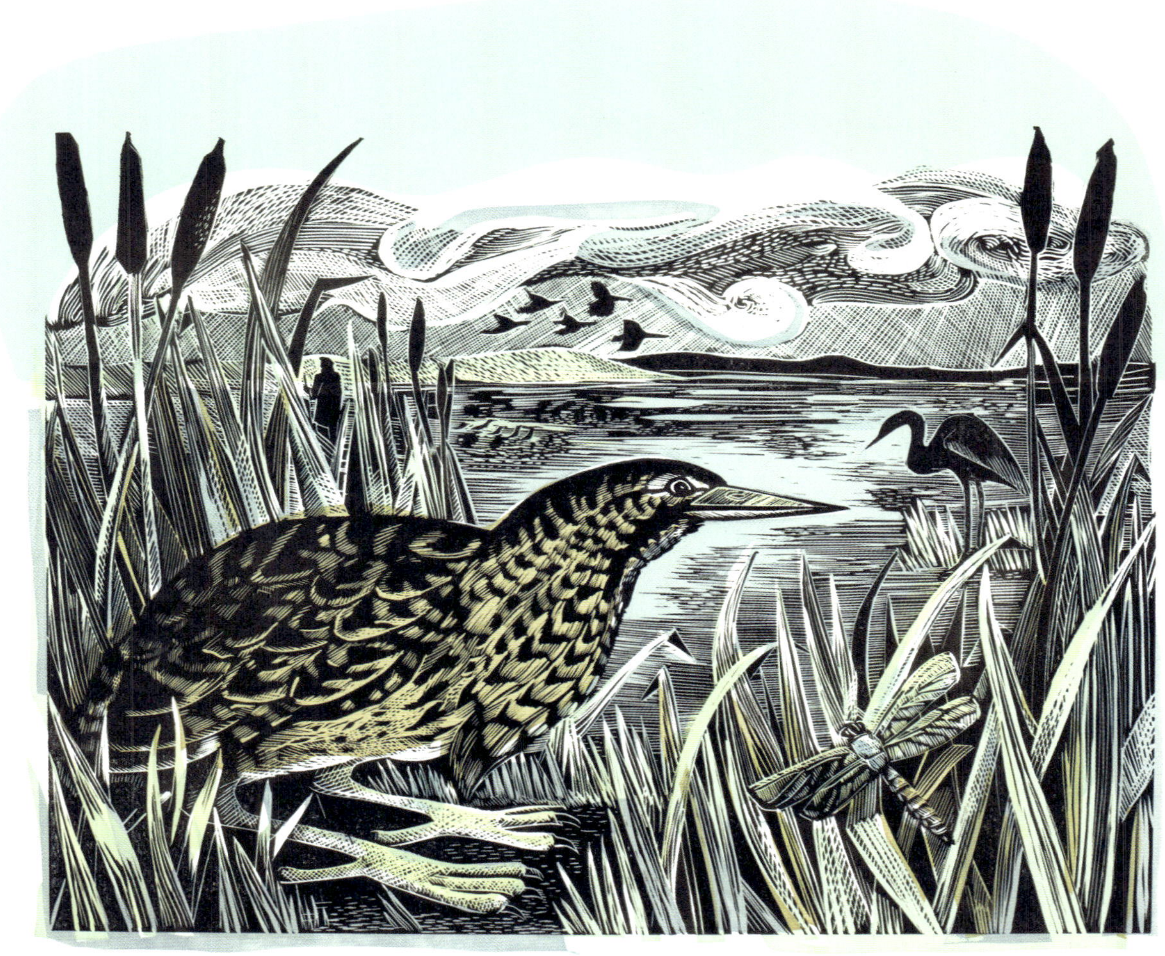

Bittern at Wetlands

Bitterns booming is the strangest of sounds: it's not a song, it is a boom of vibration that seems to go straight through you. Bitterns – once incredibly rare – are thankfully making a comeback and the bird hides at Minsmere bird reserve are the perfect place to hear and see them. You have to have sharp eyesight as they blend so perfectly with the reed beds that are their home.

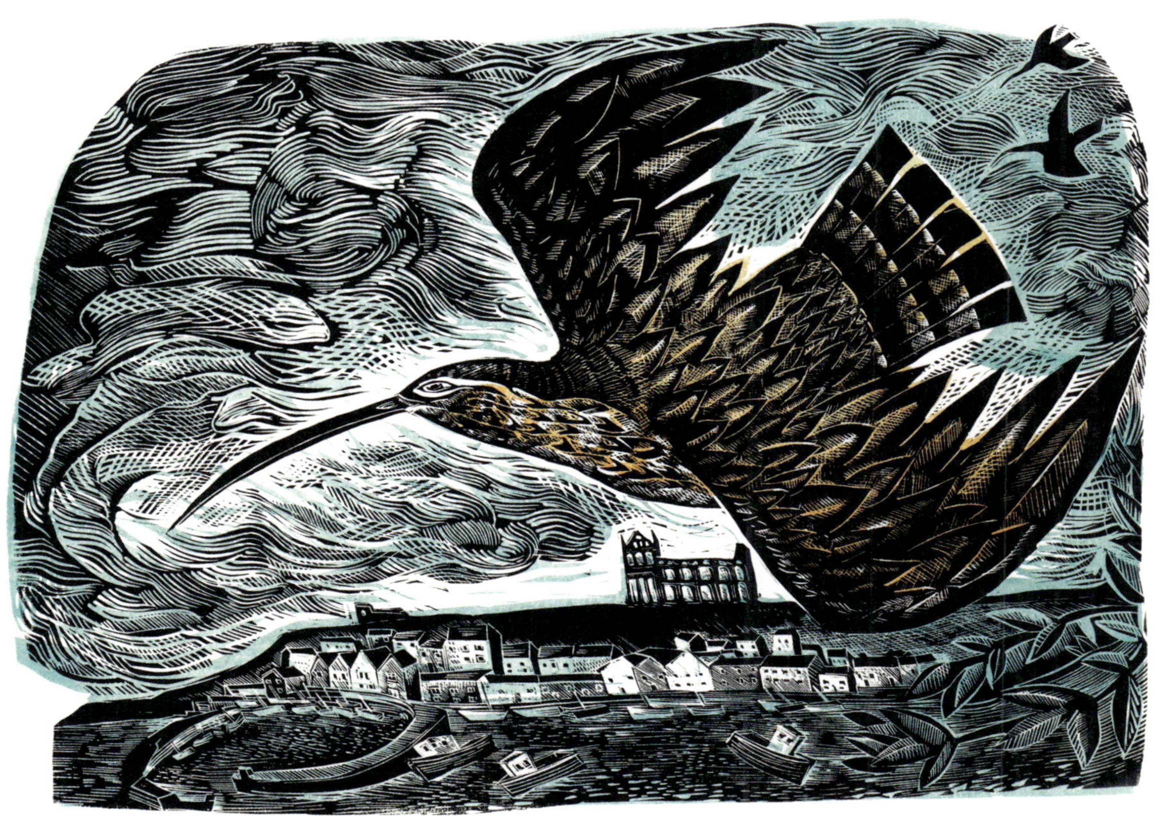

Curlew at Whitby

Curlew at Whitby is based on a memory of my youth when I spent time in North Yorkshire. In my twenties I went everywhere on a bicycle and completed a number of long journeys. A regular trip was cycling from Ampleforth (where my mother was living) to Whitby. There was no more welcome sight than that of the Abbey on the cliffs as you came down from the long ride across the always windy moors.

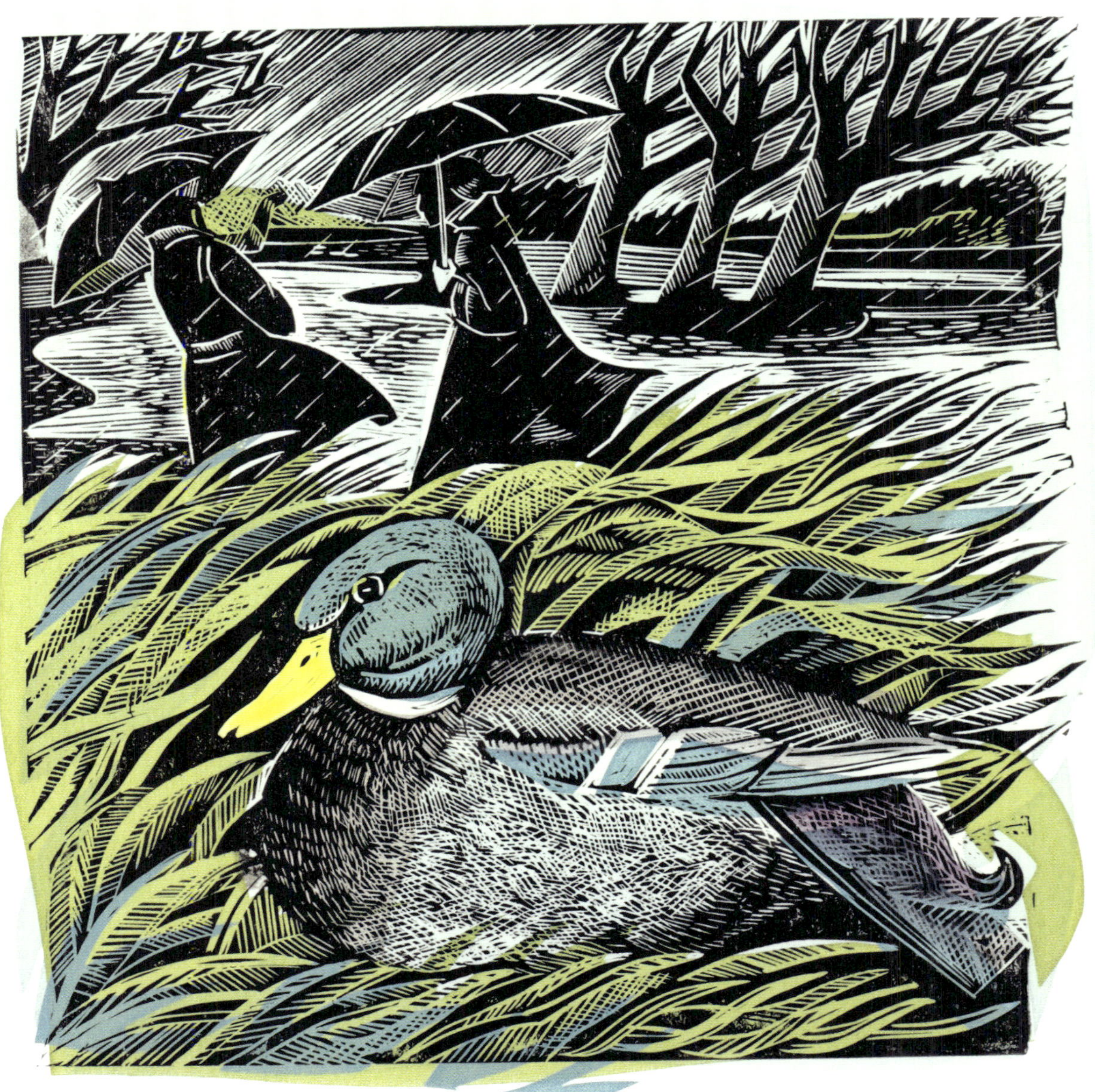

Rainy Days

When we are away on the boat it can't be sunny every day, but I enjoy rainy days just as much. There is something unbelievably cosy about being told by the weather it is a day to keep still, read a book or do some drawing. The sound of the rain on the boat's roof and the lapping of the waves against its sides is very soothing. The boat is only 24-foot long so not much space, but I have to say, as someone who is not very keen on housework, having your world reduced to one bunk, a small cooker, a kettle and a table is a treat! Birdwatching in the harbour is also a lovely thing to do; cormorants, herring gulls and swallows are a common sight. One afternoon we saw the less common sight of a cormorant catching an eel. Swallows often sit on the boat lines and you can peer through the portholes and get a close look at them before they launch out once more across the water.

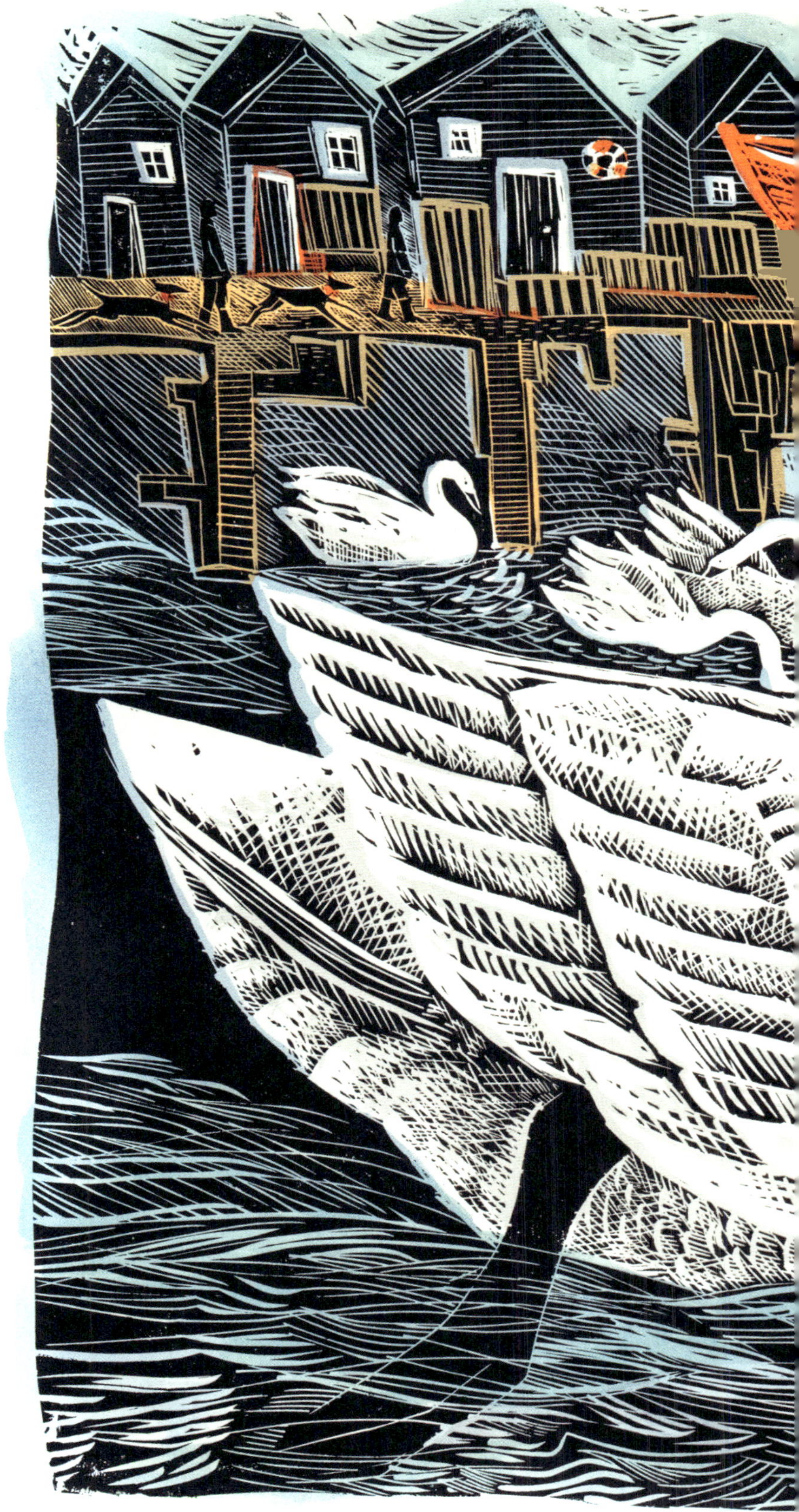

Southwold Swan

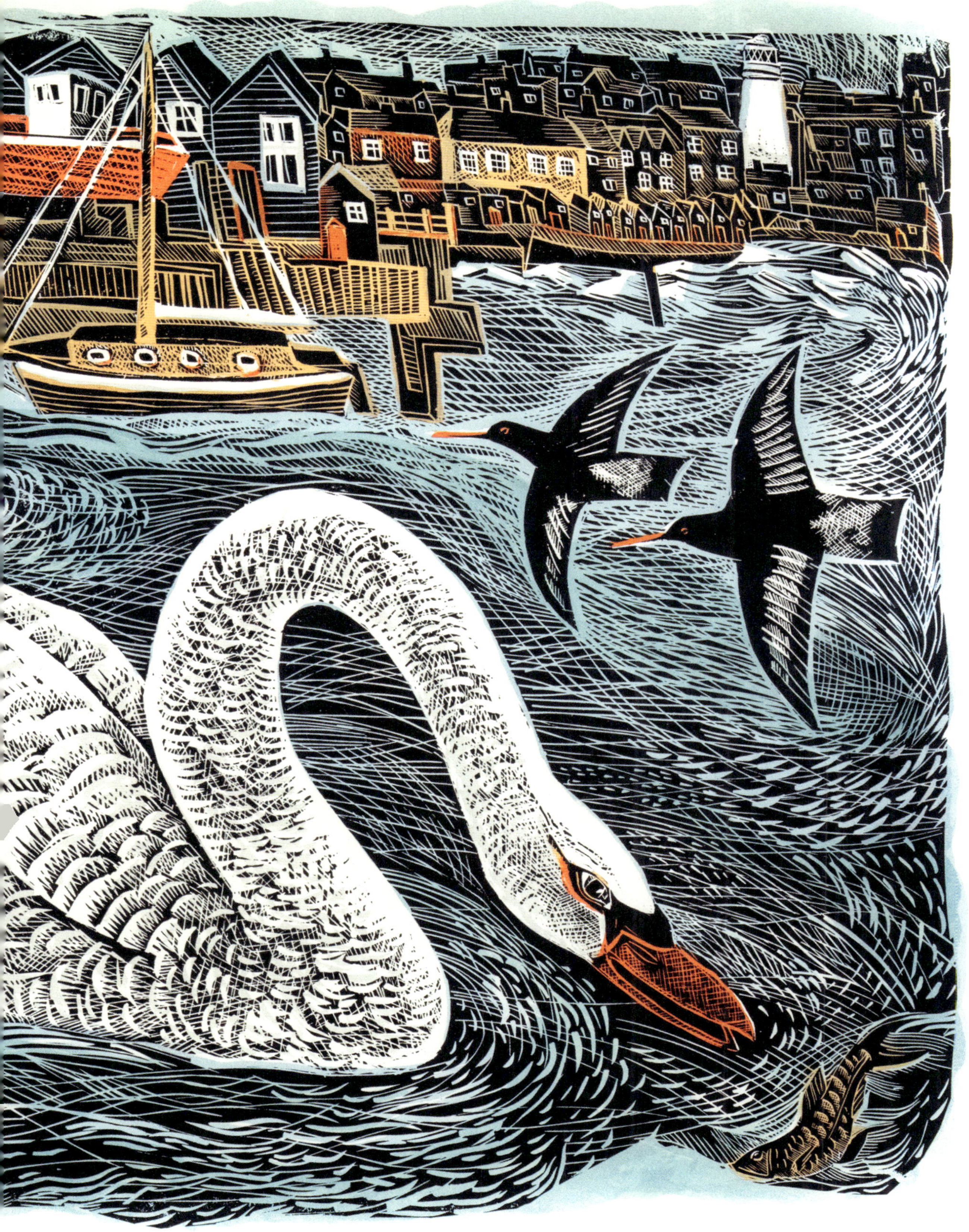

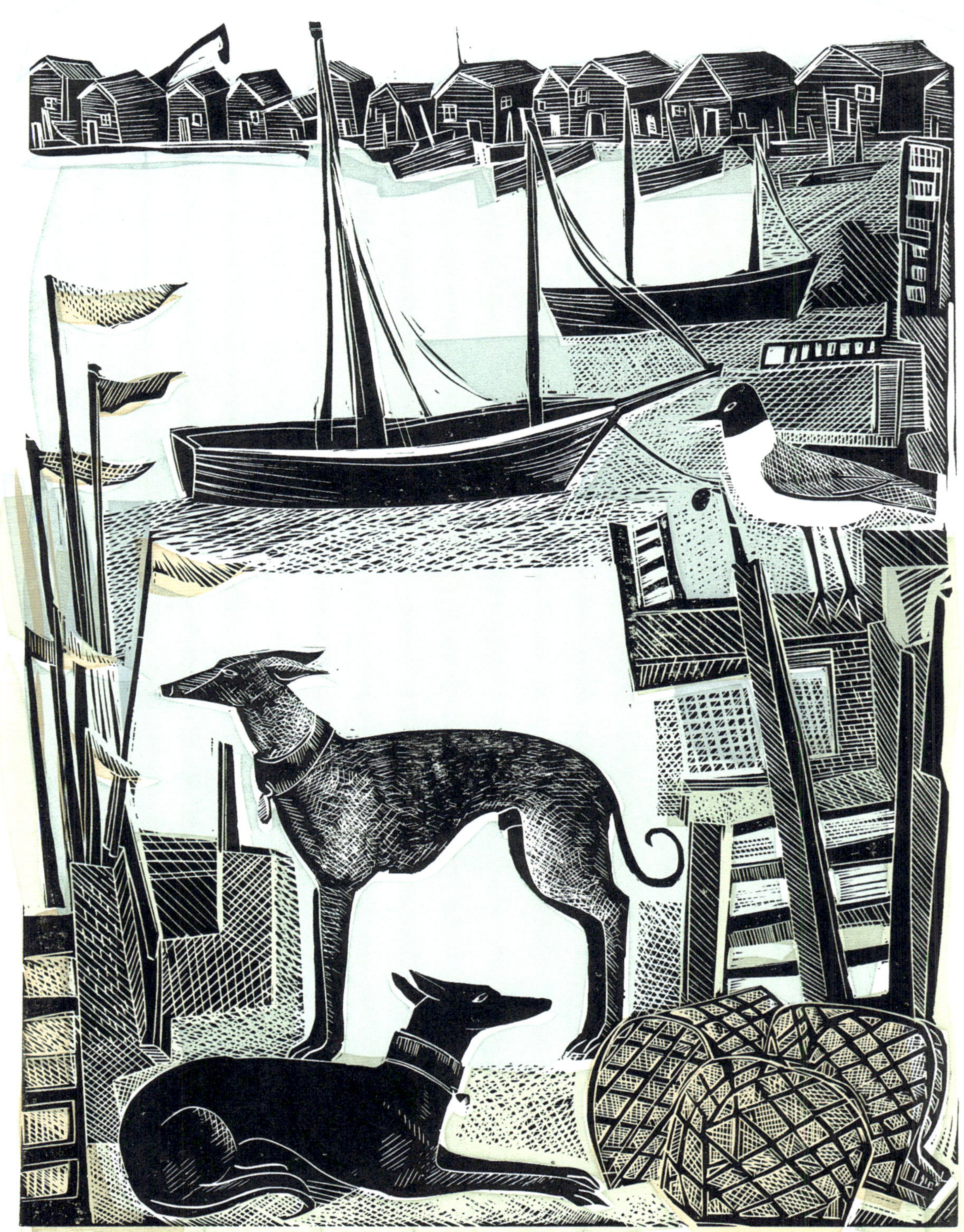

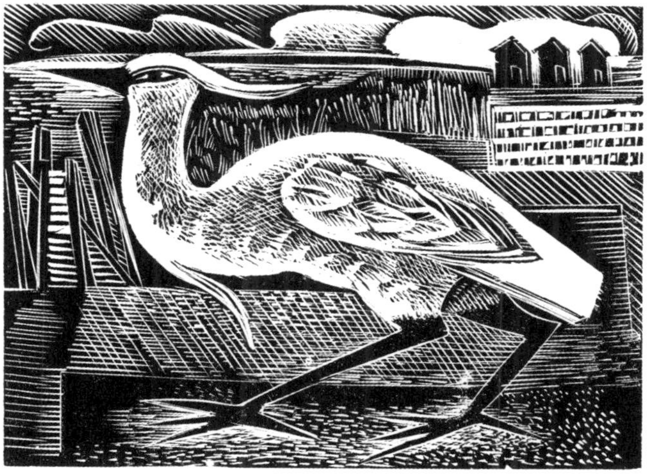

Egret

Harbour Whippets

Southwold Harbour is one of our favourite ports of call. We usually moor up on the Walberswick pontoon as it is always quieter on that side of the harbour: no road, just fields and the coastal path that leads in to Walberswick. Cattle graze in the fields beside the path and around them are white dots of egrets picking at insects thrown up by the cows' feet. The cattle egrets also appear alongside the boat and have the most fantastic yellow legs. They keep their heads amazingly still before darting forward to catch a fish. In the evening the fields fill with geese – large flocks of barnacle geese that fly in after spending the day inland. They announce their arrival with load honking calls that seem to say, 'Watch out, low-flying geese approaching.'

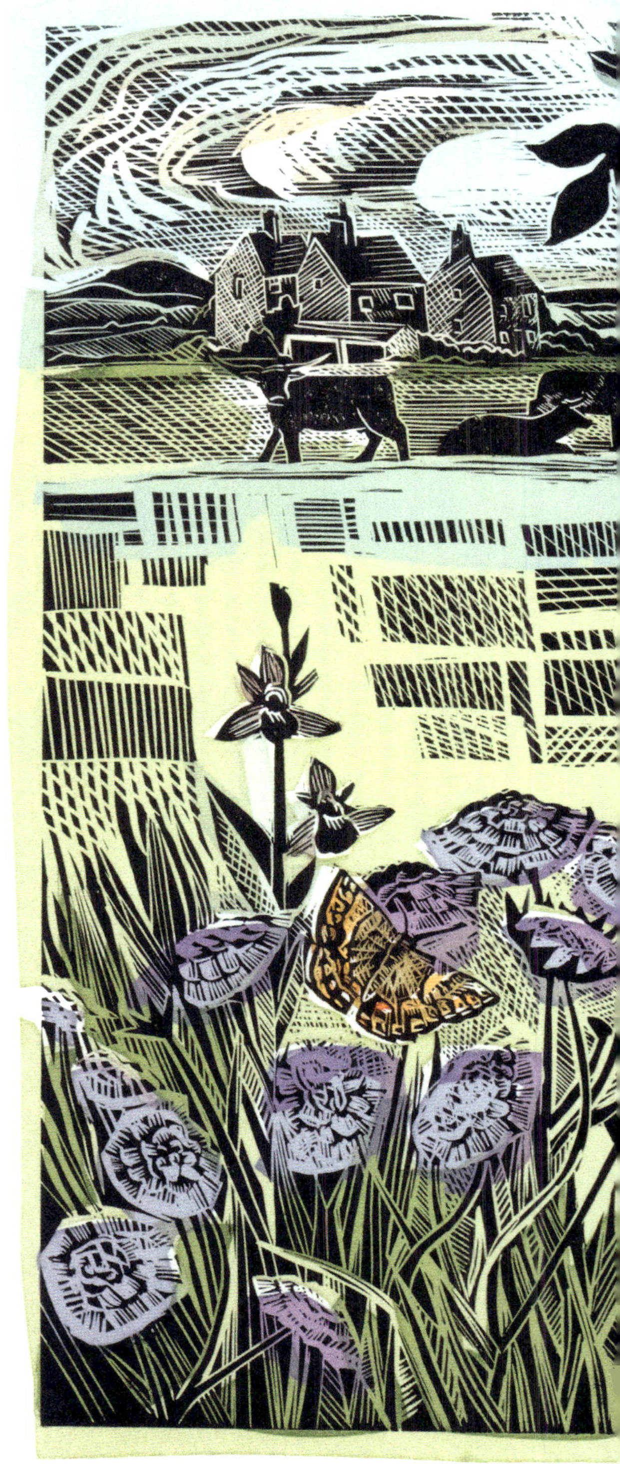

The Common

The Common close to Minchinhampton in Gloucester is a curious place as it seems to be both town and country in one. The road cuts across the chalk land which is home to orchids, rare blue butterflies, meadow pipits and cattle. All seem at home with the fact they live in a commuter belt.

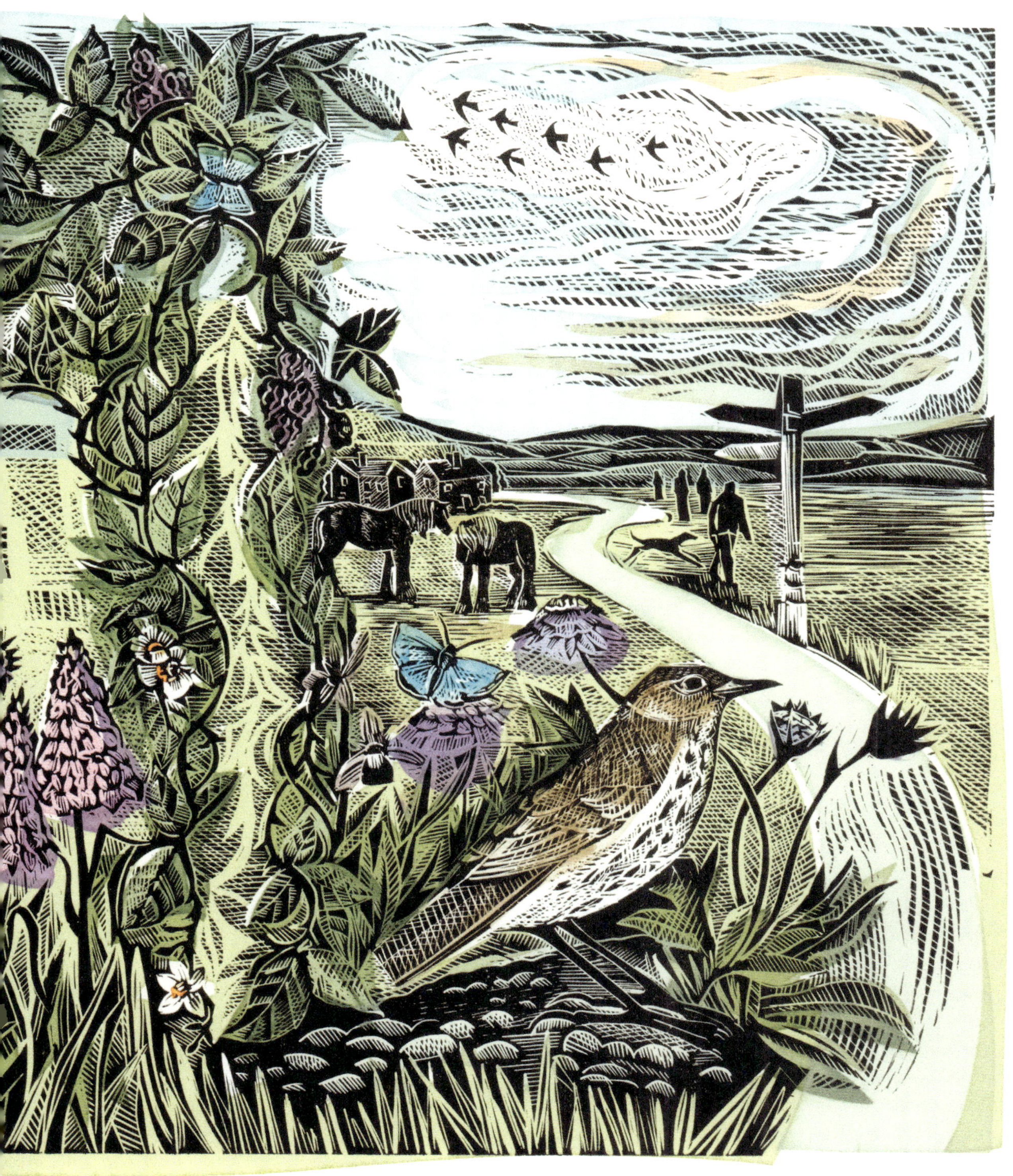

Terns at Sea

Arctic terns have the longest migration of all birds – a round trip of up to 35,000km (22,000 miles) each year. This is an illustration of them in flight through the waves, created for my RSPB book. Arctic terns feed in shallow coastal waters on small fish such as sand-eels, and nest on beaches and off-shore islands. We see them on our Suffolk trips but more often it is the common terns that we watch fishing from our boat. Roseate terns are not so common, but we once saw a large colony of them on Coquet Island, which is just off the Northumberland coast. We sailed out to the island on a beautiful blue-skied day and you knew you were getting closer as the bird noise intensified. We kept our distance, watching the birds from the boat, but the cacophony of noise was tremendous. There is only a lighthouse there and the occasional volunteer who counts the birds. I cannot see how they do that as the island was covered in a blanket of terns, guillemots, puffins and other sea birds. I would have thought there were simply too many to count. What it shows is how nature can swarm if it is given a chance and some space.

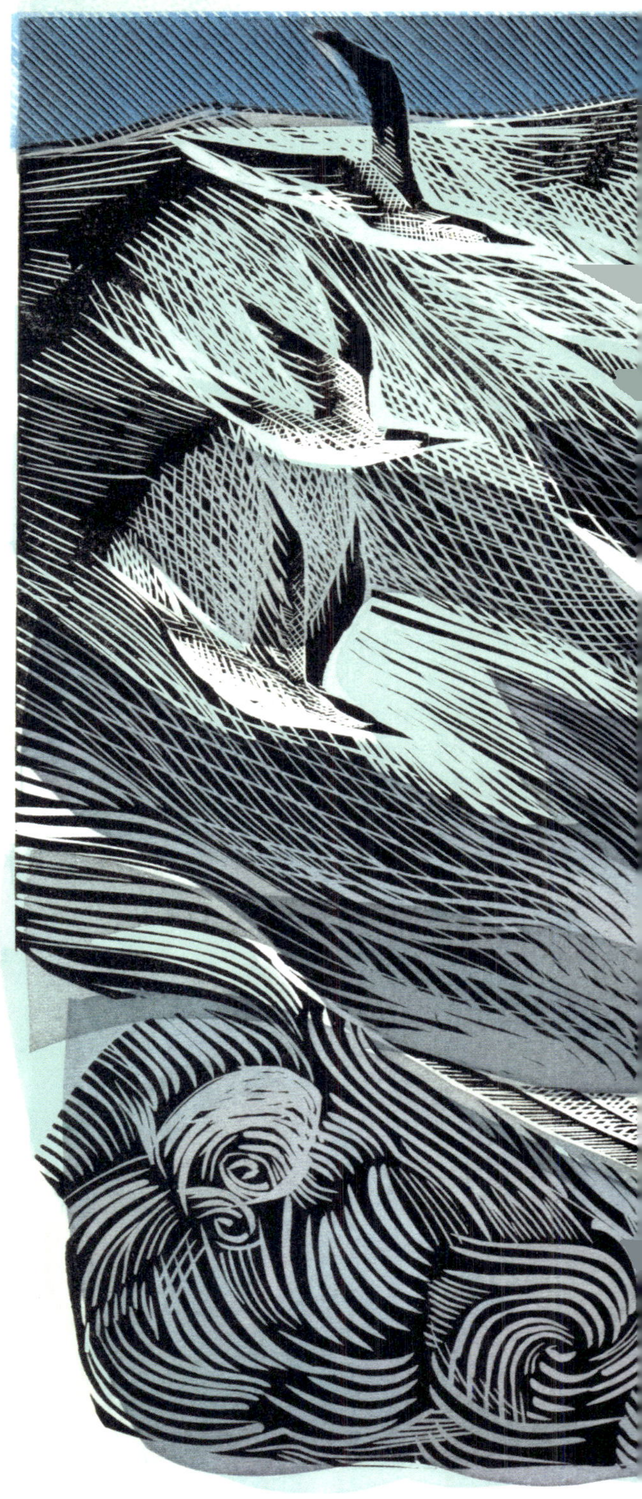

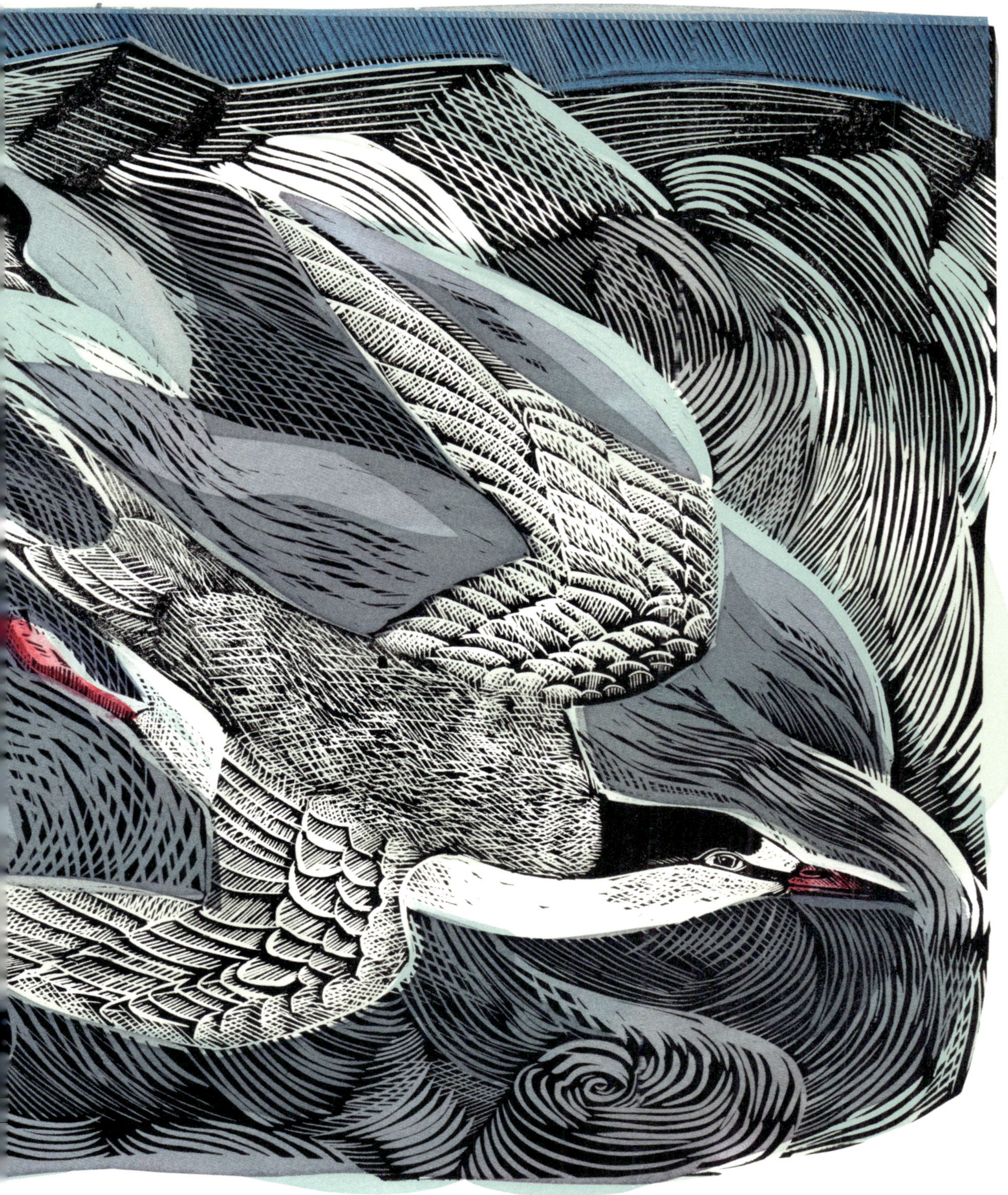

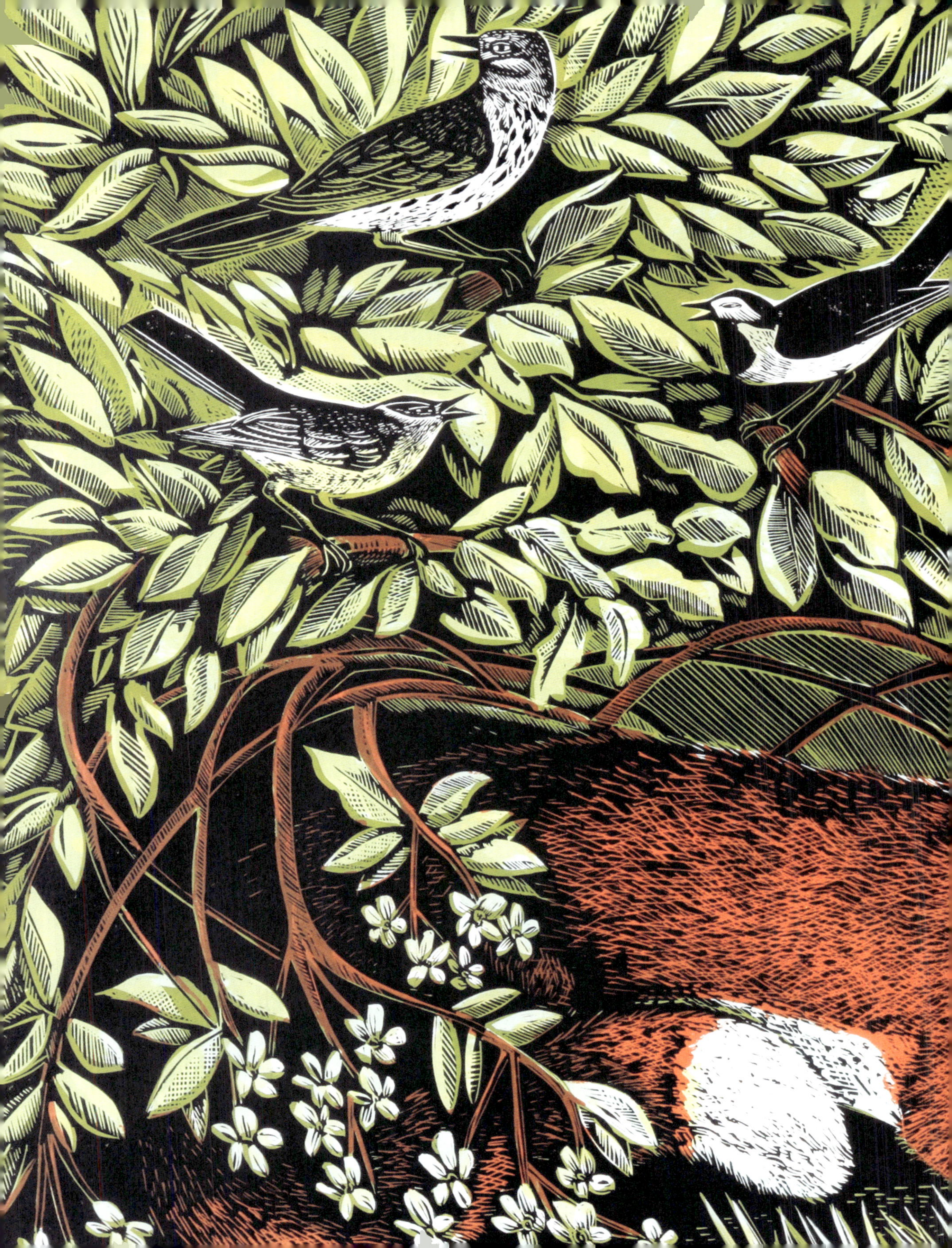

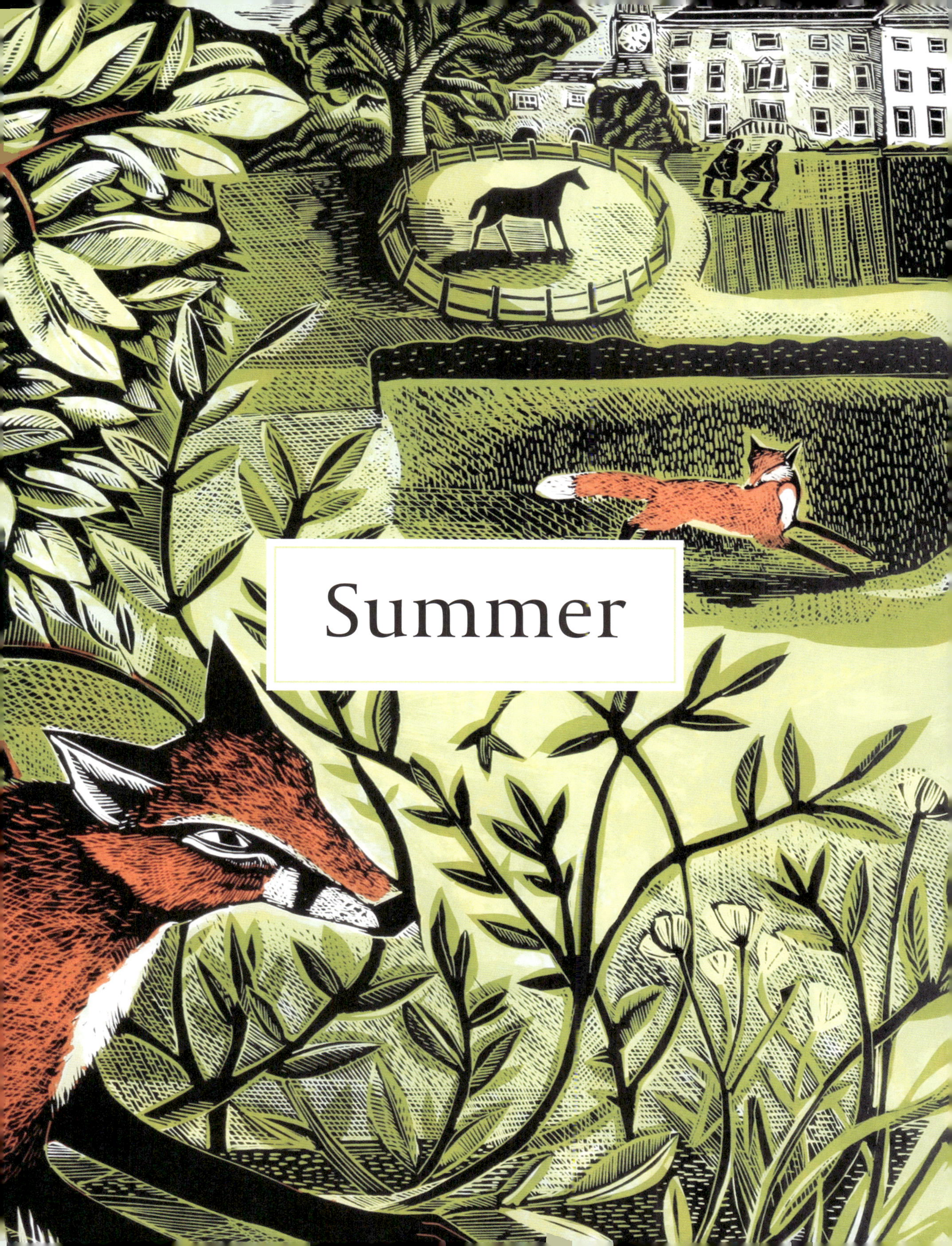
Summer

Tall nettles cover up, as they have done
These many springs, the rusty harrow, the plough
Long worn out, and the roller made of stone:
Only the elm butt tops the nettles now.
This corner of the farmyard I like most:
As well as any bloom upon a flower
I like the dust on the nettles, never lost
Except to prove the sweetness of a shower.

Tall Nettles
Edward Thomas

Summer

Blackbirds and Mulberries

Not all of my summer is spent the coast. I return home to catch up with work, the dogs and the garden – which manages to grow weeds at an almost astonishing rate! It suits us both to have time together and time alone. I am much more of a home bird than my husband and there is a great sense of freedom in knowing we are both happy in our worlds, together but with a hundred miles of breathing space – just for a few weeks before we catch up with each other again. When I get home there is always the garden to sort and the dogs for company, and by early summer the flock of Jacob sheep all have growing lambs. I am not sure what they have been crossed with but the lambs are all jet black. They are defiant markers of the year's progression as they change from long-legged wobbly infants to a gang of high-speed ramblers, all able to leap surprisingly high. They are indeed joyous but just a bit distracting from the work I need to do.

The other distraction that is always in need of some attention is the garden. As we are away for so much of the summer I do not grow many edibles, but a section of the garden is laid down to raised beds that have always been intended as use as a kitchen garden. There are strawberries, artichokes, bronze fennel, red and blackcurrants. Though these are intended for our table they are mainly eaten by the birds. I know you can net them, but I think the birds need them more than we do!

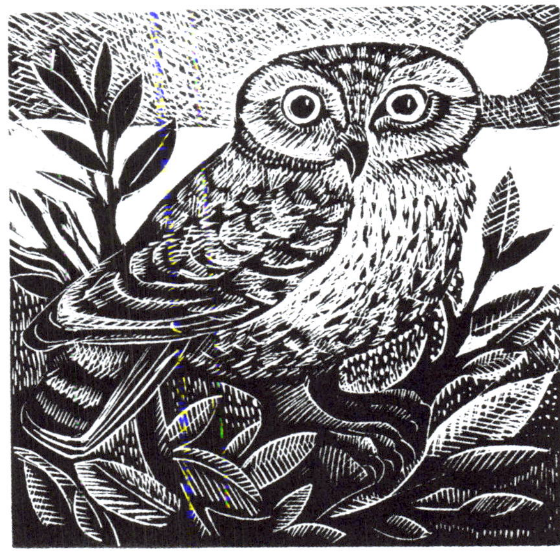

Little Owl

Moon Walk

An English summer has long days of sunlight and warmth – which is such a contrast to winter when the sun has gone by 4pm. Warm summer nights mean watching nature at night time can become a preferable activity. A few years ago, I was commissioned by BBC *Countryfile* magazine to do two images about night walking without a torch. The writer described how if you go out at night without a torch your eyes soon become accustomed to the light and you will see much more than you would have thought possible. The illustration called Moon Walk is a bit of an exaggeration of what you might hope to see on one night, but I have tried to give that sense of adventure. The woodland at night is not a place of rest but a hive of activity, filled with snuffling badgers, hunting foxes and hooting owls.

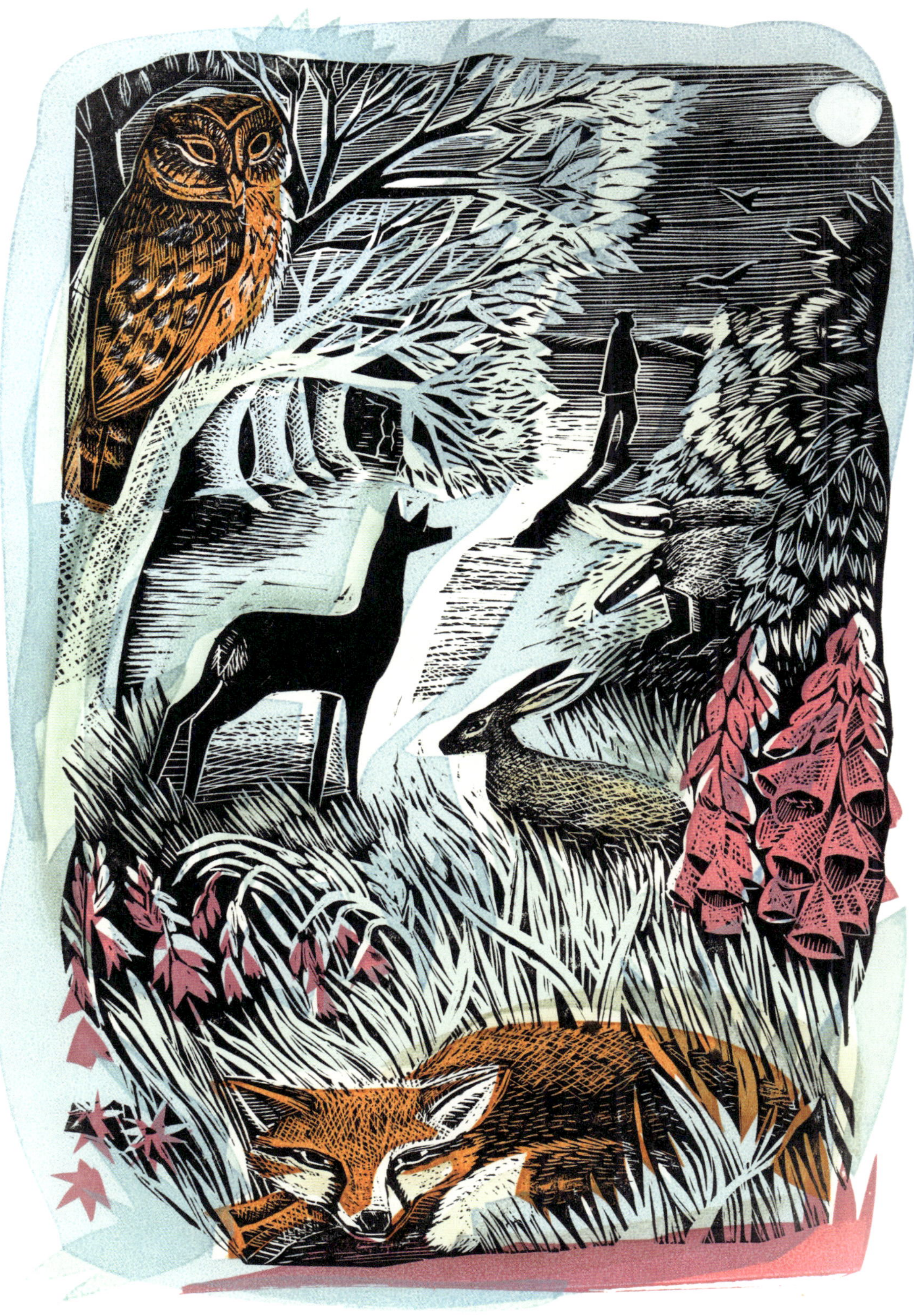

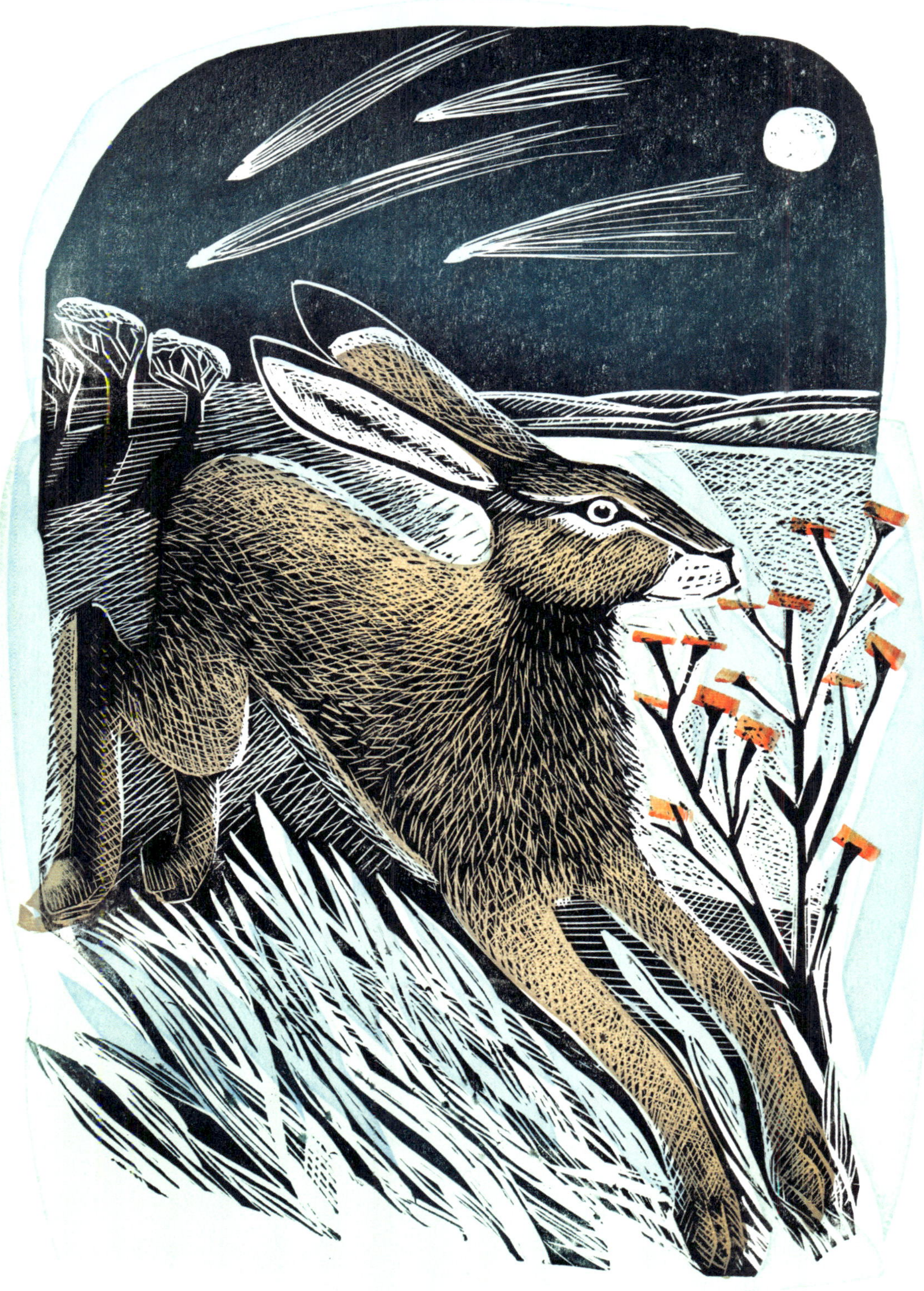

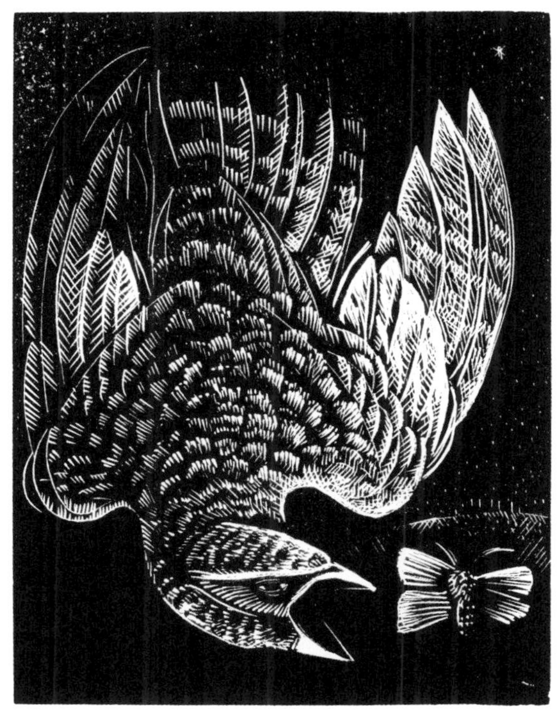

Nightjar

Shooting Stars

Shooting Stars was also commissioned for the same article. In this illustration I have portrayed a leaping hare set against a sky of shooting stars. This is because the writer described lying down in a field to watch shooting stars – he lay so still that much to his amazement a hare leapt over him.

Fishing Otter

One British wildlife experience I have not yet encountered is an otter. They are notoriously shy and even though you can be close they are hard to see. So, when Mark announced he would be sailing to Shetland I felt certain I was bound to see an otter. Mark sailed up the East Coast then up to Orkney, Fair Isle and then moored up in Lerwick Harbour on the Shetland Mainland. I went my usual train and bike route: Oakham to Aberdeen, a quick pedal up the Dene way and back before getting the overnight ferry to Shetland. Mark was waiting in Lerwick Harbour as he was staying a month touring the main and surrounding islands, but I just had a week. High on my list of what I wanted to see was otters, but it was not to be. The rest of the wildlife was stunning though, particularly the birdlife, and I will never forget seeing the gannet colonies on Noss, literally thousands of birds soaring and diving into the most beautiful clear turquoise water. The charm of being so close to puffins who have so much character and beauty – but no otters. We went to all the recommended places but not a one.

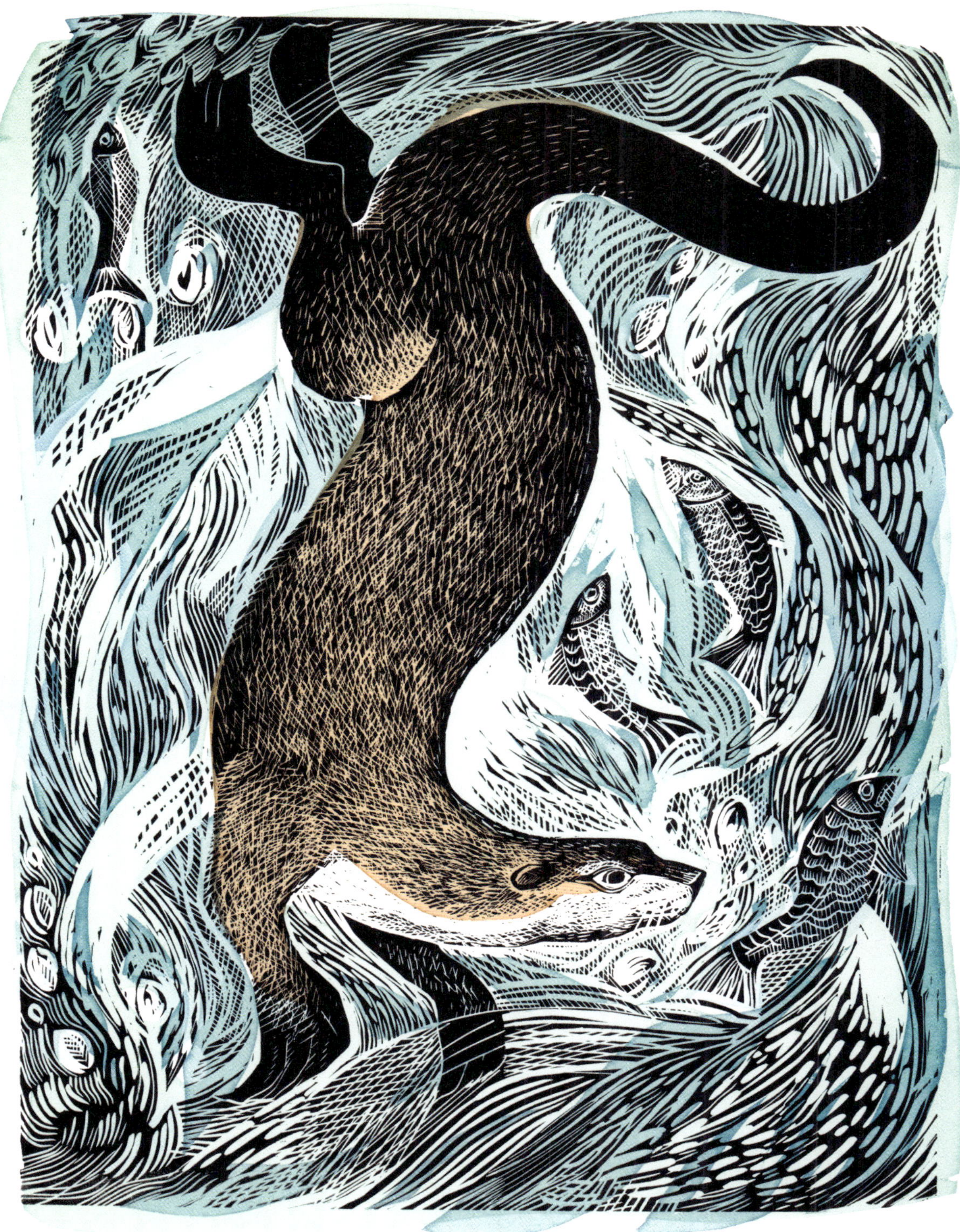

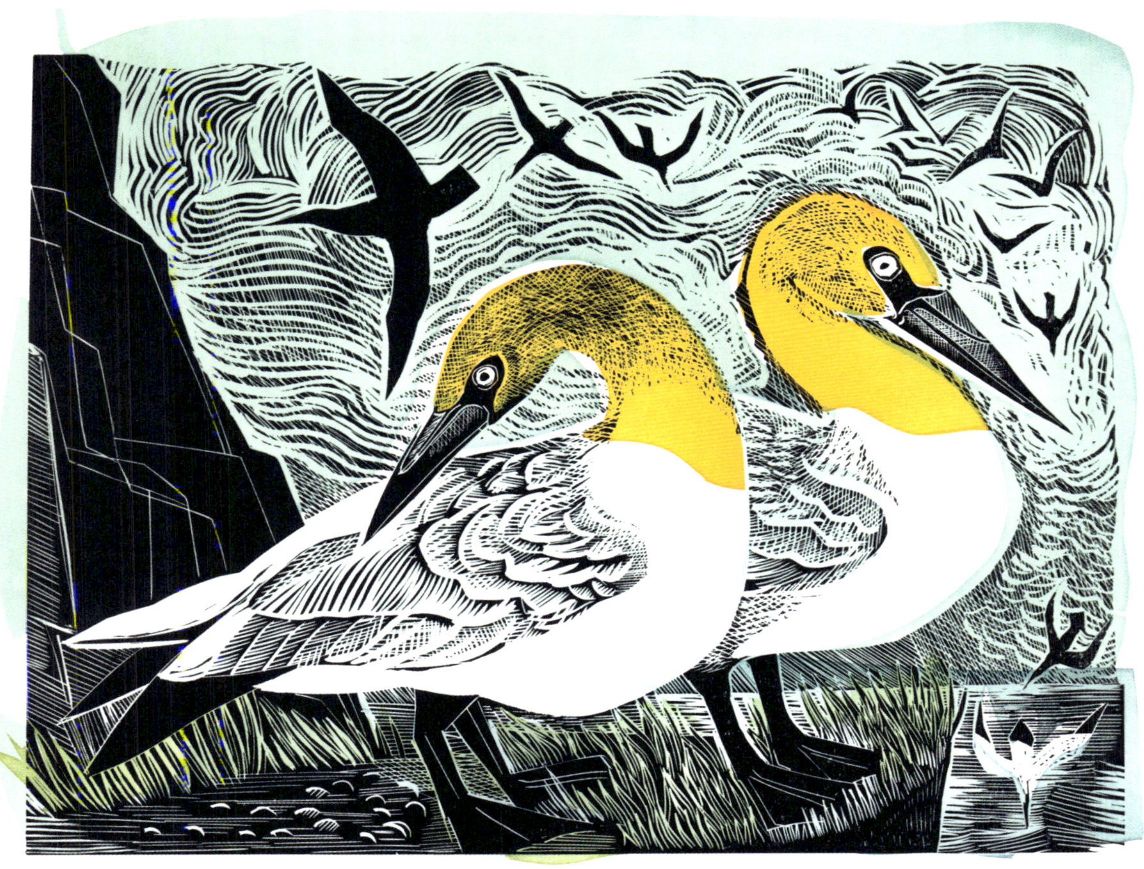

Two Gannets

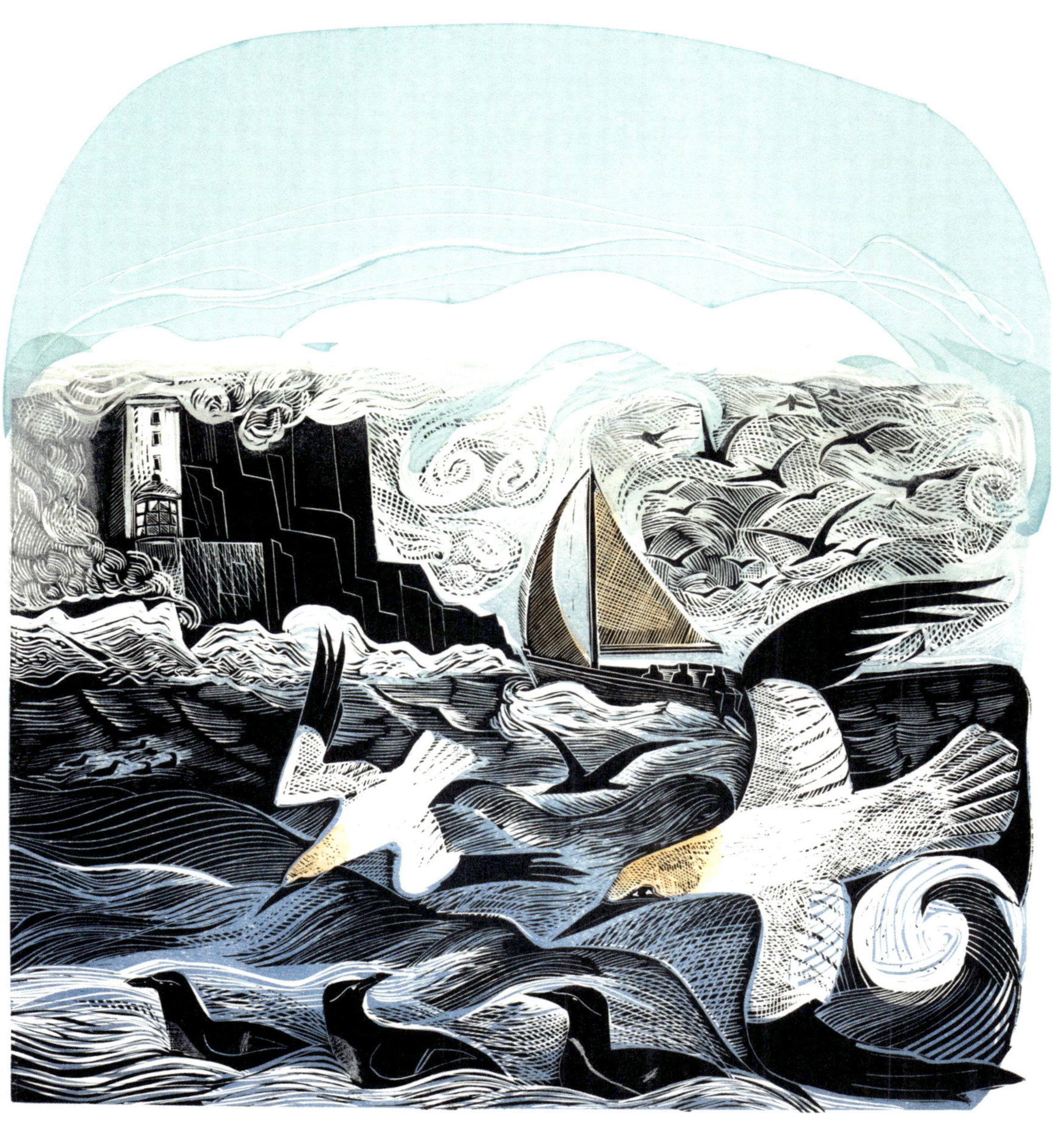

Gannets at Rathlin Island

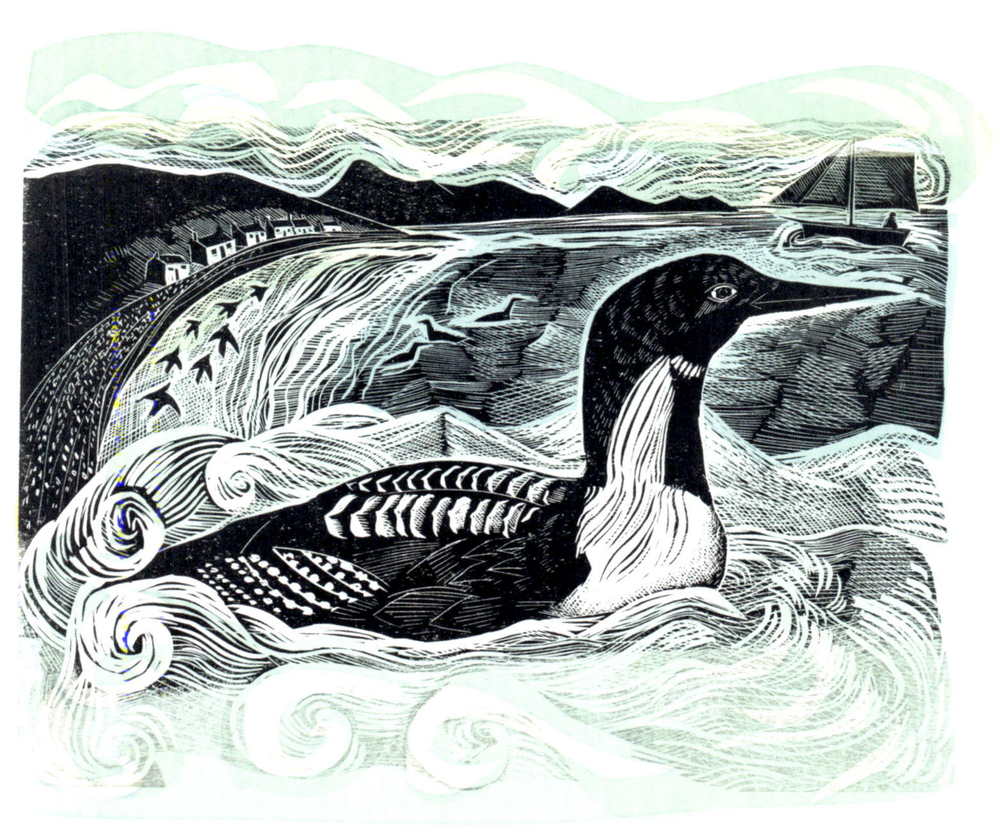

Black-Throated Diver

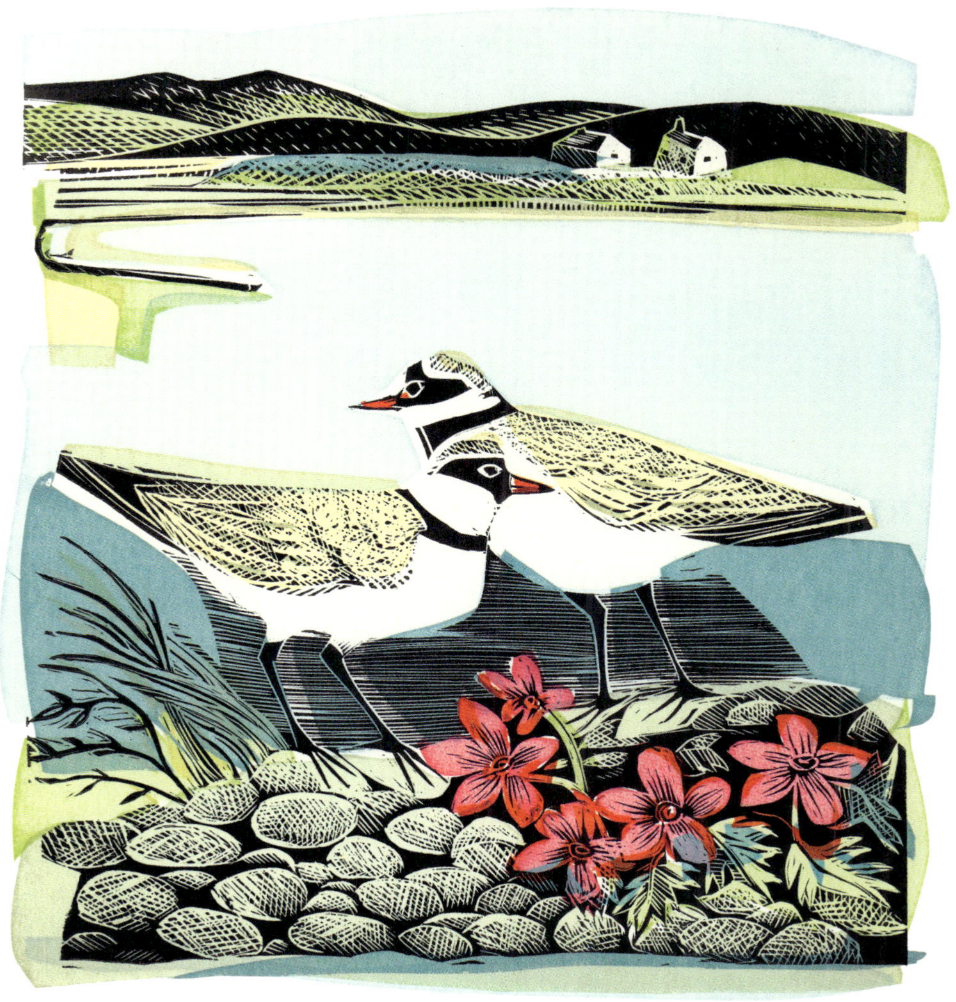

Plovers and Pinks

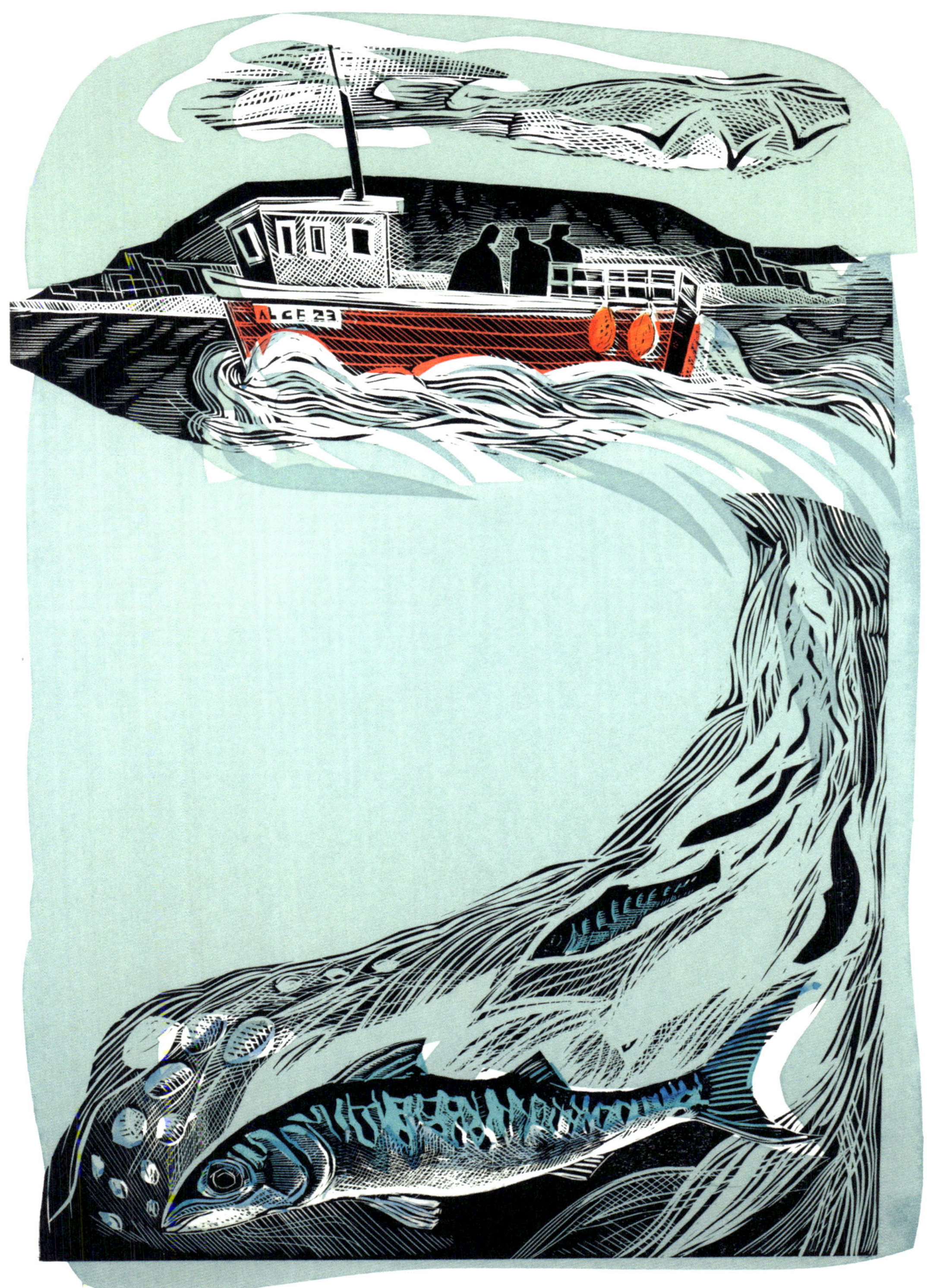

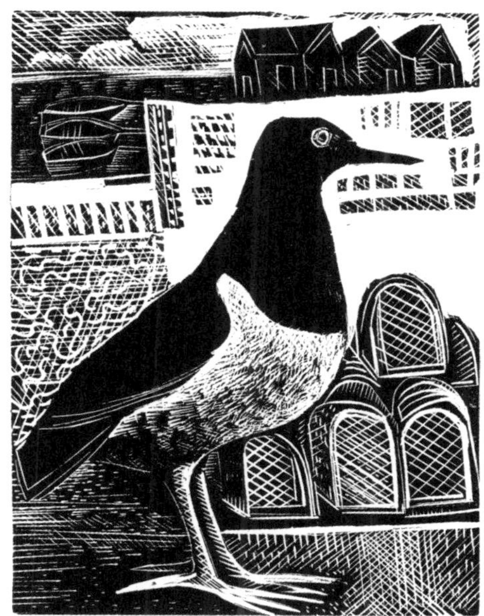

Oystercatcher

The day came when I had to head home for work and leave Mark to sail back. When I got home I rang to see if all was well. 'I'm not sure I should tell you this,' said Mark in a rather worried voice. Oh dear, what had happened! I was imagining all sorts – the boat gone – but no, all was fine. Mark was back on *Windsong*, still moored in Lerwick which is a busy town. He had been having his breakfast as usual on the back of the boat when he looked up and at the end of the pontoon was an otter also having breakfast. Mark said the otter was so close you could smell its fishy breath (I think that is an exaggeration myself!). He then went and asked the harbour master if this happened very often. 'Oh yes – most days! But the best place if you want to be sure to see an otter is the roundabout just outside Tesco . . .' The Tesco roundabout had not been mentioned in the wildlife guides I had read!

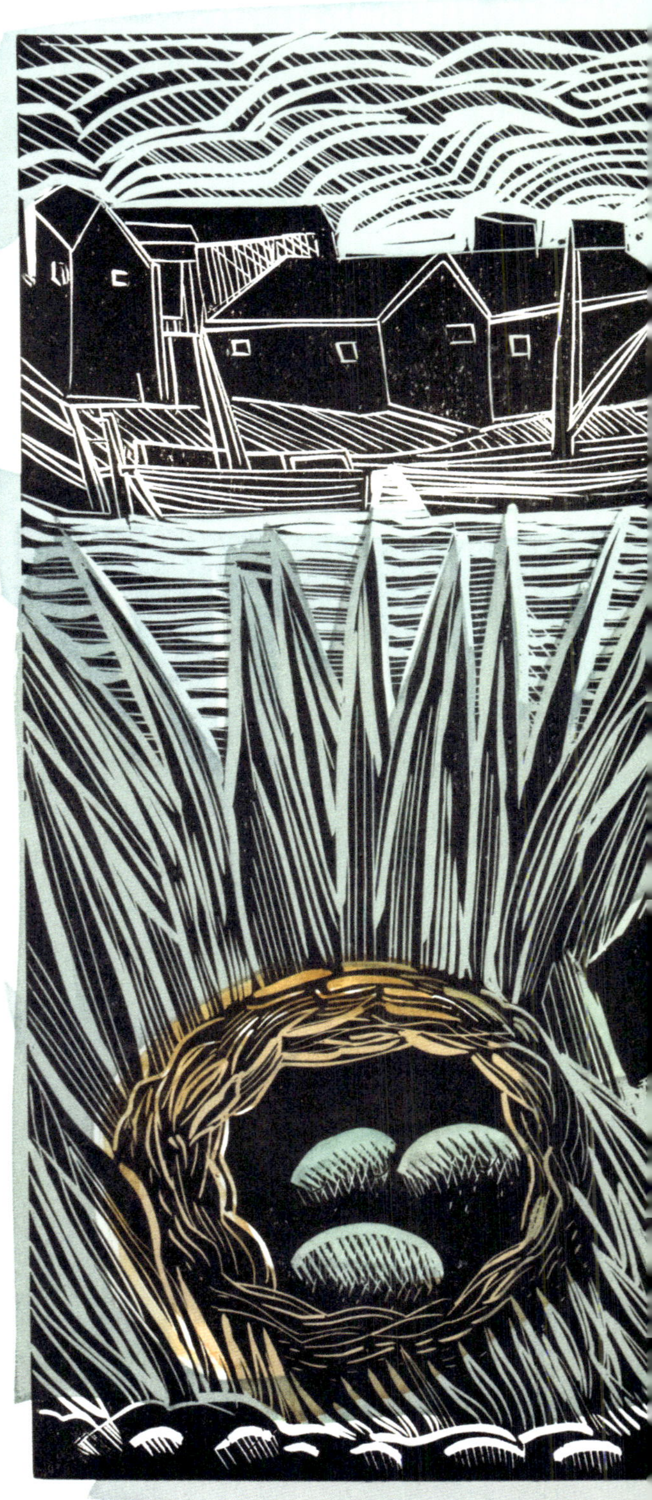

Snape Maltings

A regular summer stop on *Windsong* is visiting Snape Maltings in Suffolk. We are able to do this as *Windsong* has a lifting keel. She was built for the Essex rivers, so her shape allows us to use rivers that have quite shallow water. Mark is very good at navigating through winding thin strips of water that are marked only by wispy withies (willow sticks). Even though we have done this a number of times it does mean the occasional grounding on sand banks and quite a lot of swearing from my husband. Moving through the reed beds that spread out in all directions is fantastic for watching wildlife. In the evening as the light dims we often see barn owls hovering over the marsh, the beautiful colours of the barn owl echoing the colours of the reeds, and if we are very lucky we sometimes see merlins hunting moths.

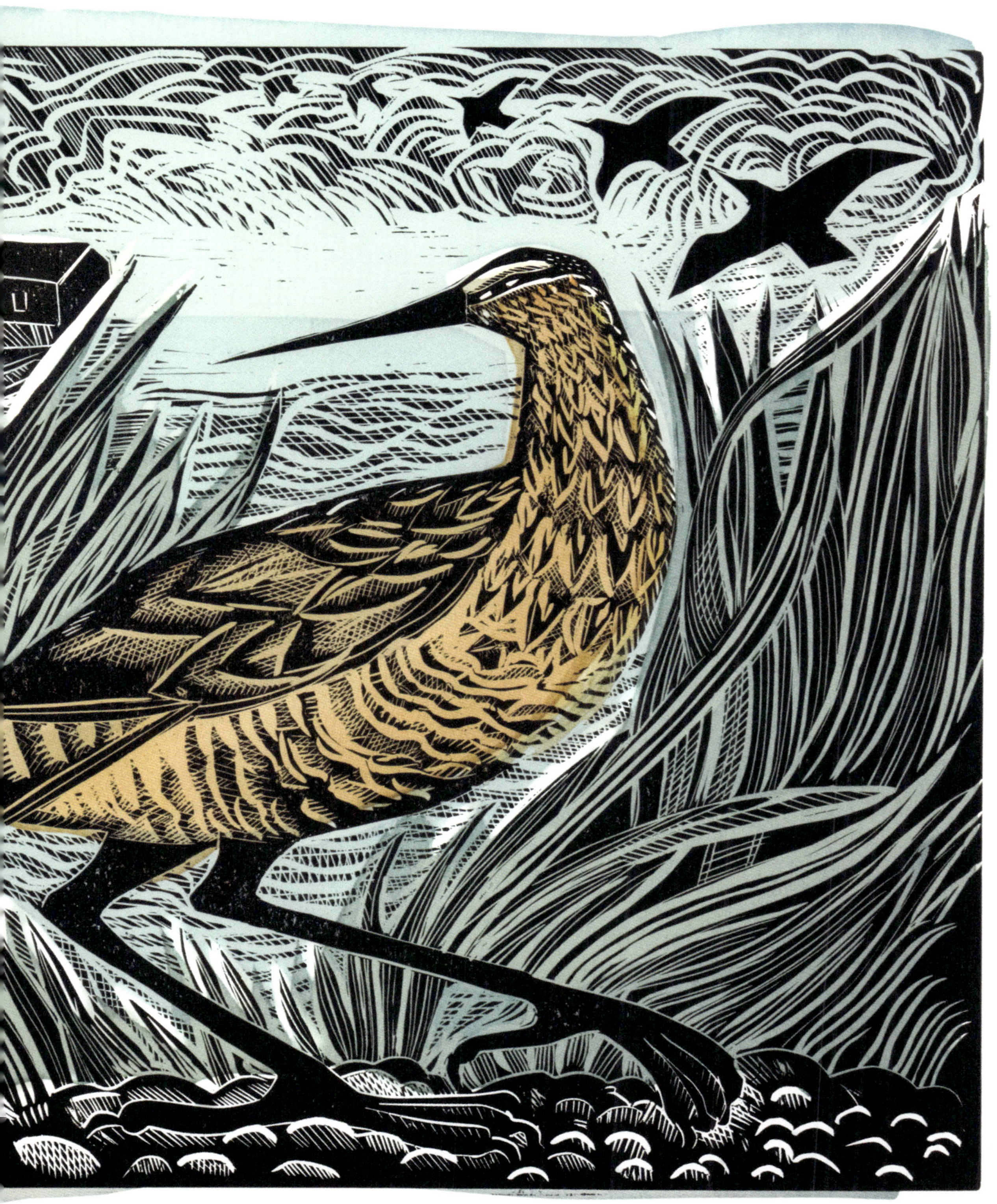

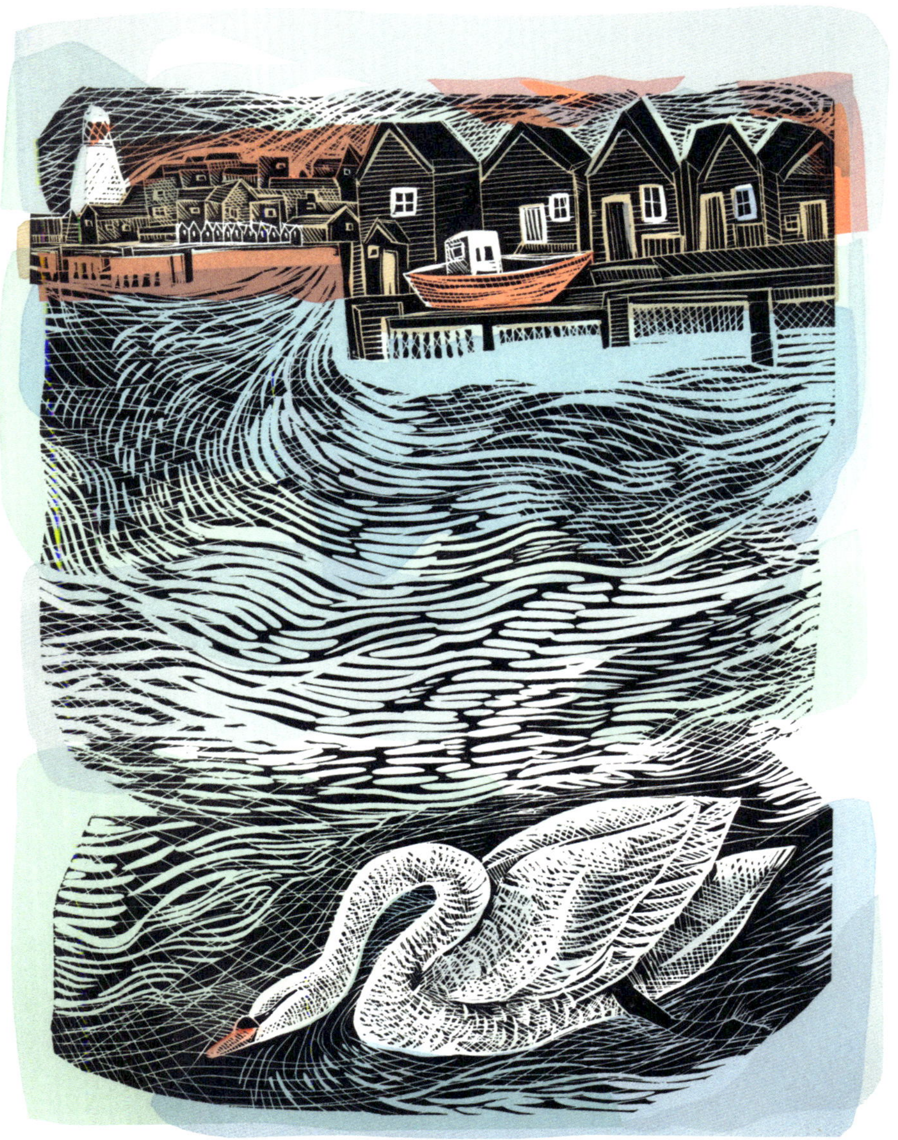

Summer Swans

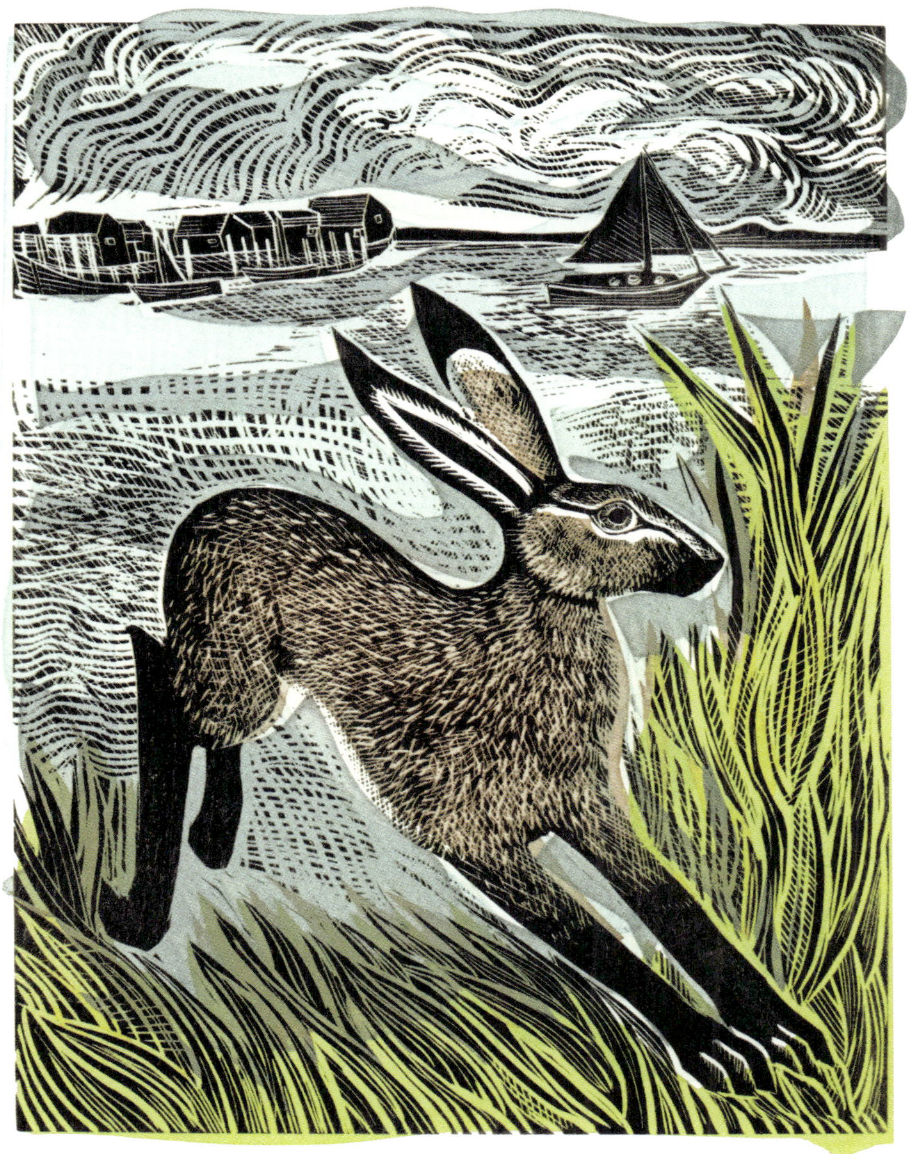

Young Hare

Summer Foxes at Marske Hall

In the 1960s my family moved to North Yorkshire where my father was to take up the headship of Richmond primary school. The house my parents had bought needed some renovation, so we took up temporary accommodation in Marske Hall. The hall sounds very grand indeed, but it was a tumbling-down old wreck. The Hall dated back to the seventeenth century and was still beautiful, but it had been turned into flats. I was only five or six at the time but I still remember it vividly. The main hallway was full of stuffed animals. An old coach house in the grounds still had coaches in it with blue velvet seats. Memory is a strange thing and as you grow older you are not sure what you really remember and what is invention. Summer Foxes at Marske Hall is an illustration of this memory. It was only after I completed this print that my now ninety-year-old mother told me that when we lived at Marske I would sit on her knee and watch the foxes run across the lawns outside our window.

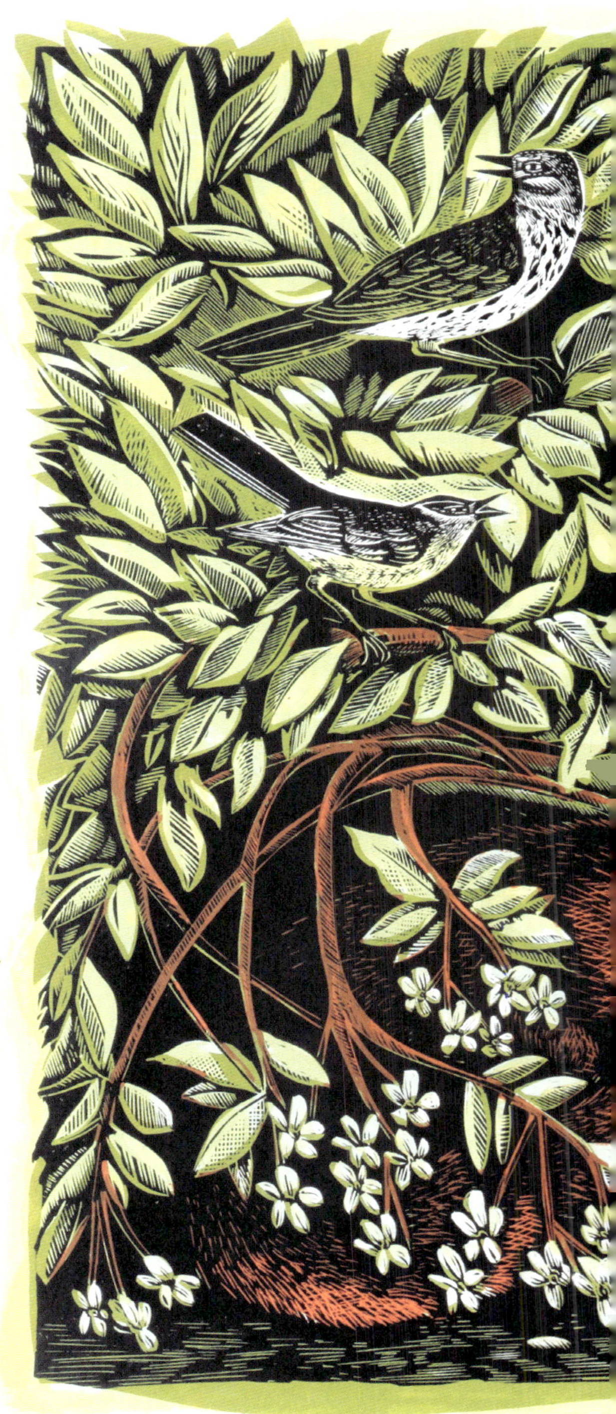

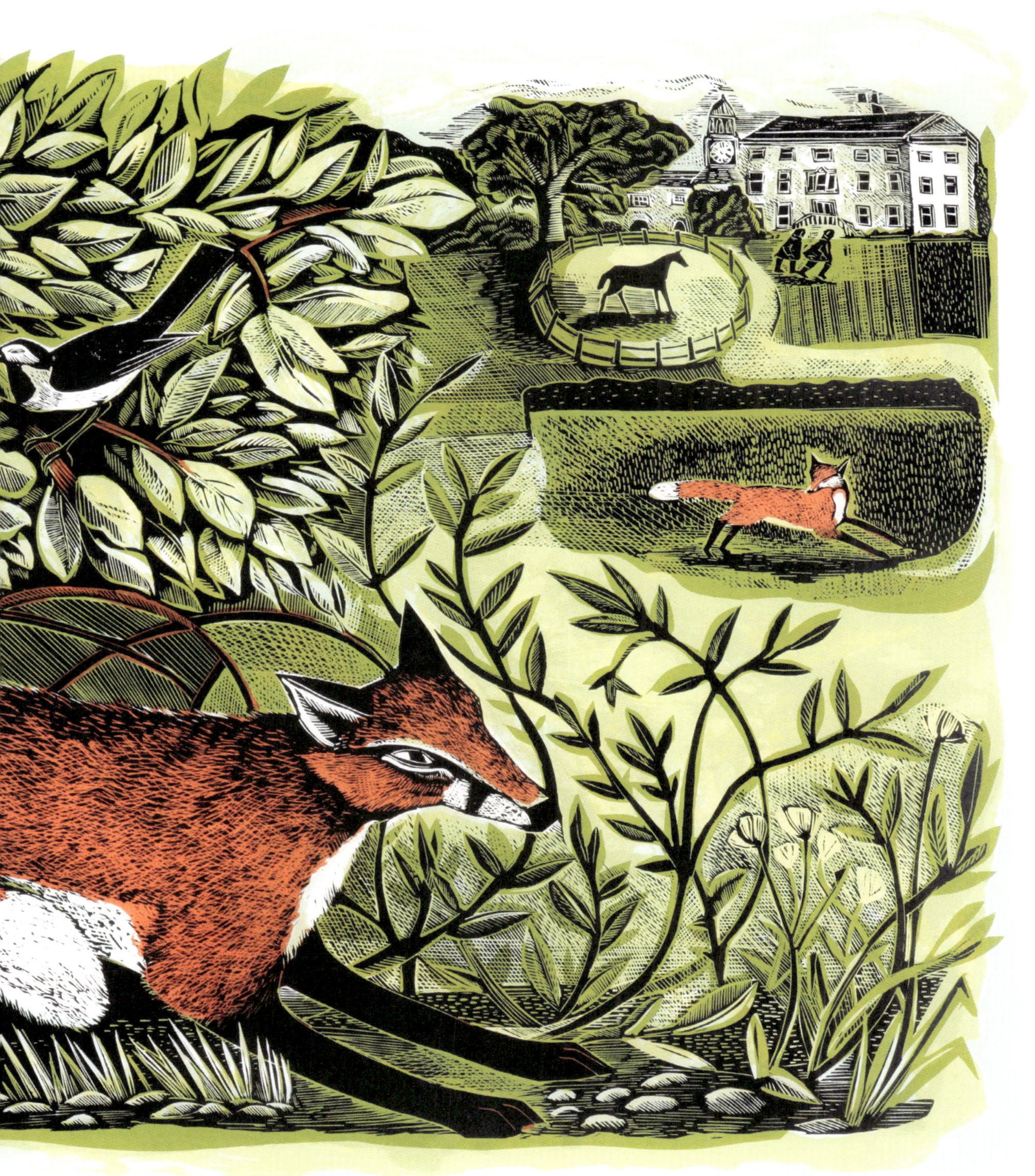

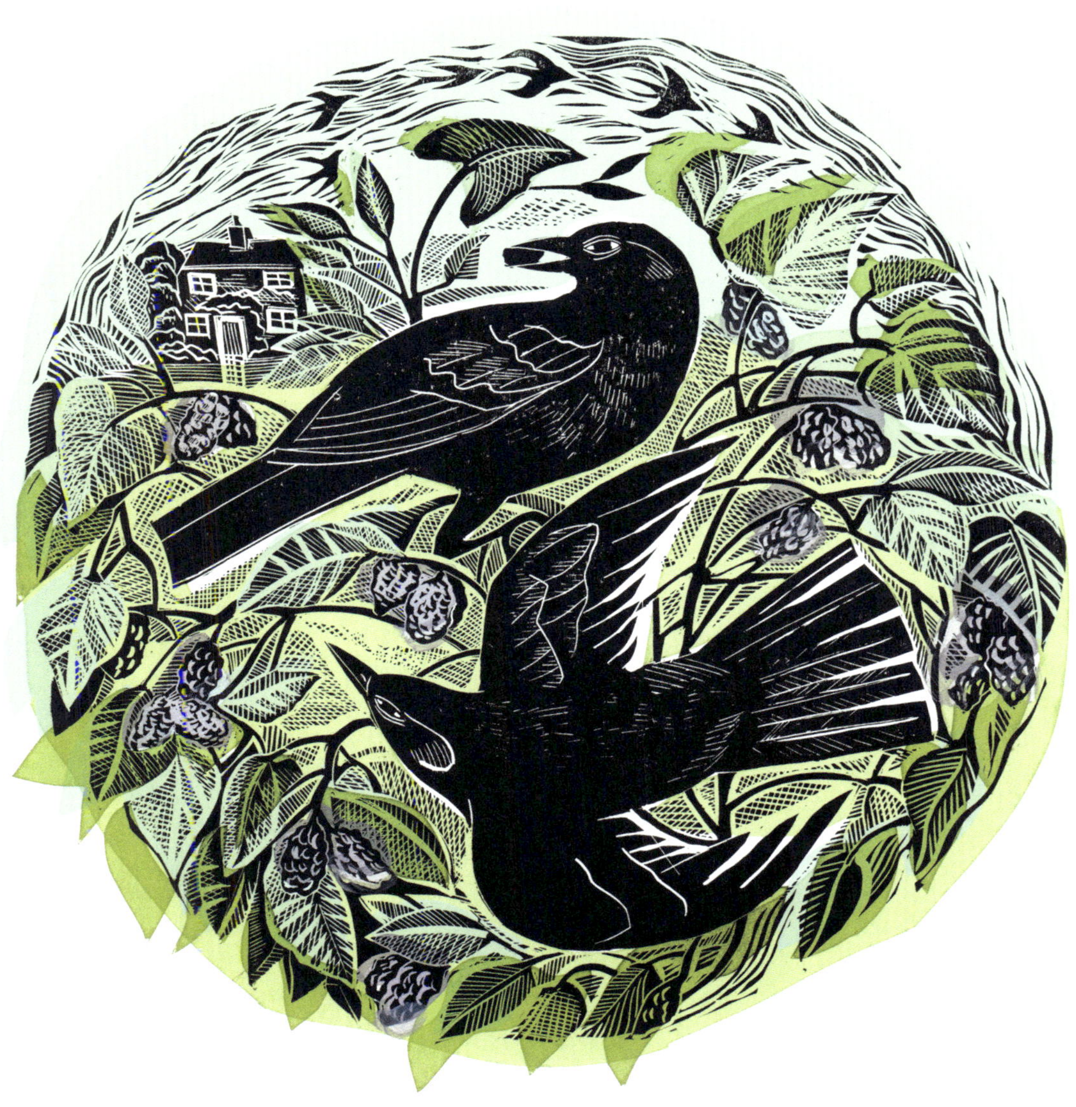

Blackbirds and Mulberry Tree

In August an English garden starts looking tired and mine is no exception. There is still plenty of colour – English roses have their second blooms, the dahlias are flowering, nasturtiums tumble over the edge of the veg beds; the colours in the garden are reds, oranges and browns. As the autumn season progresses this is reflected in the colours of the trees as their leaves begin to turn. The garden still has charm but a different charm to spring and summer. By the end of August, the mulberry tree is thick with mulberries. Mark and I planted the mulberry within the first year of arriving in Wing, to remind us of when we first met. We met in 2004 when I was doing a wood-engraving course at Gainsborough House in Sudbury. I would take a tea break in the garden there and chat to Mark and in the garden was the most magnificent mulberry tree. It is said that tree dates from the time when Gainsborough was living in the house himself. They are very slow growing and can live to a great age, so we promised ourselves one for our own garden. The fruit has the most remarkable flavour and the one in our garden fruits really well – the lovely black berries are delicious. There is nothing better than picking them from the tree and putting them straight onto your breakfast cereal. You have to battle the blackbirds for them; they seem to know as soon as they are ripe and are able to eat a tremendous number every day.

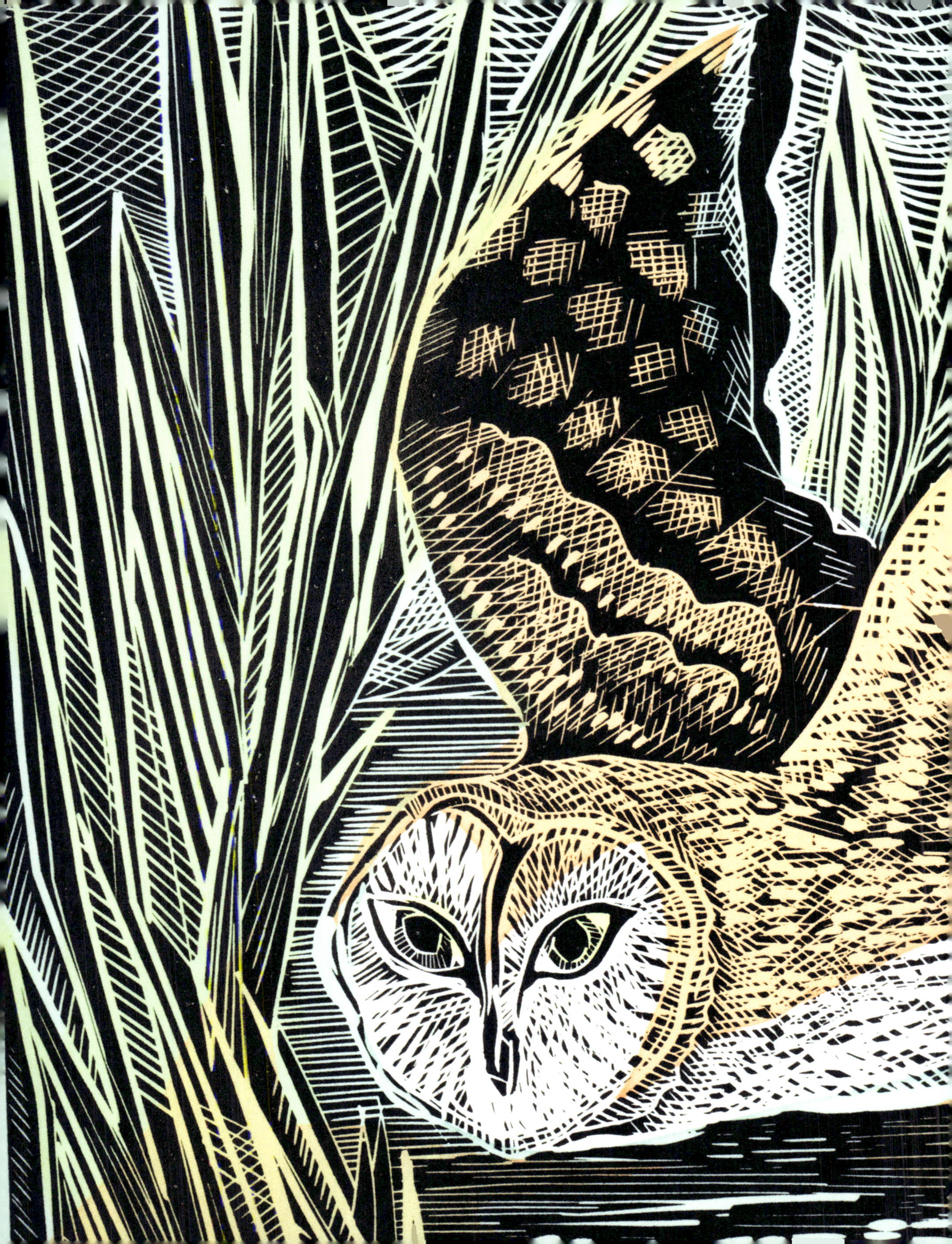

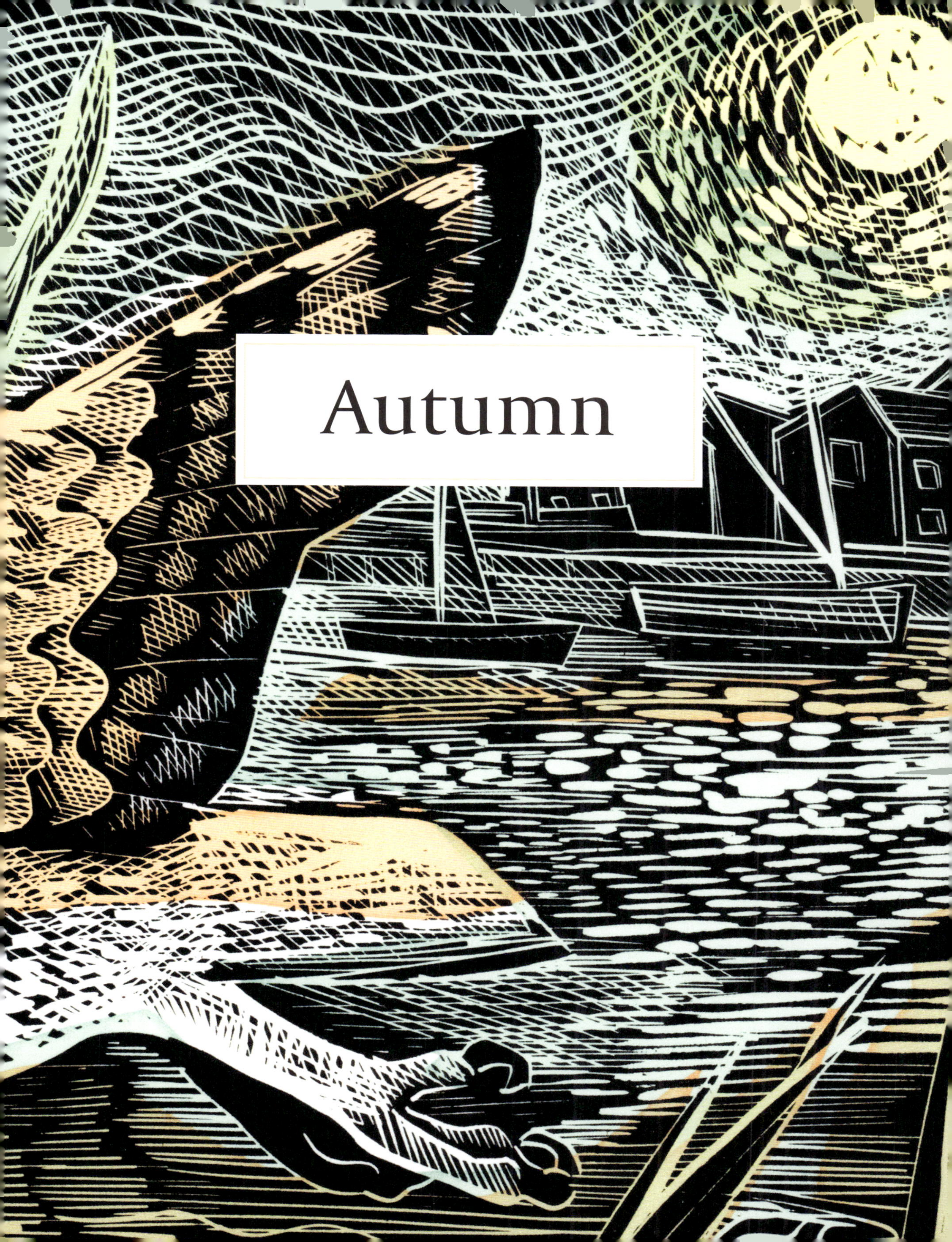

Autumn

The green elm with the one great bough of gold
Lets leaves into the grass slip, one by one, –
The short hill grass, the mushrooms small milk-white,
Harebell and scabious and tormentil,
That blackberry and gorse, in dew and sun,
Bow down to; and the wind travels too light
To shake the fallen birch leaves from the fern;
The gossamers wander at their own will.
At heavier steps than birds' the squirrels scold.

The rich scene has grown fresh again and new
As Spring and to the touch is not more cool
Than it is warm to the gaze; and now I might
As happy be as earth is beautiful,
Were I some other or with earth could turn
In alternation of violet and rose,
Harebell and snowdrop, at their season due,
And gorse that has no time not to be gay.
But if this be not happiness, – who knows?
Some day I shall think this a happy day,
And this mood by the name of melancholy
Shall no more blackened and obscured be.

October
Edward Thomas

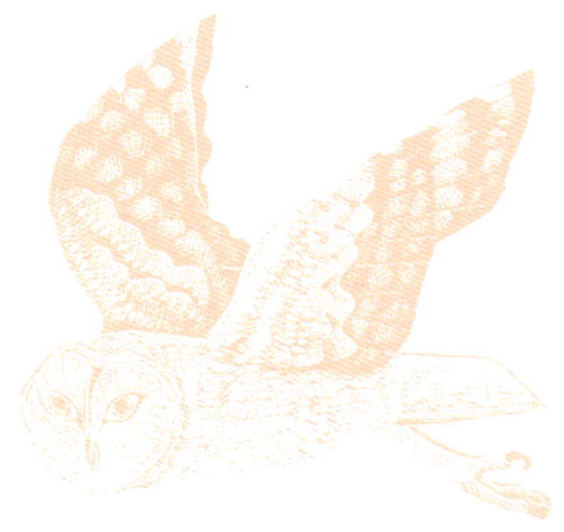

Autumn

Owls in Flight and Feathers Found

Many years ago, when I was a small child of about seven, I started collecting feathers. I collected them on woodland walks or from the garden. Once found they were identified as best as I could and kept in a small orange suitcase. The case contained an assortment of wing, tail and breast feathers of all sorts. One of my friends at primary school was a butcher's daughter who kindly supplied me with an assortment of game bird feathers. Long pheasant tail feathers and shimmering mallard wing feathers had an intensity of colour and detail that seemed much sharper than it does today. The day I found a jay's wing feather is still the sharpest of memories in my mind. The bright blue feather was in an autumn wood. Perhaps it was the contrast of the aqua blue lying on the orange leaf that drew me to it and made it so memorable. I do not have that suitcase any more; as children we moved many times so I expect as I moved from child to teenager the once much-treasured suitcase was left behind.

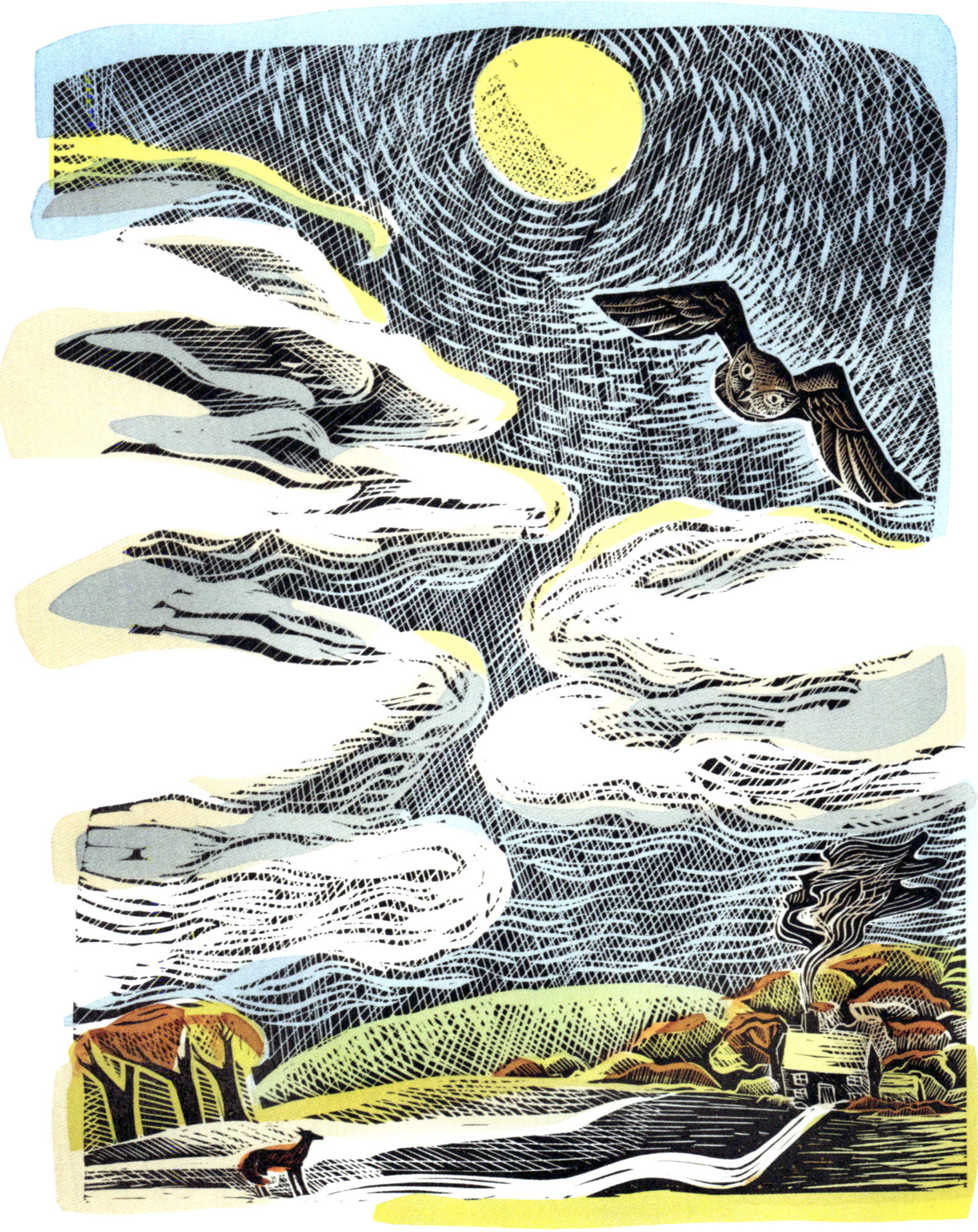

Autumn Flight

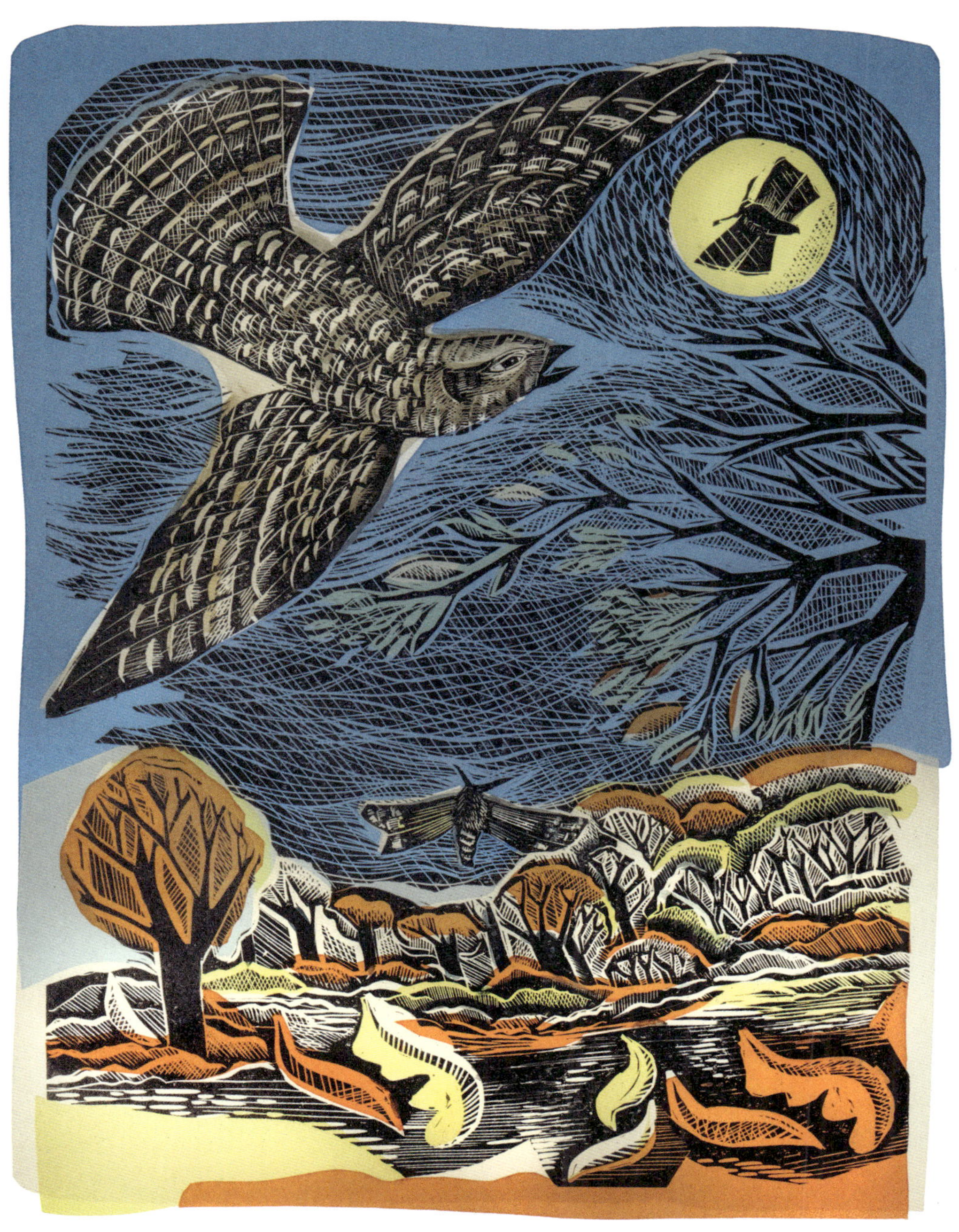

Autumn Nightjar

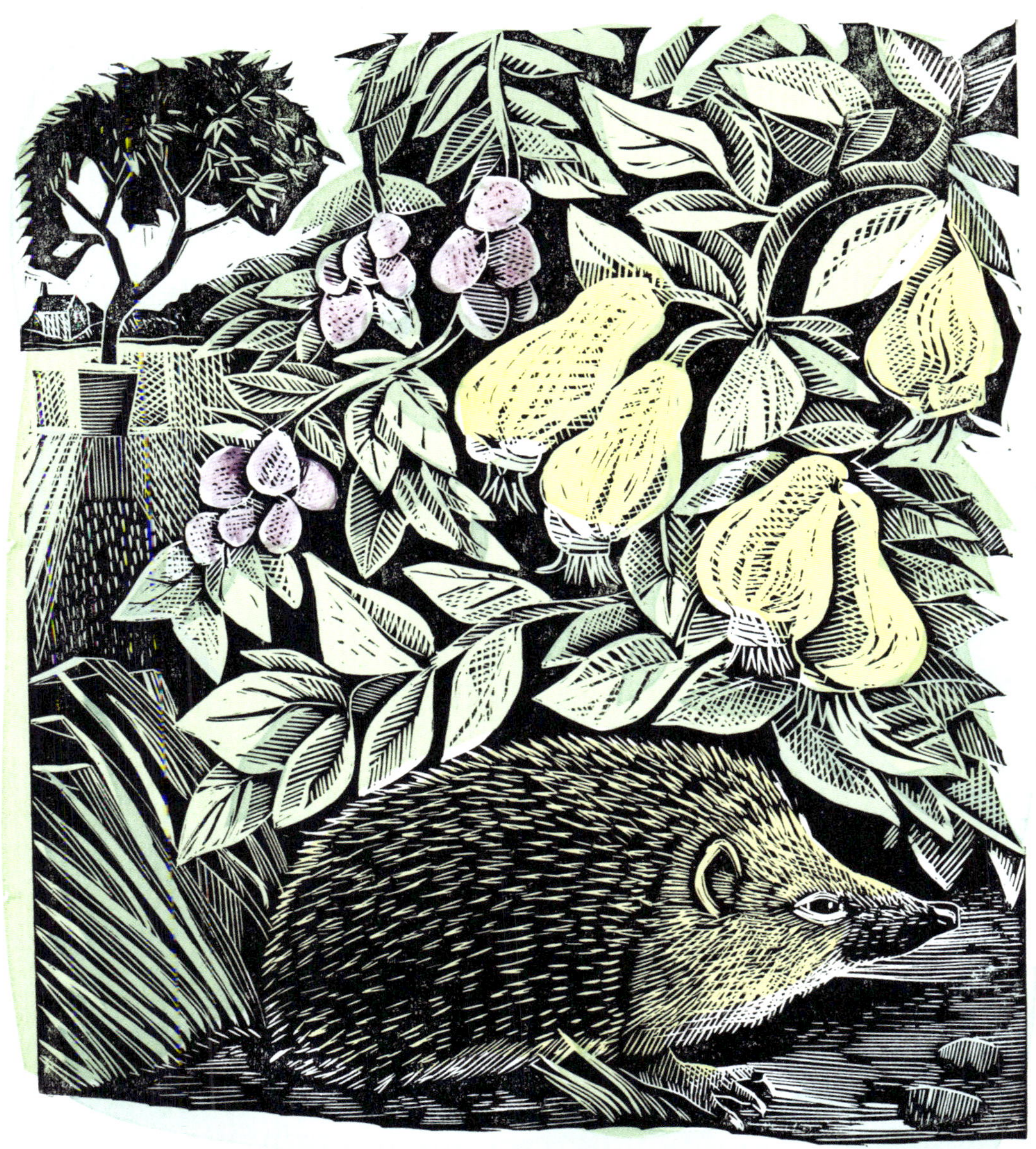

Hidden Hedgehog

Since lockdown there have been many stories of people enjoying their gardens and the wildlife they support in a new way. This very much applies to two friends of mine, Sara and Jules, who also live in our village. Sara runs a catering business and like so many people during the pandemic, has not been able to work. This led to us working together on a gift product: I produce the illustrated tin and Sara the most amazing brownies. It has been a positive of lockdown that such projects arose, but more importantly we got to know each other better.

Sara and Jules are normally great travellers and have been all over the world watching wildlife: gorillas in Africa, sloth sanctuaries in Costa Rica, diving with sharks and scaling mountains in Bhutan. Lockdown has of course put paid to their travels. When Covid rules allowed they invited me to their garden to enjoy a homemade pizza. It was fantastic to see that their enthusiasm for wildlife had not waned but had moved to observing the local game of their garden. A very professional looking telescope was poised and ready in their conservatory – this was for the viewing of their resident hedgehogs. Their in-depth knowledge of the daily routine of their now growing family of hedgehogs was very impressive. On this particular evening no telescope was needed; as if on cue the wonderful hogs trundled into view just next to where we were sitting. Their two favourites had been given names – Hettie and Hogpot. We could hear the sound of munching as they came out to feed – delightful hogs munching as we munched too.

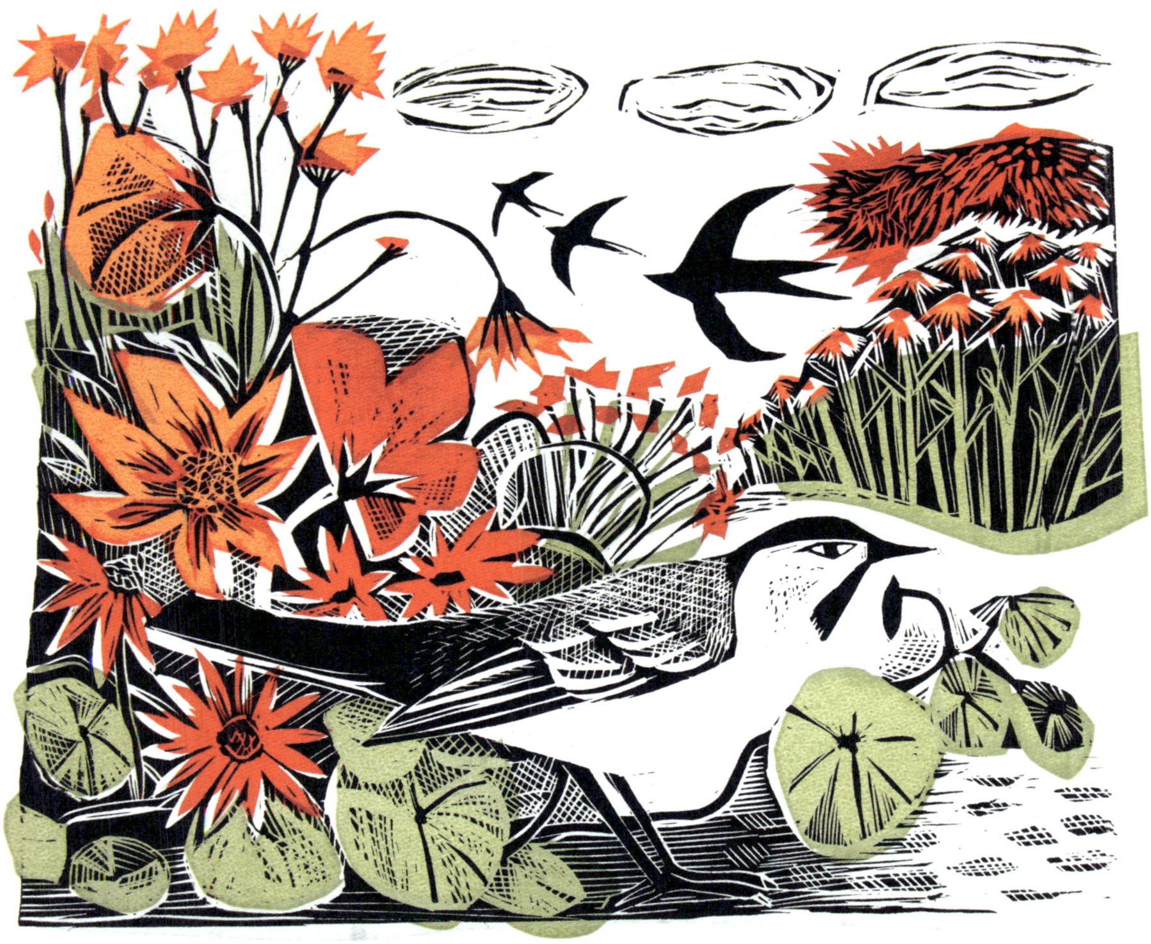

Heading Home

As summer draws to a close, the swallows and house martins gathered on the telephone wires outside the studio. The adults and juveniles practised their flying skills in preparation for their long journey to Africa. Last year's breeding must have gone well as there were a large number of young birds. They looked like a complex musical score – dots of swallows and house martins swaying on the wire. But then one of them decided to take flight, and in a whirl of wings and a mad chattering panic they all took to the sky. It soon became apparent why they were behaving in this way – there was a hobby! A hobby is a small bird of prey about the size of a kestrel but it is much faster, with thinner arching wings. The hobby swooped through the swallow mob, and the adult swallows showed their protective nature towards their young as they dive-bombed the hunter. No swallows were caught by the hobby on this occasion so the wires quickly filled again with the young birds – a musical score once more.

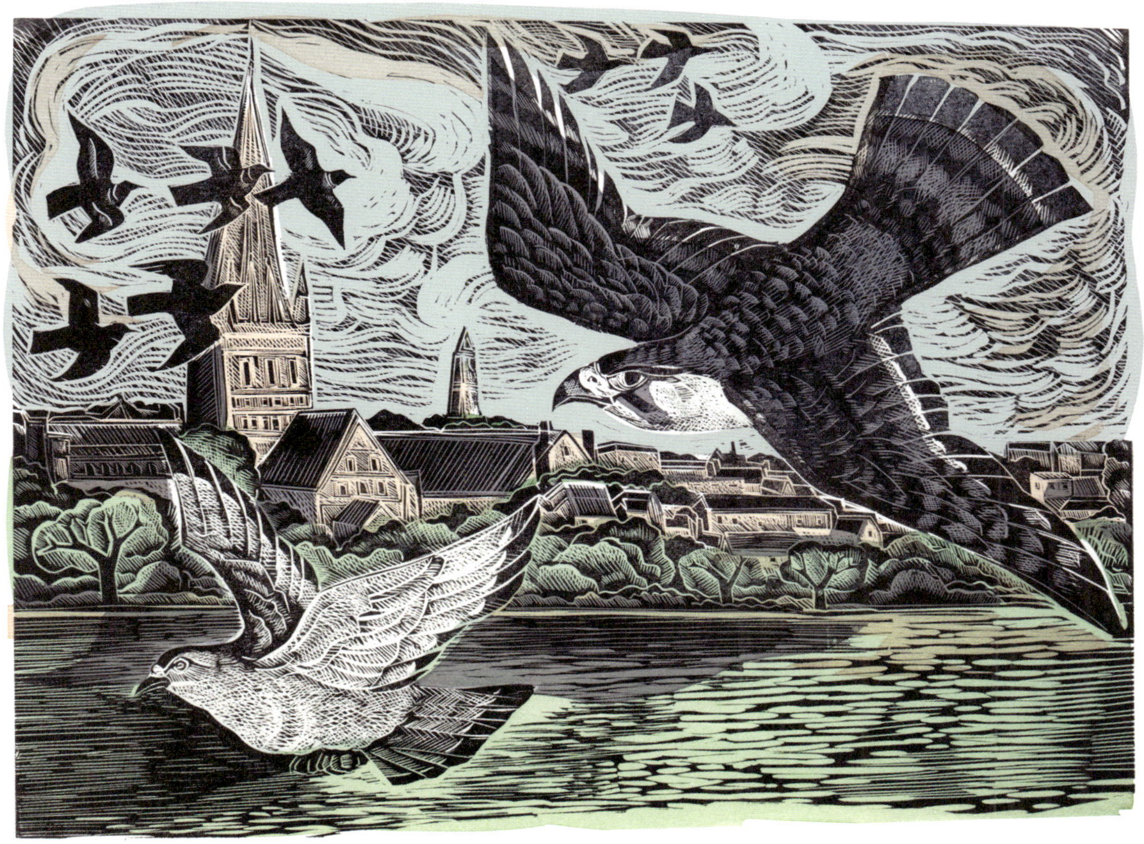

Peregrine and Pigeon

Cathedrals and churches have become breeding places for the peregrine falcon – All Saints Church in my local neighbourhood and Oakham have a breeding pair. The illustration above is a peregrine I saw in Norwich chasing its usual prey of pigeons. Their chosen town homes seem so different from the cliffs of Cornwall were I have watched them many times hunting rock doves and other small birds.

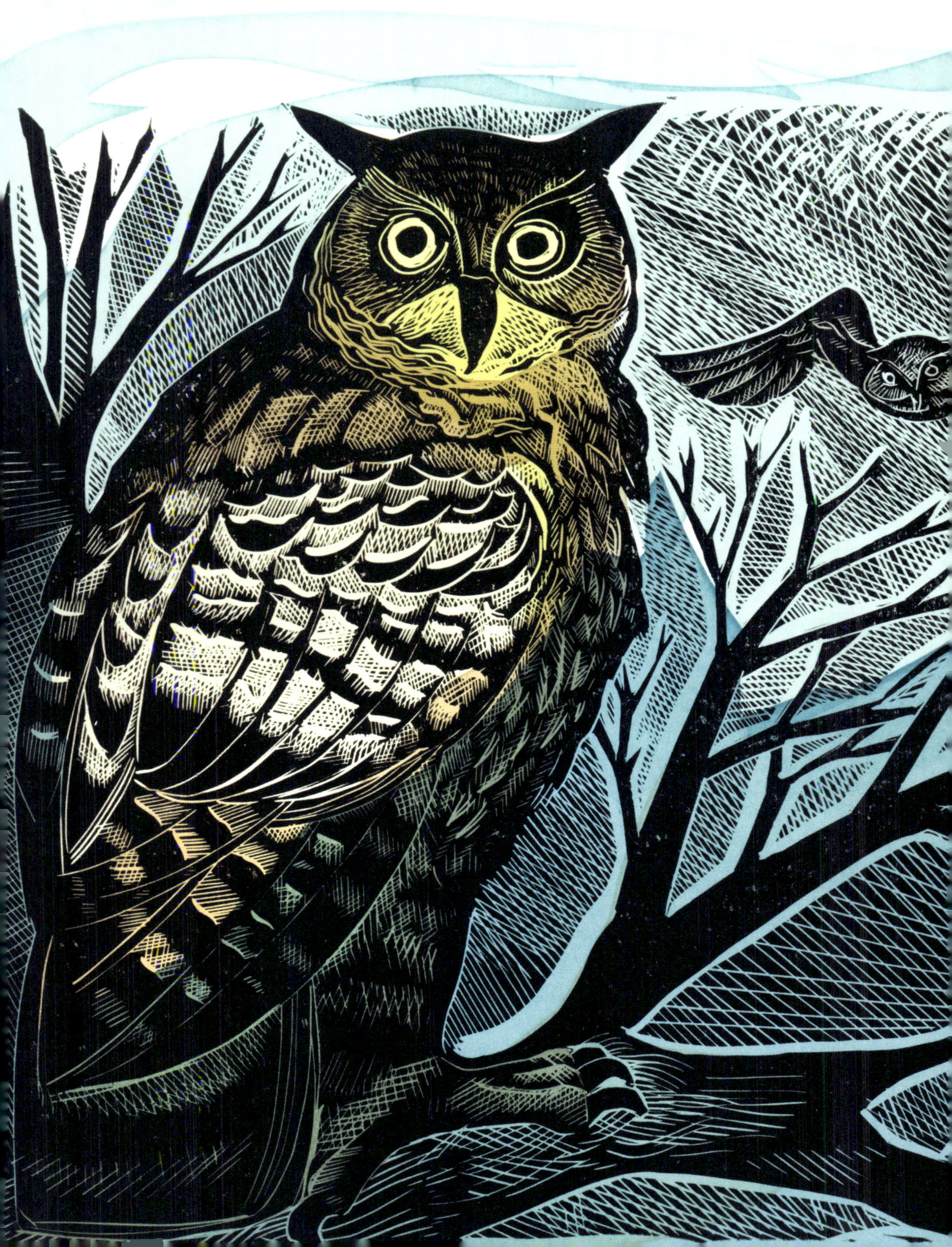

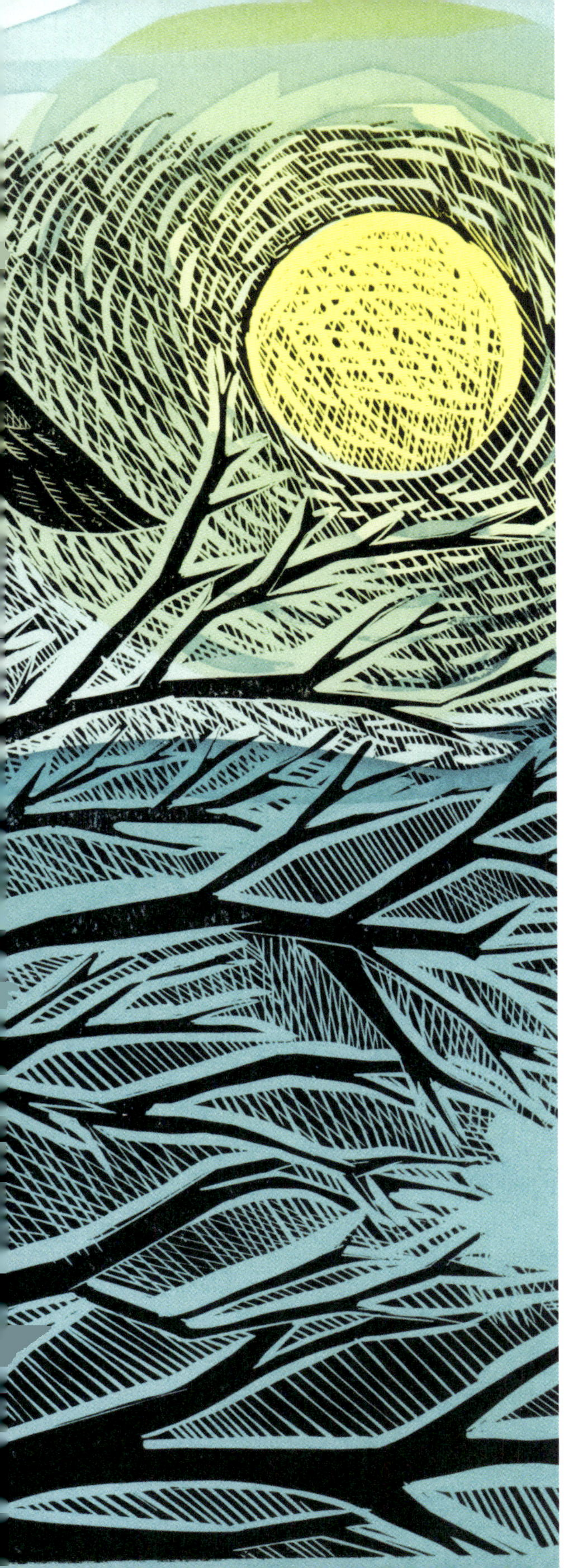

Owl and Moon

Swallows and Seas

Goodbyes – the gathering clouds of swallows, geese in storms flying over the boat, the ghost of a barn owl over the water at Snape …

When sailing is done it seems to coincide with the time when we say goodbye to the swallows, house martins and swifts.

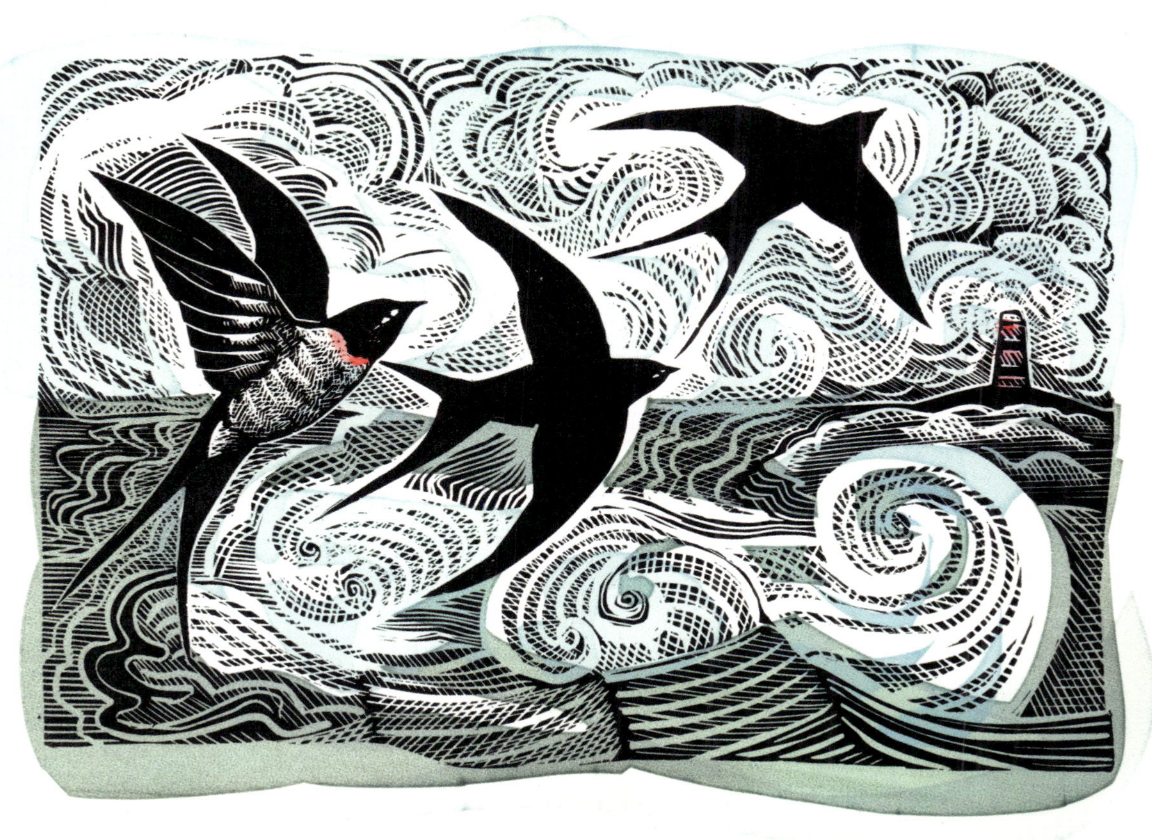

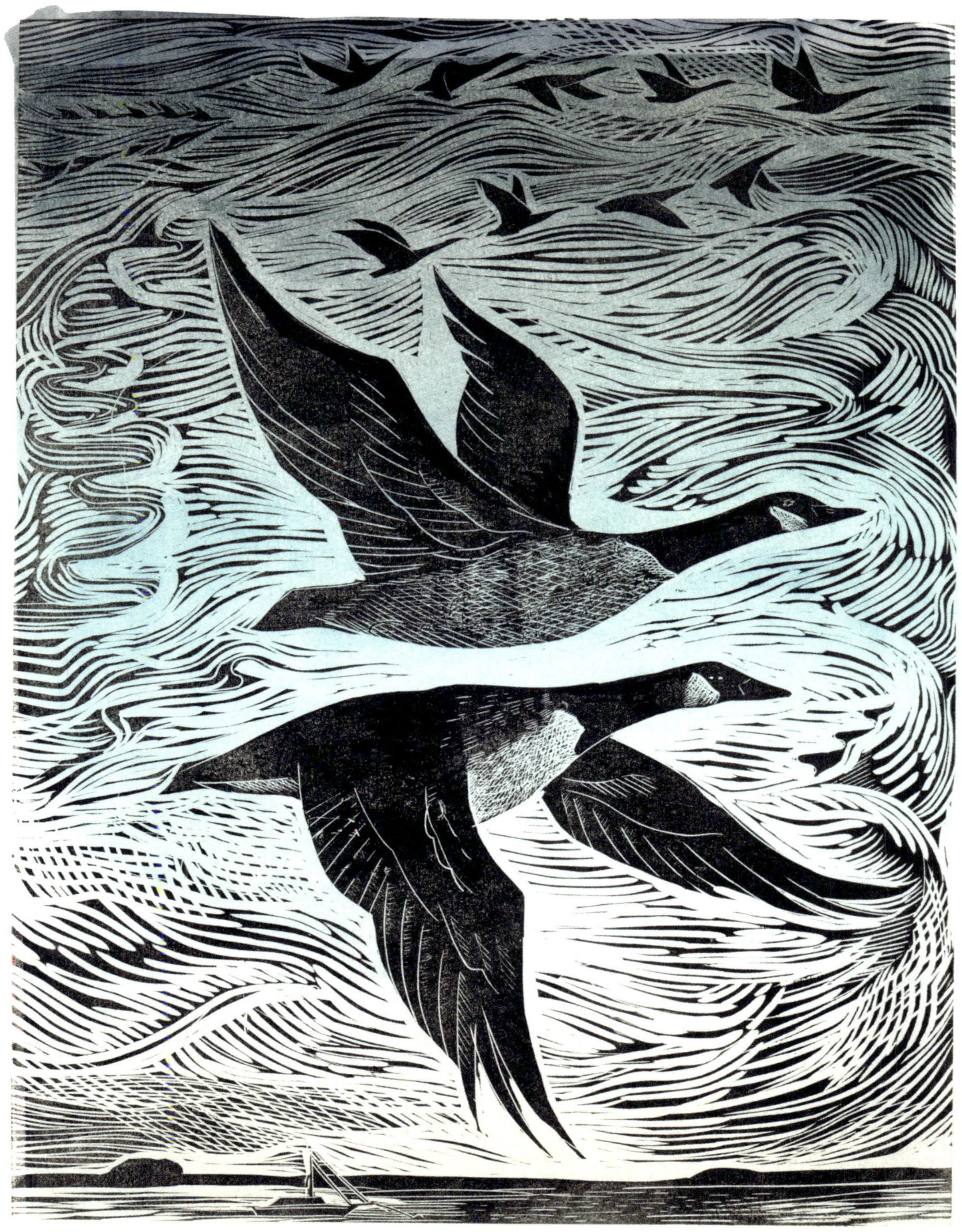

Canada Geese at the Butely

Early autumn offers the last weeks to join Mark on *Windsong* before winter sets in. The days are already getting shorter, but these last days of warmth are great for watching wildlife. Autumn in Suffolk or Norfolk is when geese gather in great flocks. The flocks are a mixture of pink-footed, Canada and greylag geese.

These great squadrons of geese fly in formation over the boat at what seems to be at the same time every evening with a volume of noise that it hard to believe. They follow the course of the river, looming out of the dusk, then part in formation round the mast of the boat before rejoining in the sound bouncing off the water. Contrast the incredible quiet of the day to the echoes honking off of the still water – their voices are not tuneful but play their part in the beauty of being on the River Butely. Also in Suffolk you may see marsh harriers and barn owls. While they are still not a common sight, the marsh harriers have been greatly aided by reintroduction programmes.

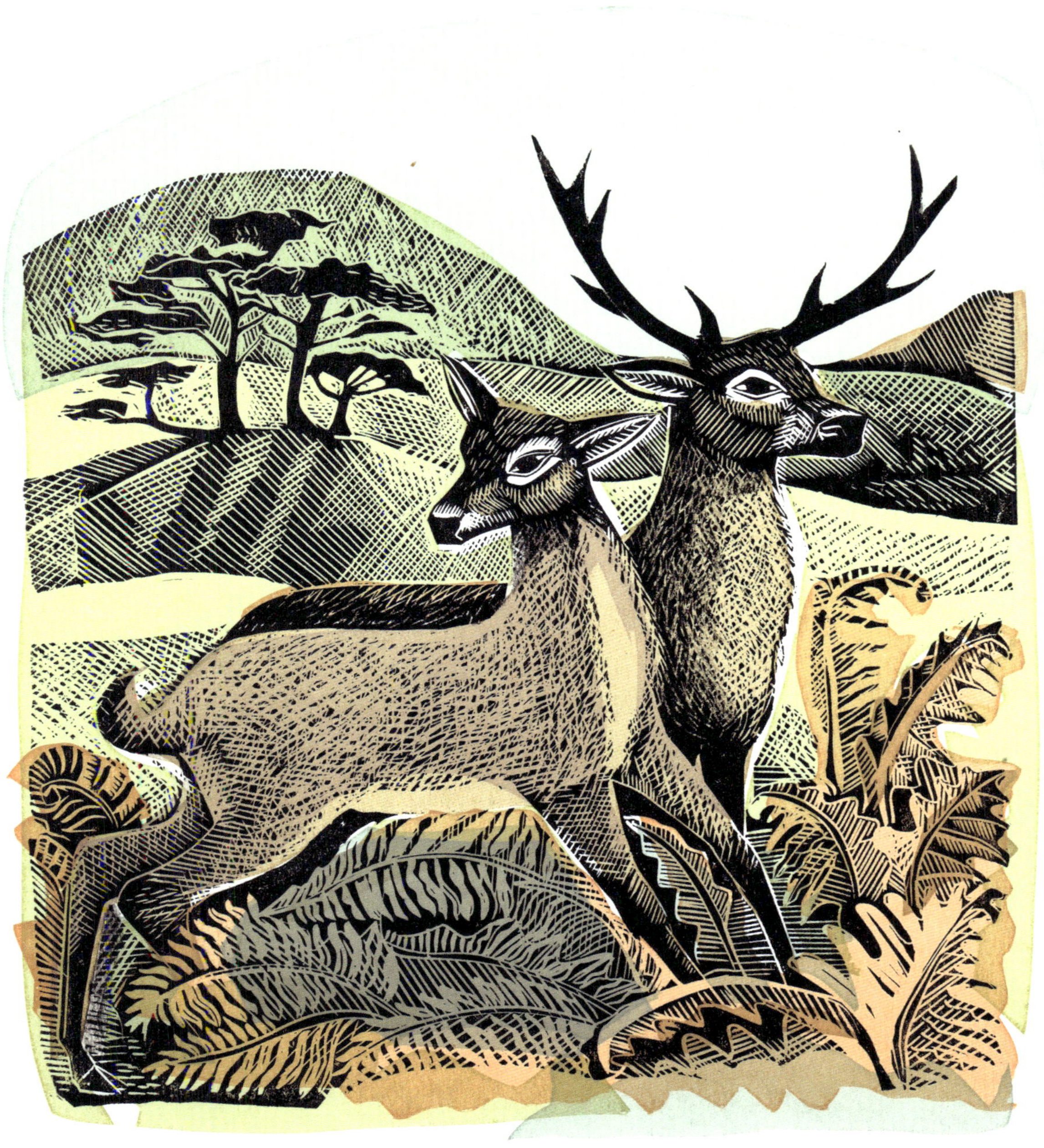

Deer and Bracken

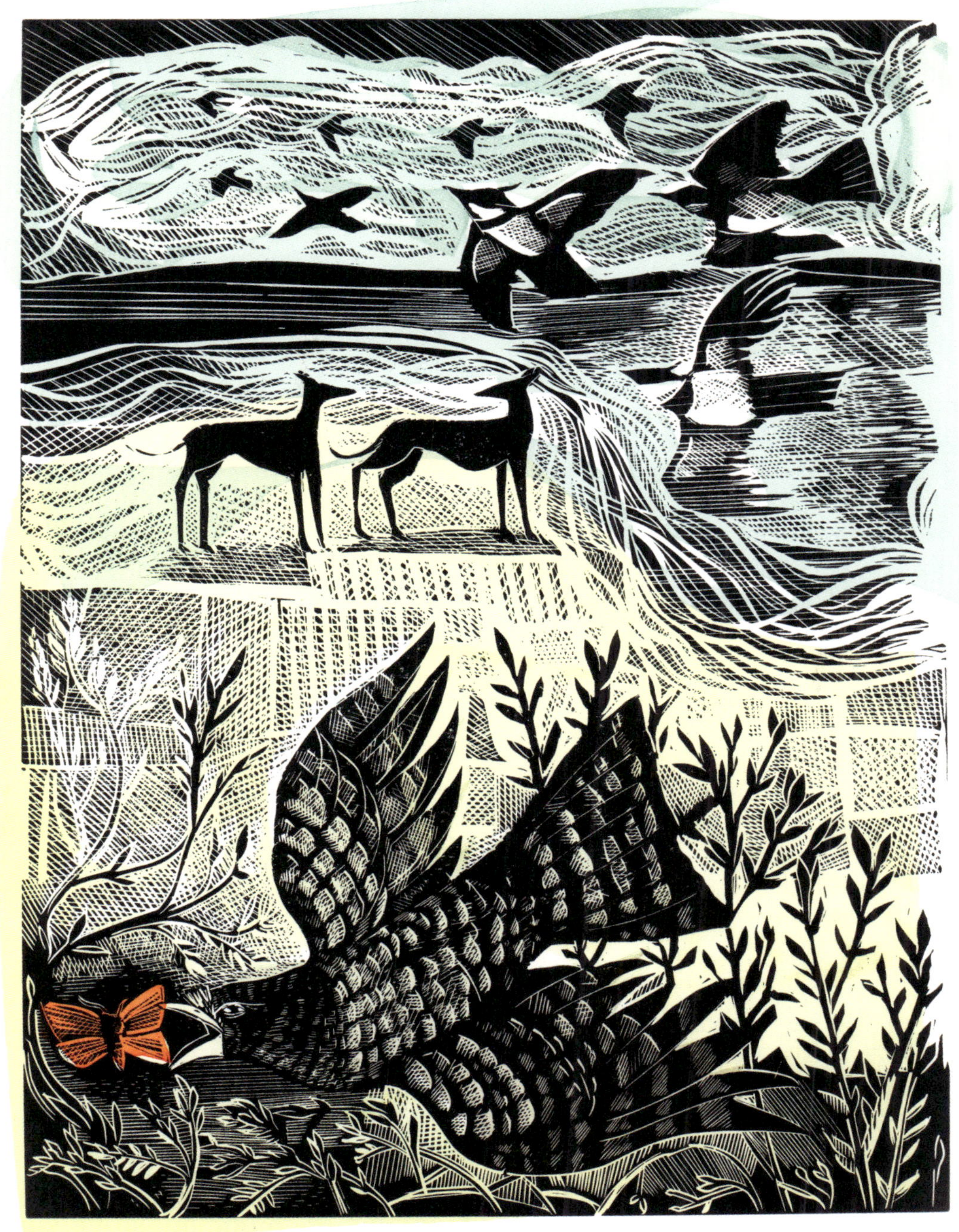

Nightjar and Sea

Rose Cottage

One of the last of the summer trips is to North Devon. I have two friends Lyndon and Matt, who live in Lee, near Ilfracombe, and visiting them is always a great treat. They live just a stone's throw from Lee Bay in the most idyllic thatched country cottage. The wooded valley shelters wildlife and it contrasts with the ruggedness of the north Devonshire coastline. A couple of years ago I was visiting, and we were all out for a walk and saw the most amazing beetle – it was huge and iridescent. I looked it up and it was one of four oil beetles, which I had not seen before and I hadn't realised there were so many varieties. On that same visit that I had another encounter that I will not forget. My friends are very keen on a daily swim in the sea – and that throughout the year! Swimming in the sea in England is not on my to-do list and definitely not in September, but it seemed impolite not to join them. Well, if you're going to do such a thing you might as well be the first one in and get it over with. As I ran toward the waves I could see what I thought at first was a pigeon. It turned out to be a storm petrel. They migrate to Spain in the autumn but it had been a particularly stormy season and due to the very high winds this one had been knocked into the sea.

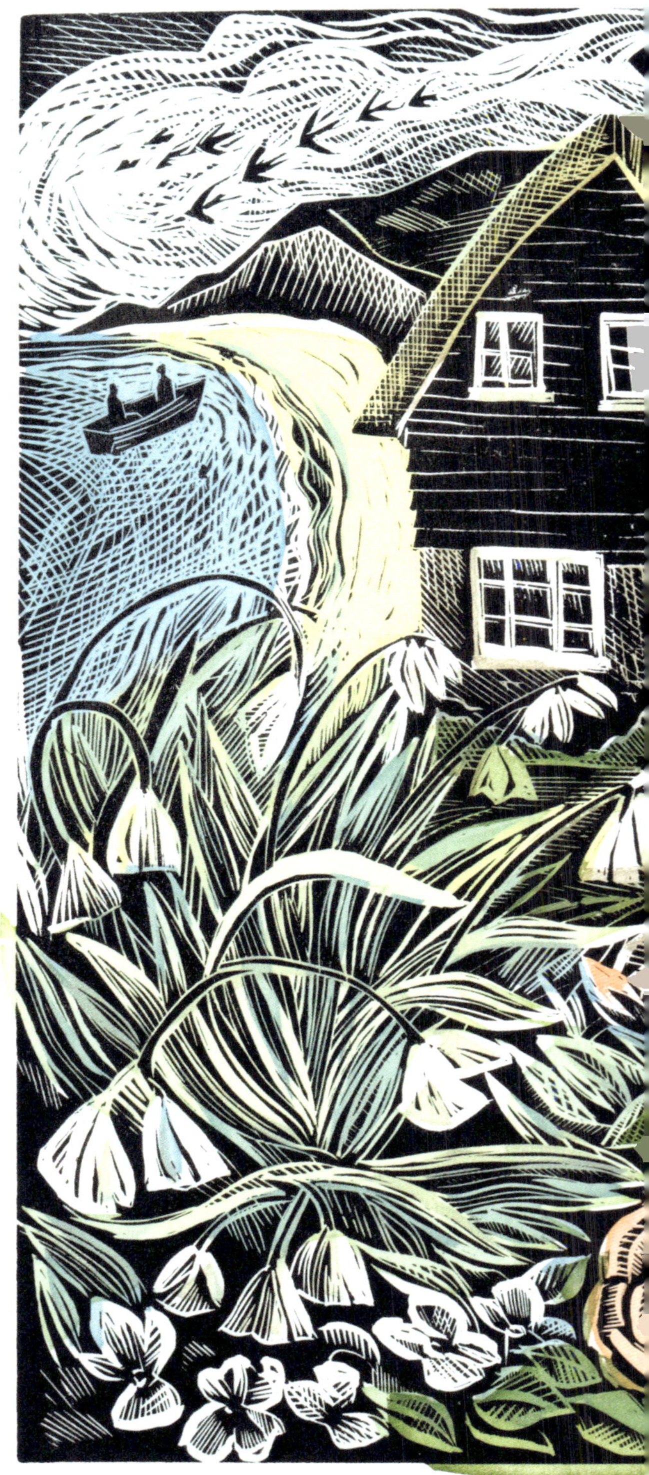

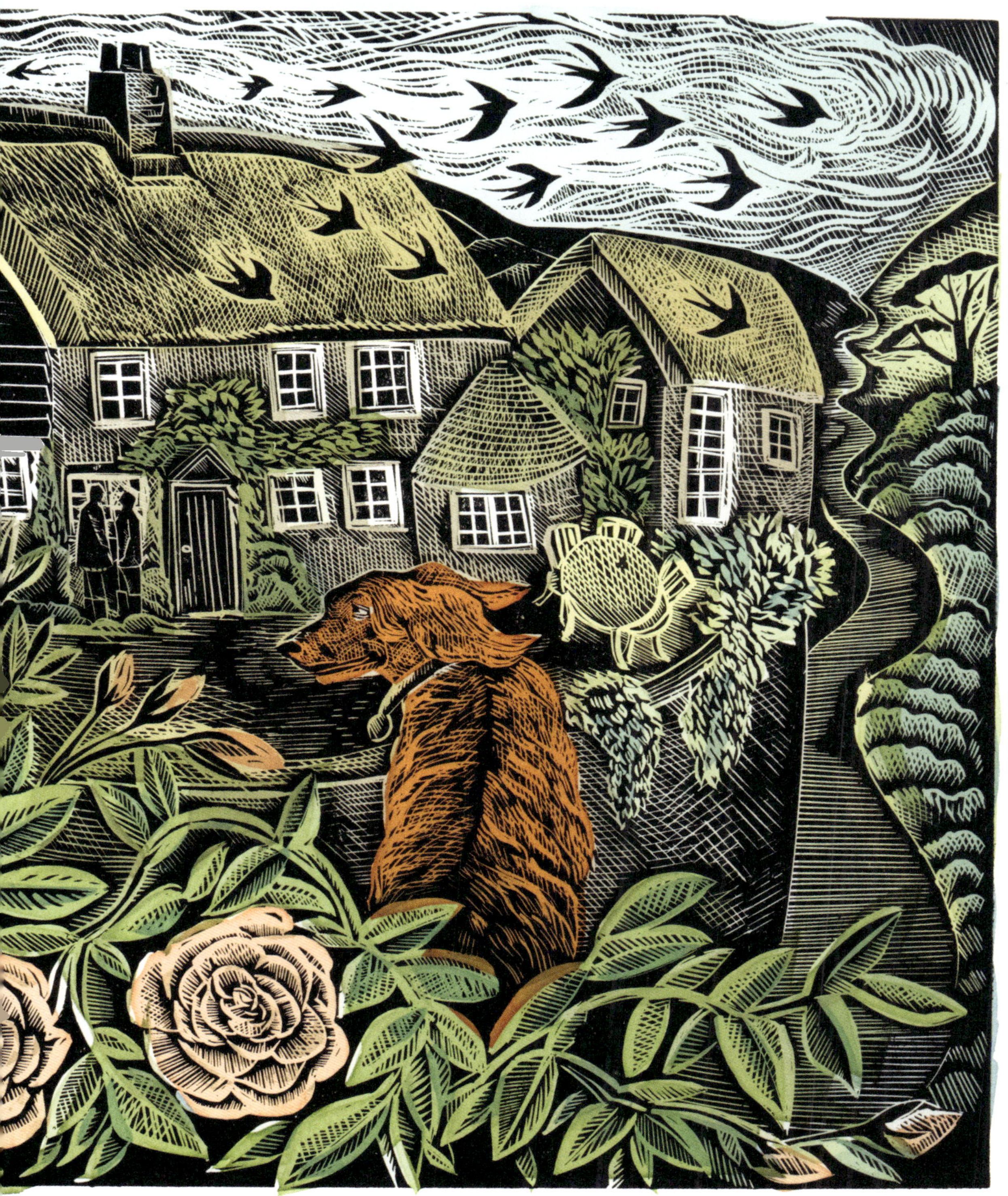

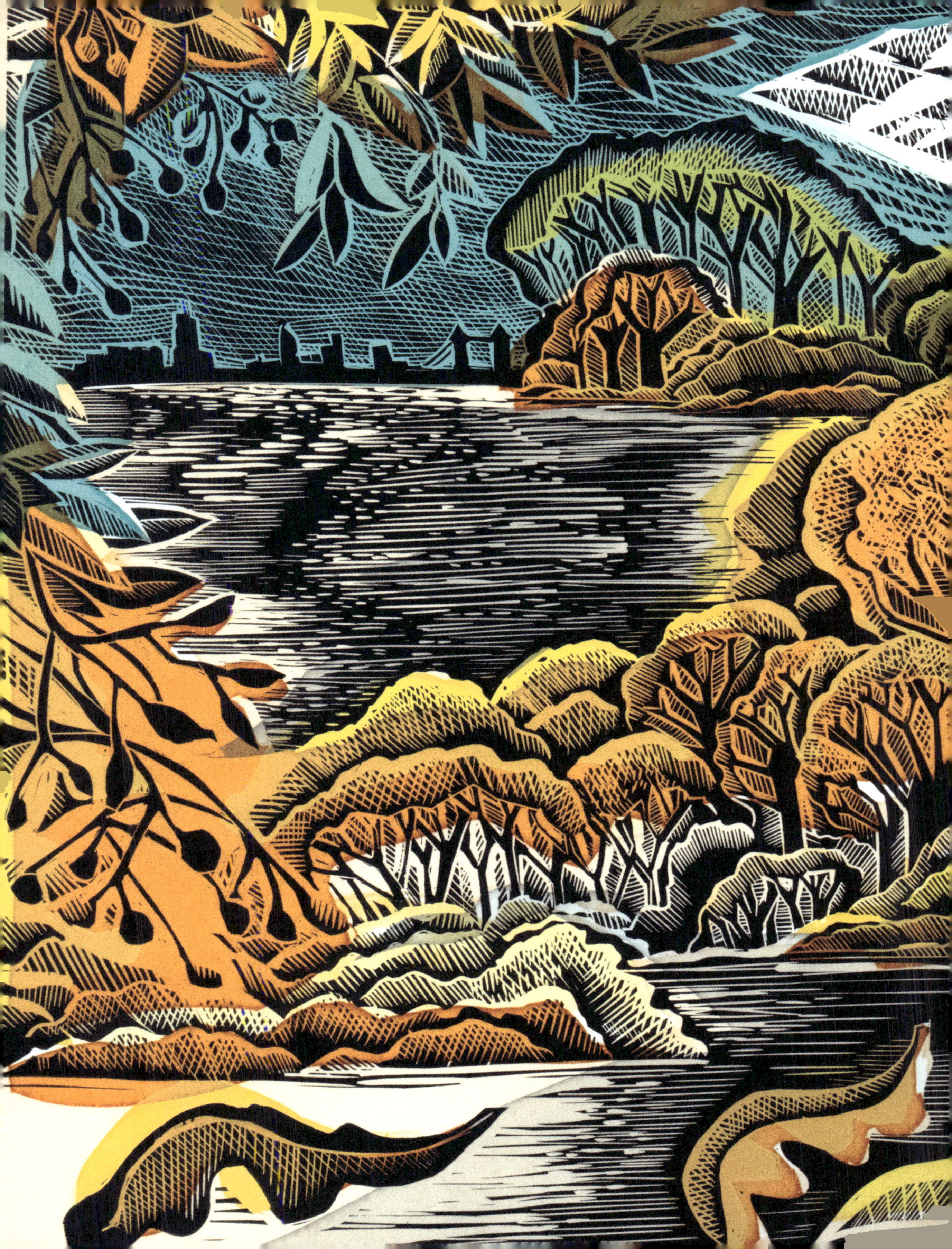

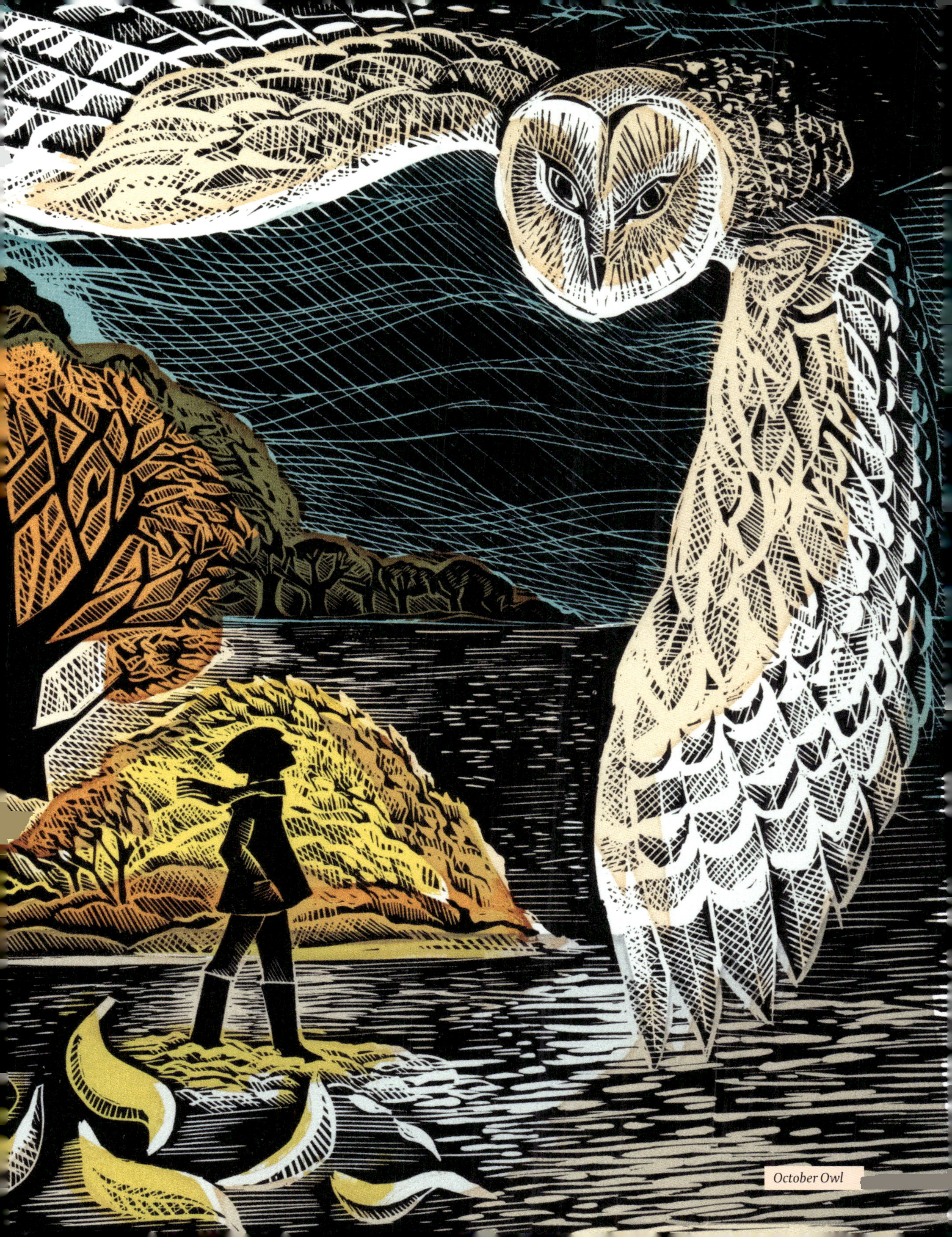

October Owl

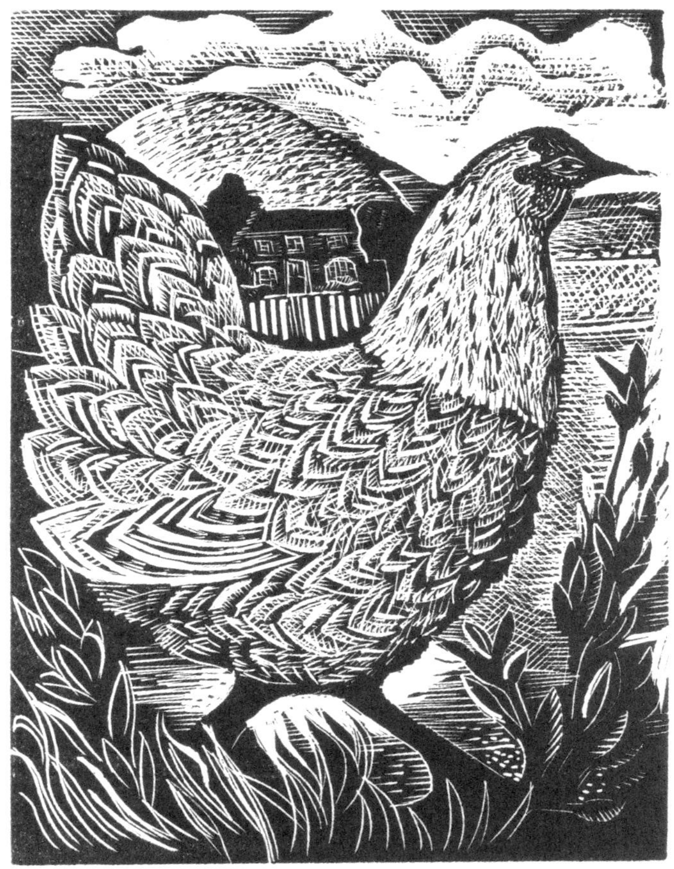

Chicken

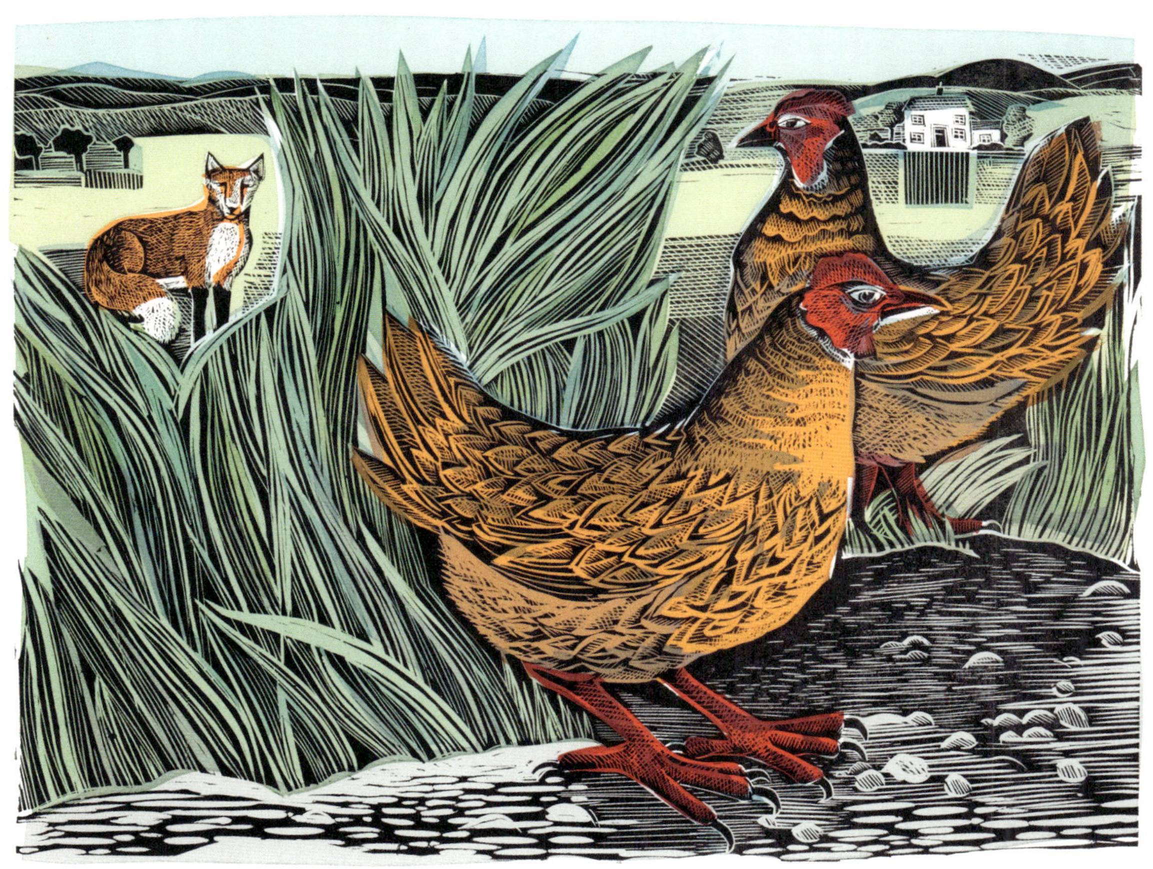

Autumn Chicken

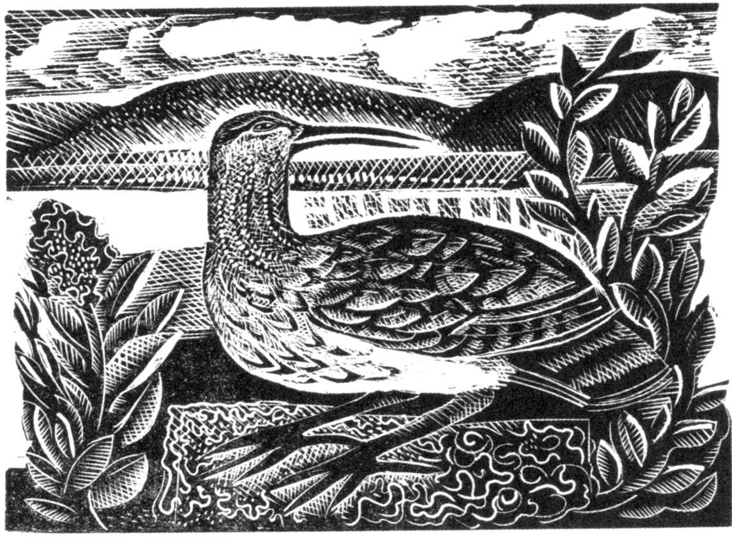

Whimbrel

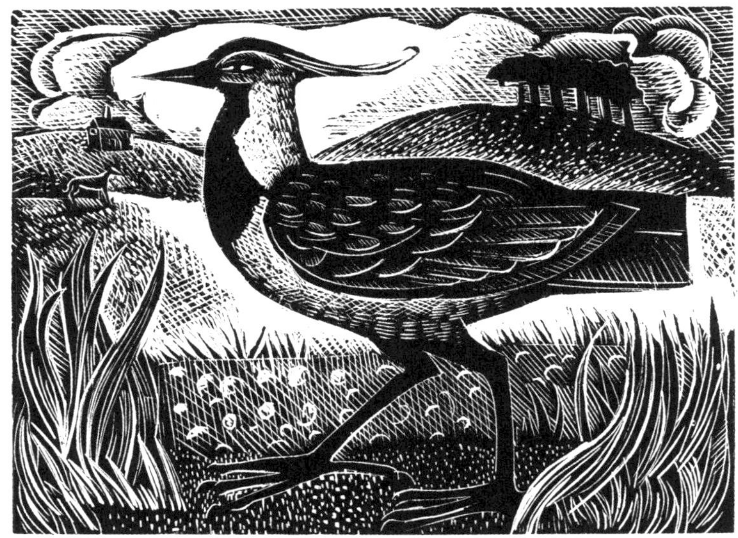

Varas Varas

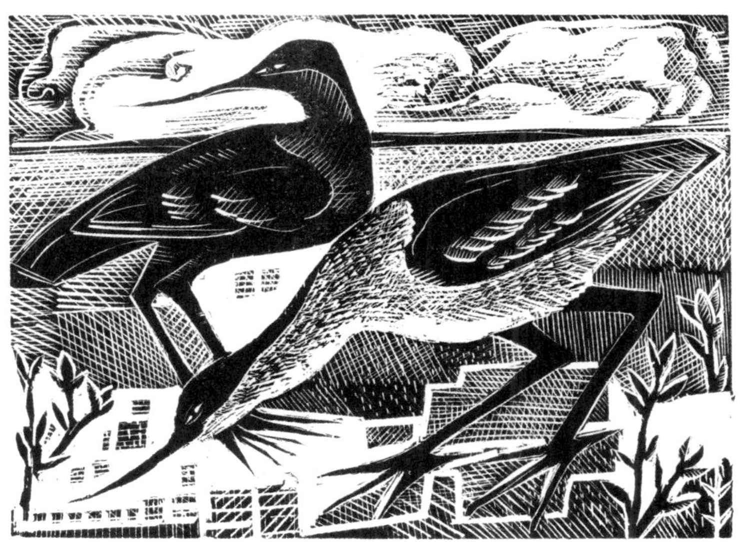

Avocet

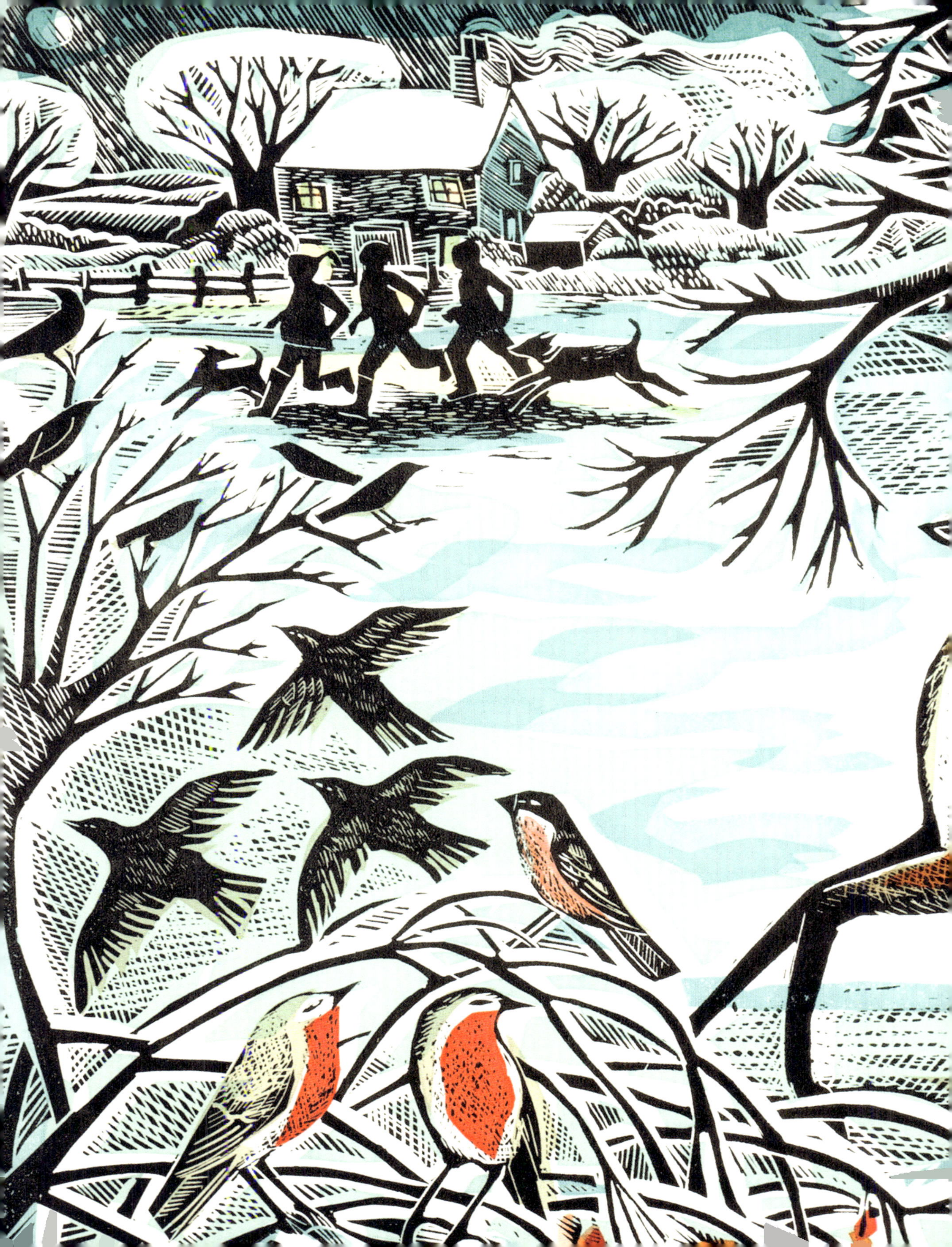

Winter

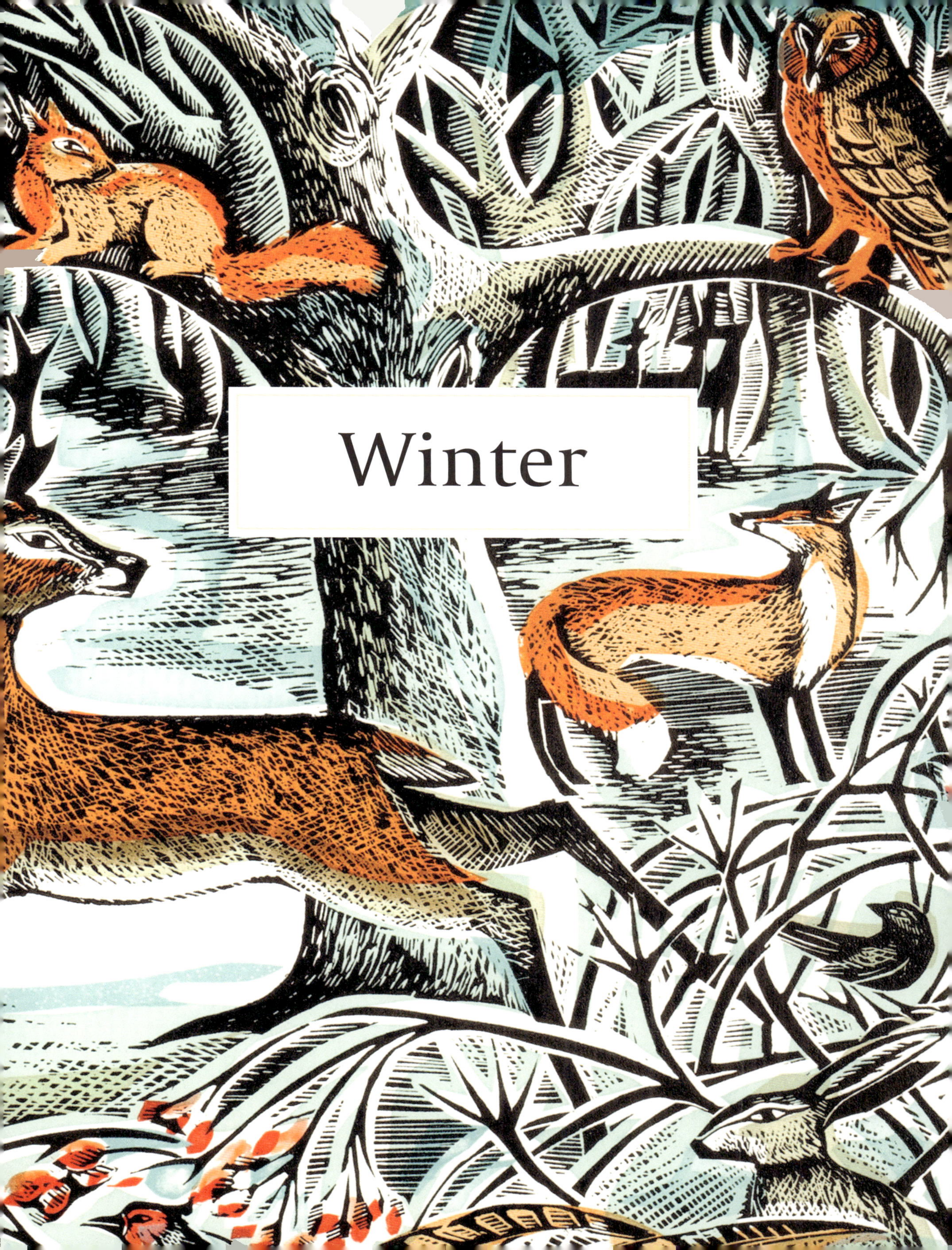

Out in the dark over the snow
The fallow fawns invisible go
With the fallow doe;
And the winds blow
Fast as the stars are slow.

Stealthily the dark haunts round
And, when the lamp goes, without sound
At a swifter bound
Than the swiftest hound,
Arrives, and all else is drowned;

And star and I and wind and deer,
Are in the dark together, – near,
Yet far, – and fear
Drums on my ear
In that sage company drear.

How weak and little is the light,
All the universe of sight,
Love and delight,
Before the might,
If you love it not, of night.

Out in the Dark
Edward Thomas

Winter

Robin Songs and Winter Hares

Robert Frost's beautiful poem 'Stopping by Woods on a Snowy Evening' is, I know, a national favourite but despite it being in common use I never tire of hearing it.

I have a print titled Stopping by the Woods; it does not have all the elements described in the poem, but I hope it has its atmosphere. I also revisited the poem for Winter Wood and I hope this image too evokes something of the mood of the Frost poem. I find winter images inspiring to create, the tree branches against the sky, and reducing colour use to a simpler palette suits the way I like to work. I also love Christmas; as a family we love all aspects of it and though my family is now grown up they all seem to have inherited this love of the festive period. Bringing home the tree is always special. Before I learned to drive at the age of thirty, I cycled everywhere – shopping, work and holidays. Bringing home a Christmas tree on a bike was no mean feat as it meant you had to strap it to the bike and literally ride it home. I wish I had a photo of that – but sadly not!

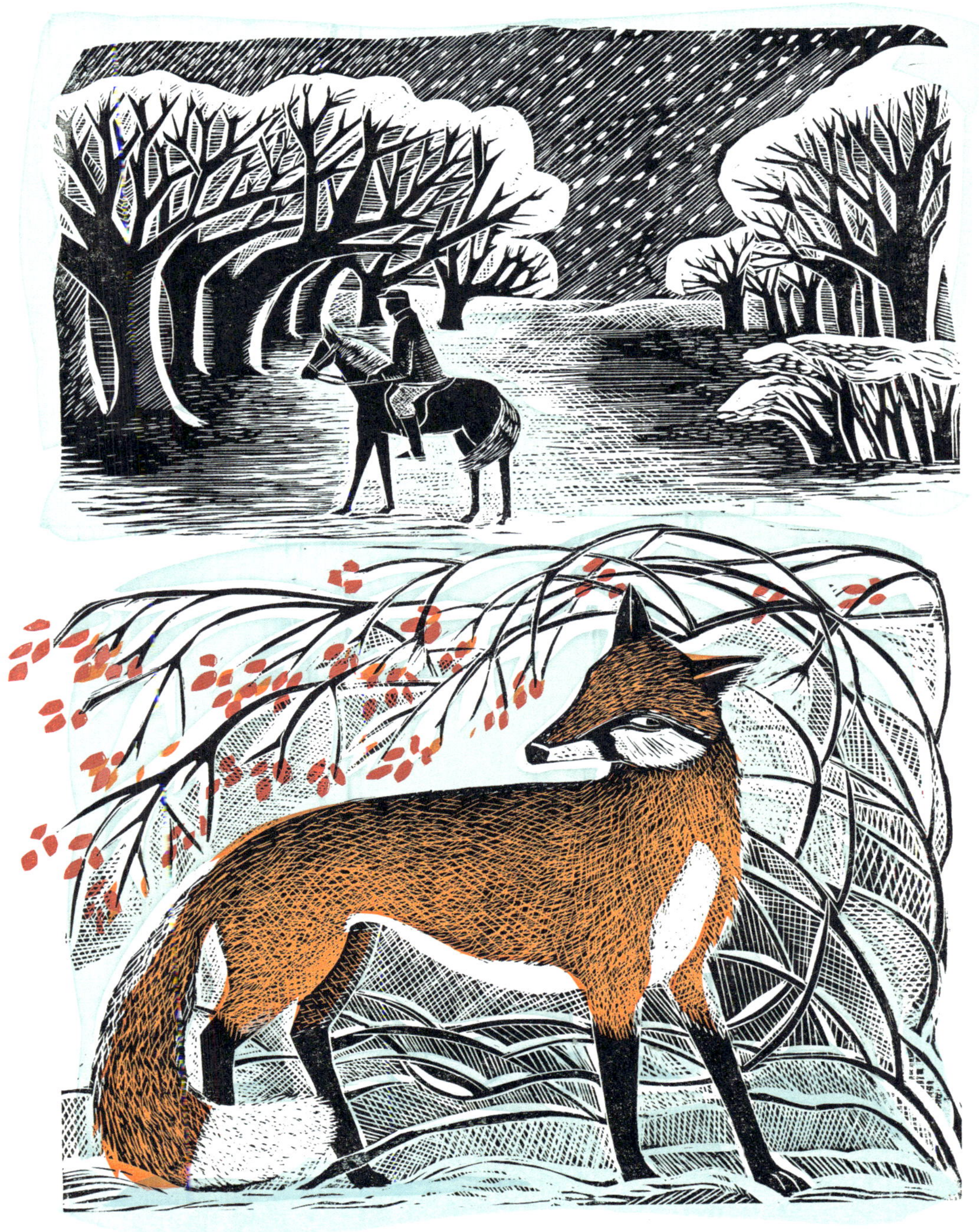

Stopping by the Woods

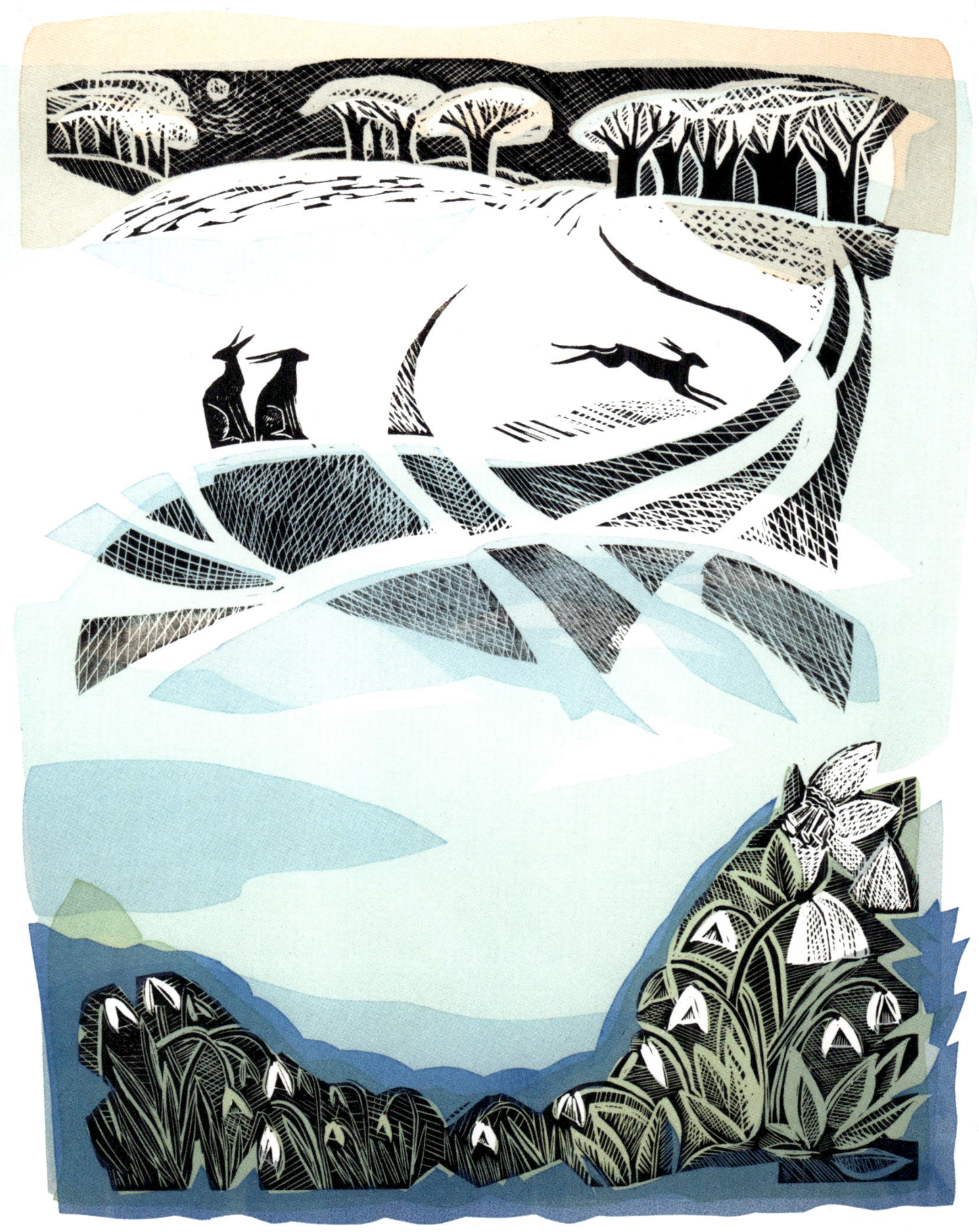

Winter Fields

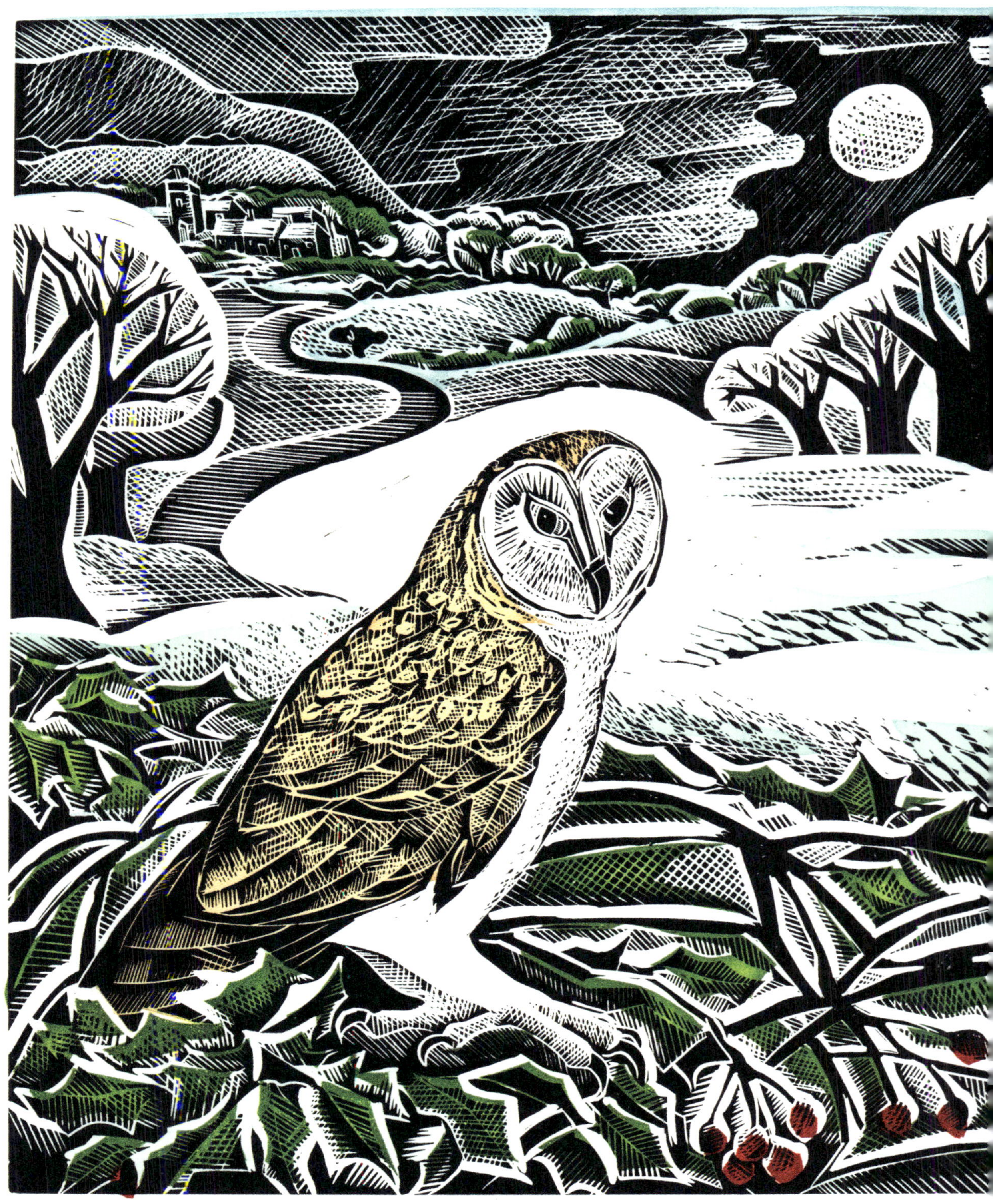

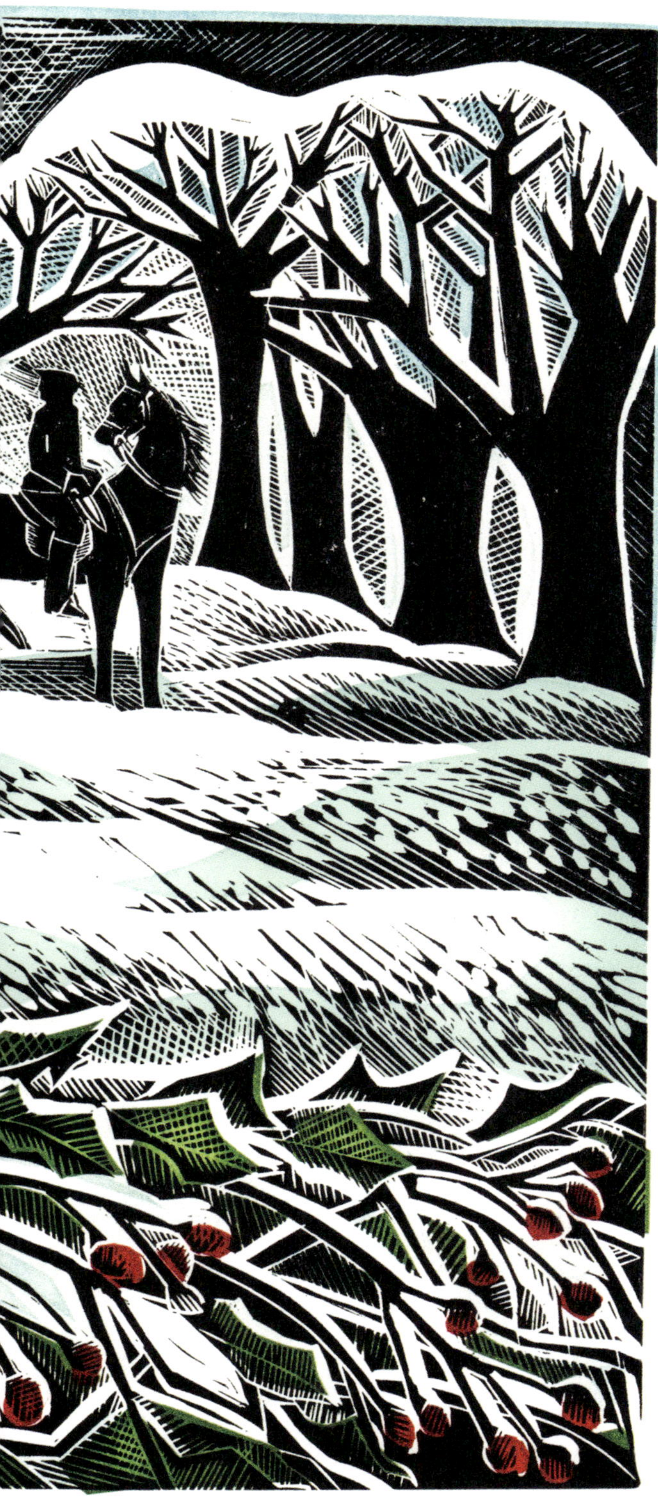

Winter Wood

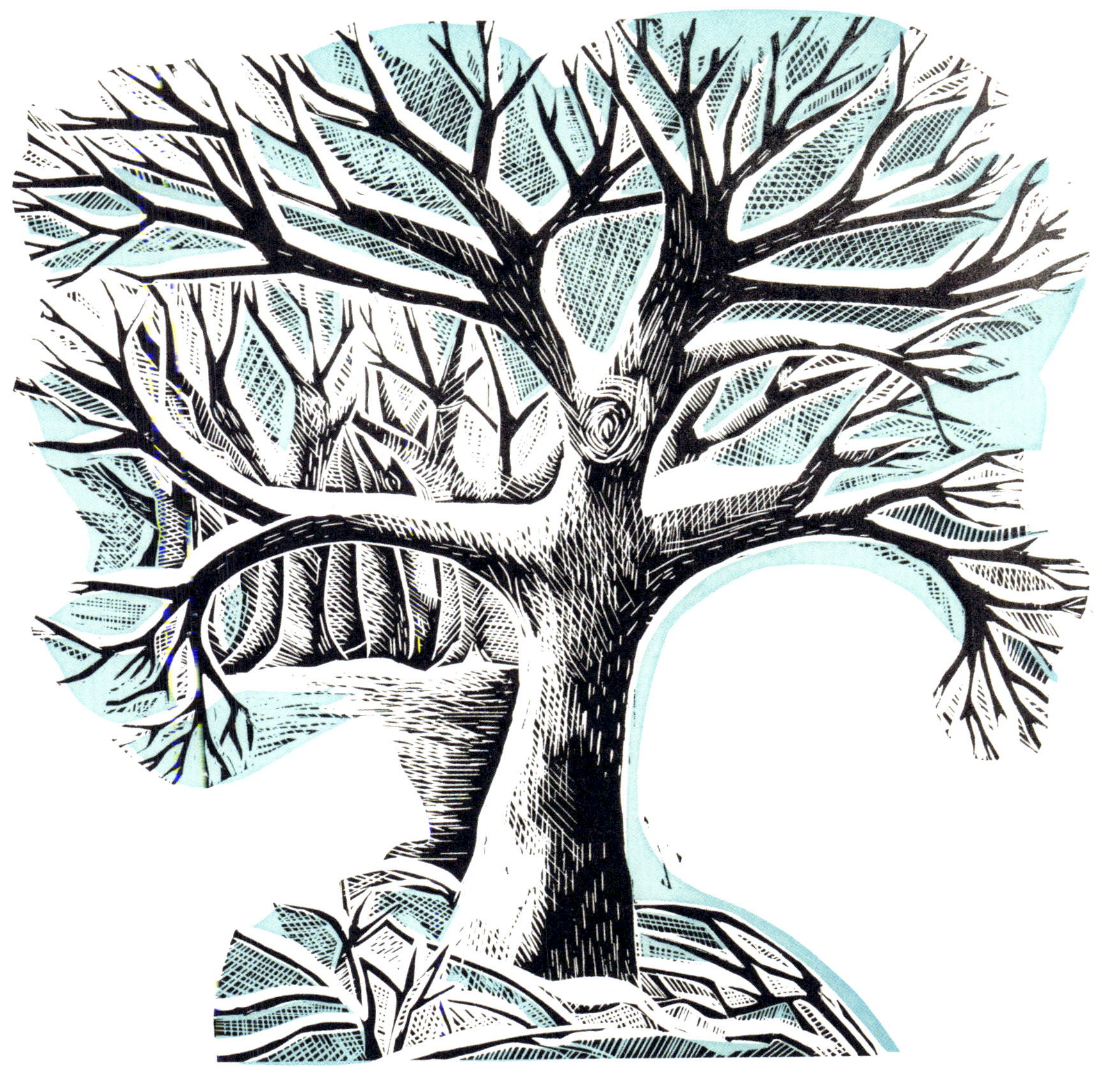

Winter Trees

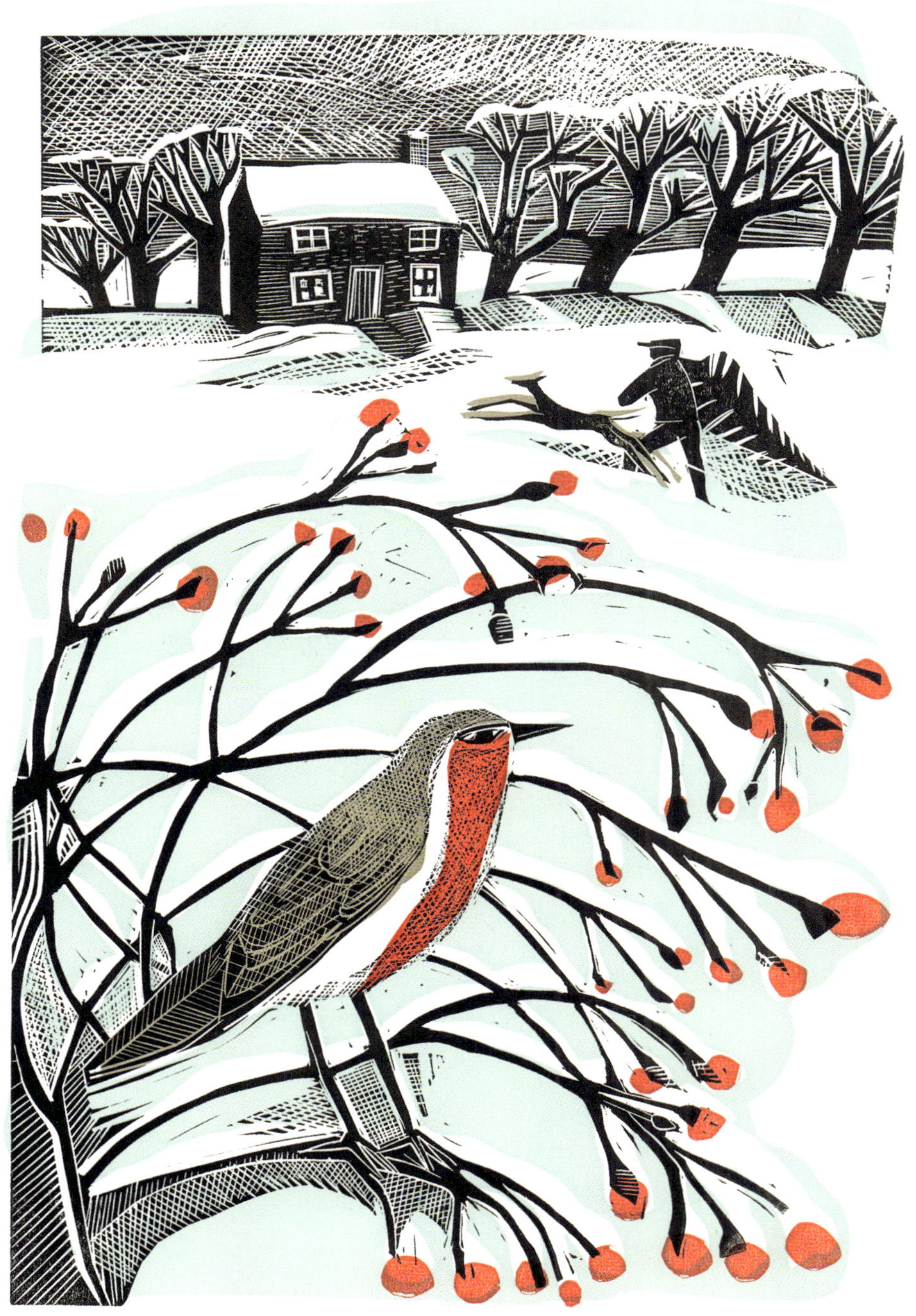

Bringing Back the Tree

Winter Fox

One of the aspects of my work that has evolved over the years is making an annual advent calendar – the ones I create are of course just pictures but they seem to be enjoyed as much by adults as by children. The images are imagined but I do add one or two aspects from my home life. Winter Cottage is based on my father's house. He died in 2019 at the age of ninety-four but he lived for more than forty years in the same cottage on the border of Wales in Shropshire. It was an iconic gingerbread cottage perched on the top of a cross roads that looked into Wales one side and then out across the Shropshire plain on the other. It was the most amazing view and according to my father it gave him a view of more than half the width of the UK – which meant he could keep an eye on us wherever we were. To the back of the cottage is Bromlow Callow – a callow is a hill topped with a circle of distinctive trees. This is an image that often appears in my prints – that and his ever-present whippets.

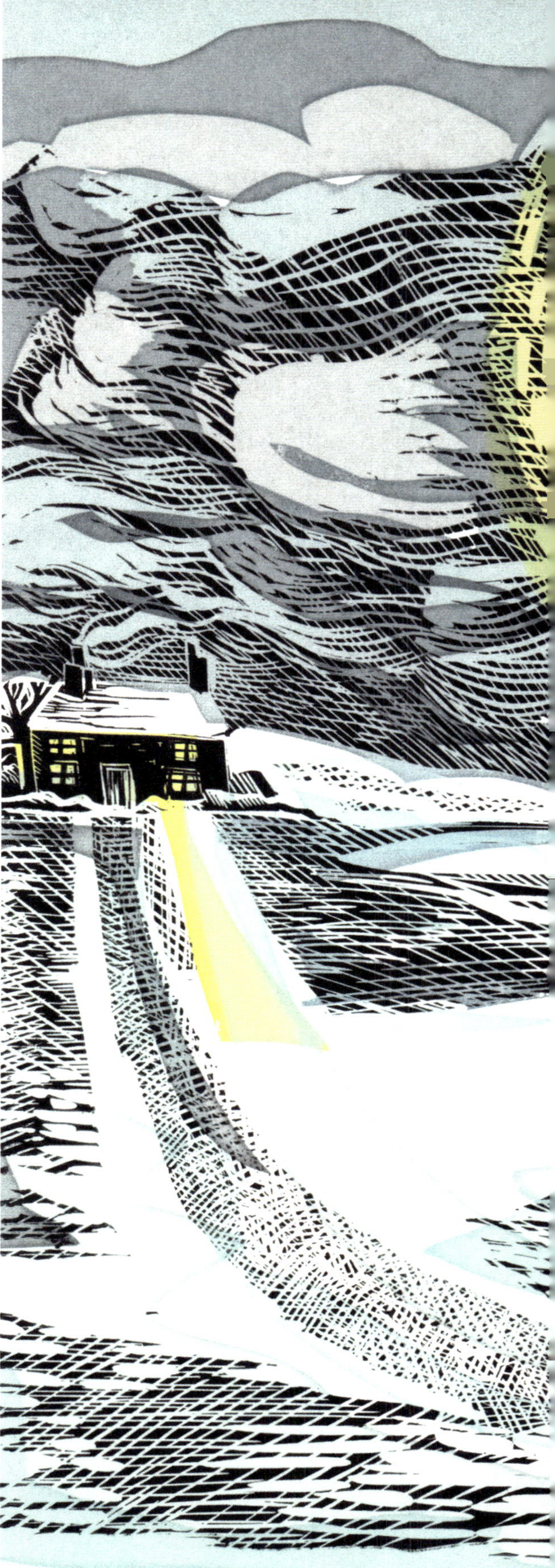

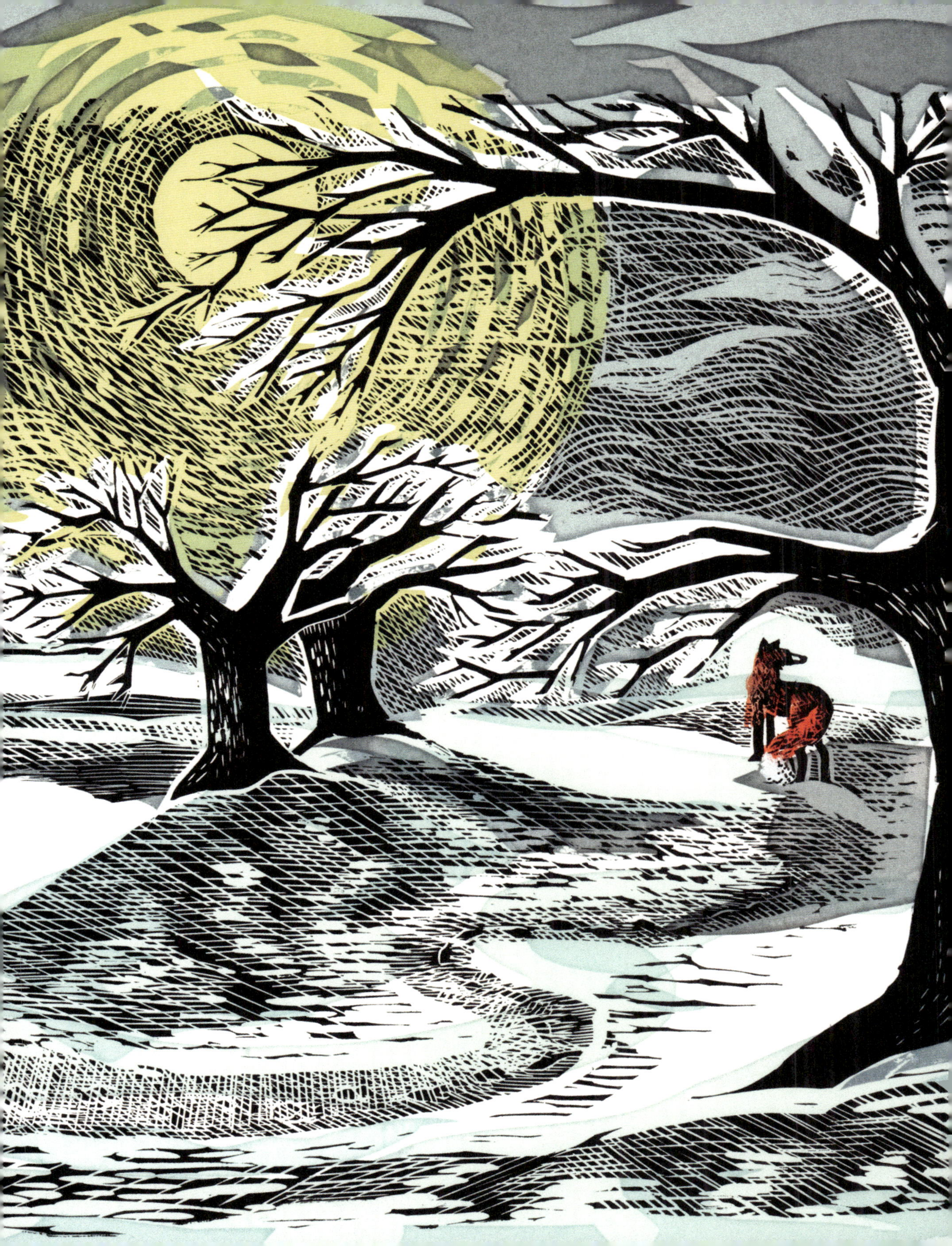

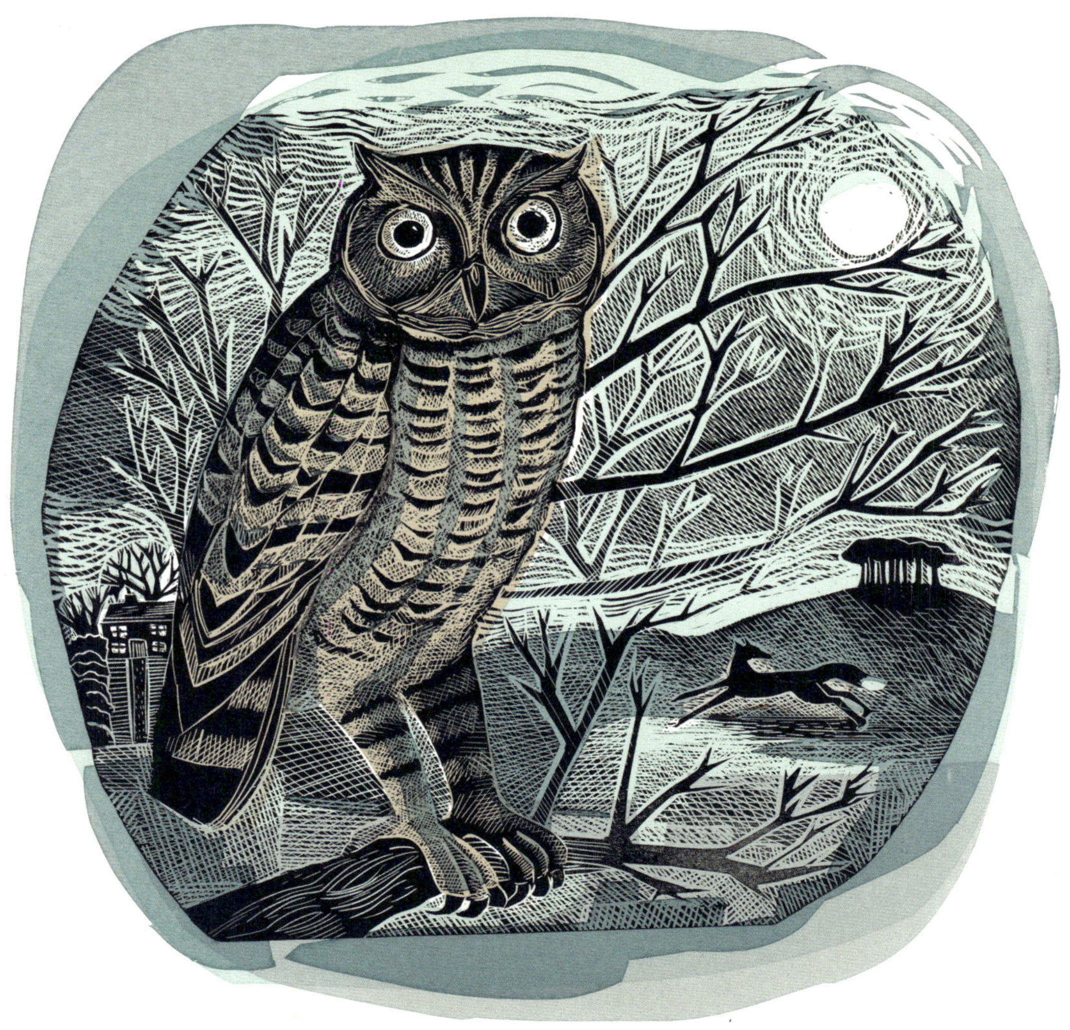

Owl, Hill and Fox

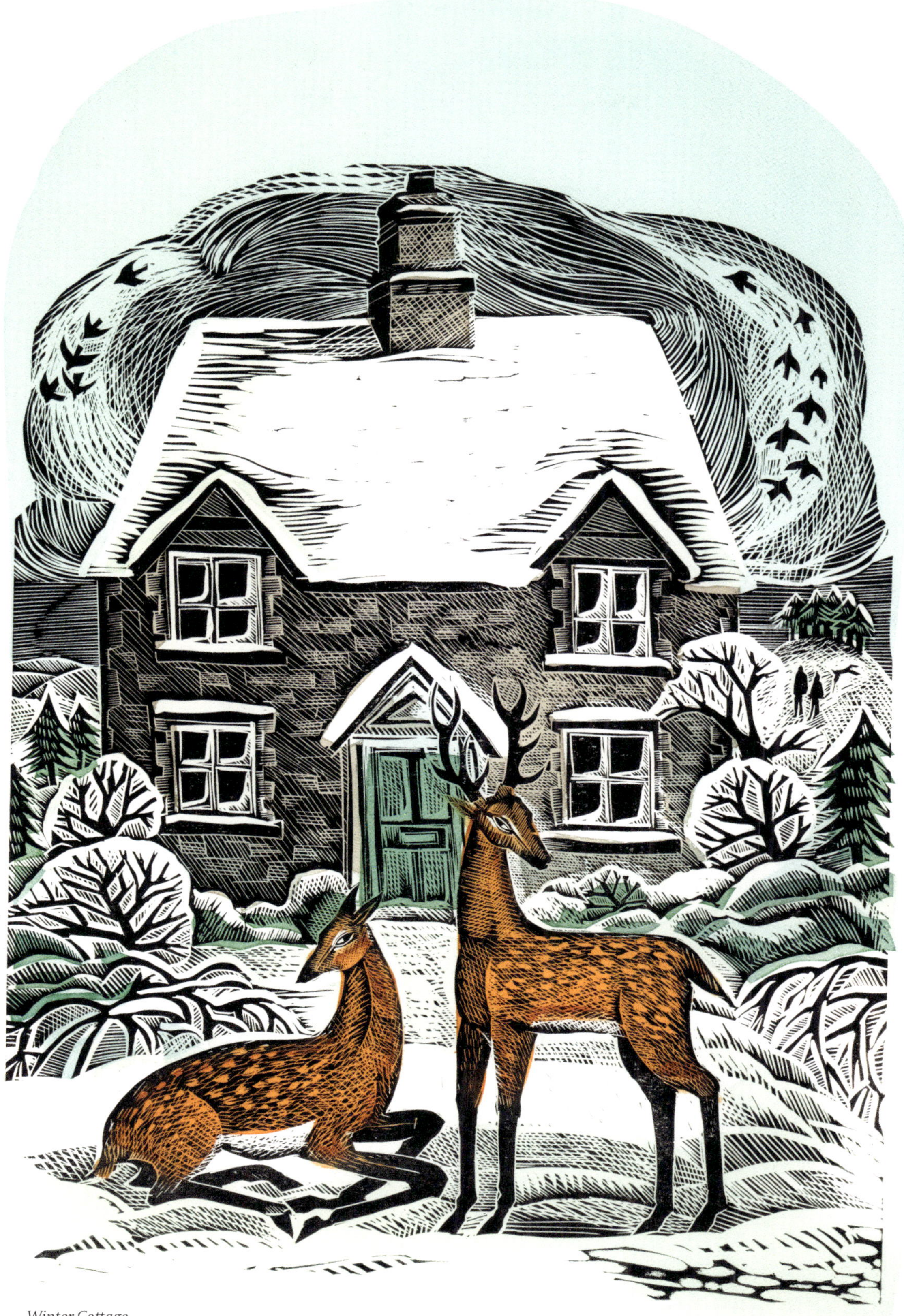

Winter Cottage

We Three Hares

Thick snow in Wing is rare – in the sixteen years we have lived here it has only happened three times – but in 2020 we had one of those snowfalls that in the course of one afternoon turned Wing into a place of true magic. As the snow falls I am instantly turned back into a child and there is no point in trying to work – I want to be in that snow. It is never with us for long, so every moment is to be enjoyed. In my winter prints I hope I convey the sense of excitement that the snow gives me. In Winter Hare you can see Mark and me trudging through the snow watched by a wiry hare. This print is not accurate because in truth even when they were young, our two whippets would not go out in the cold without a coat. So, the bounding coat-free sighthounds in the background is a bit of artistic license. Though a few years back we did own a lurcher called Syd who was much hardier, and he loved the snow as much as we did.

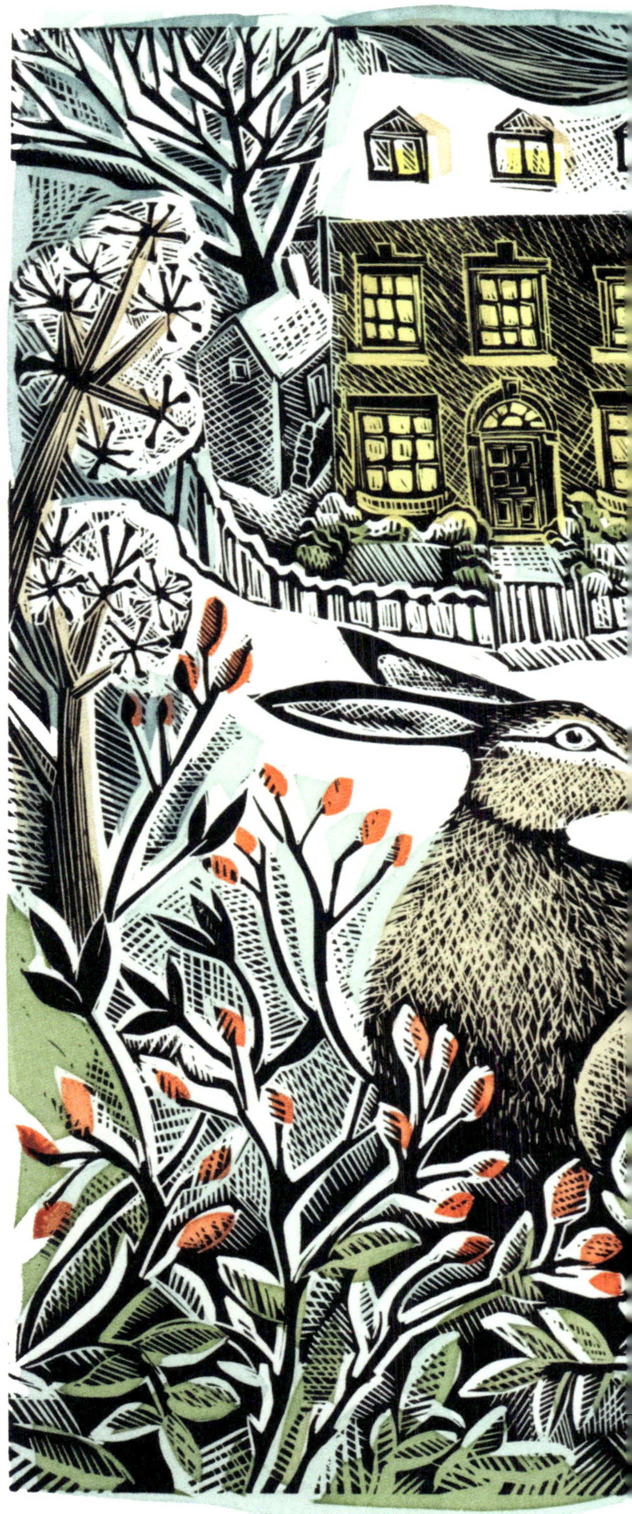

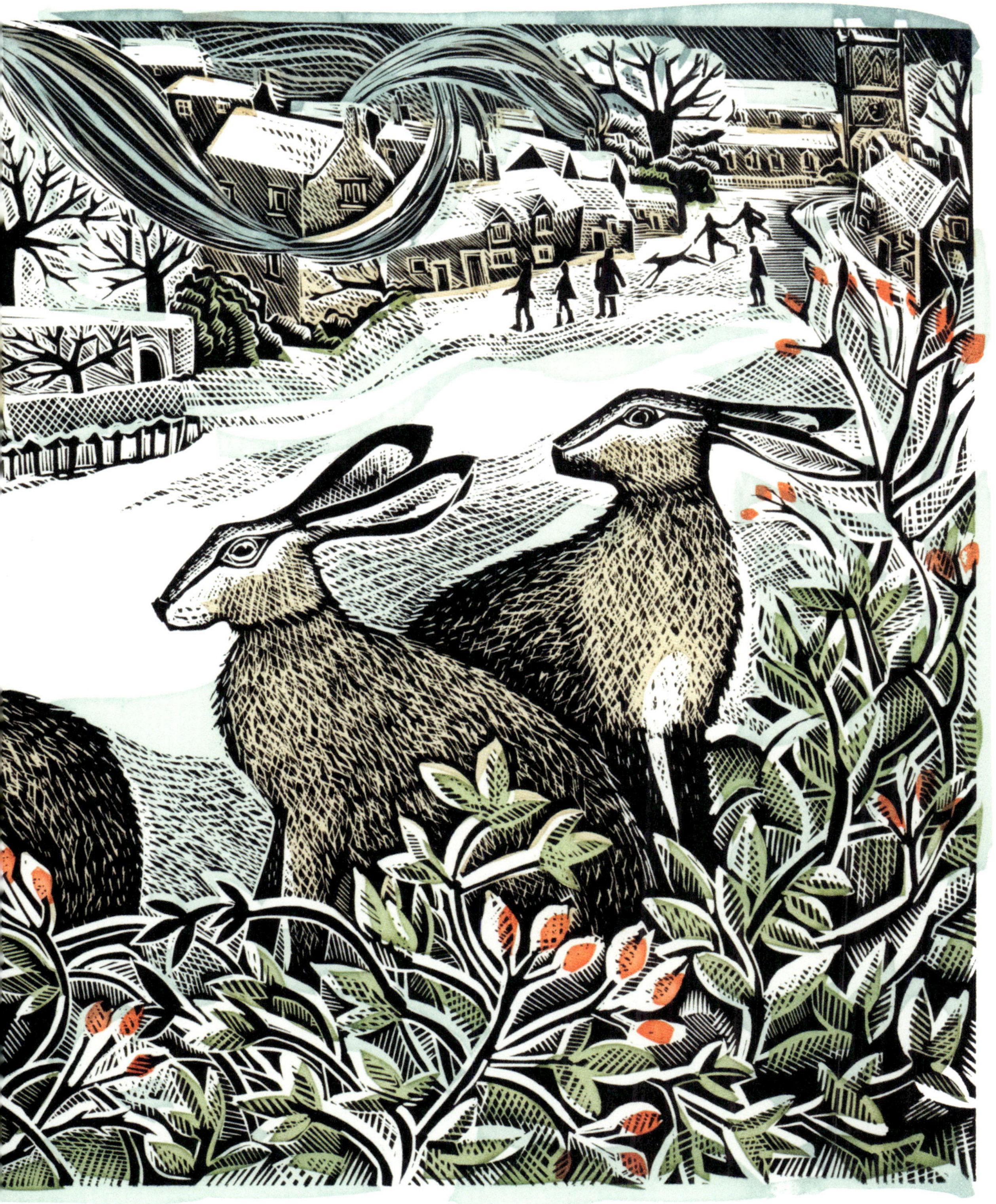

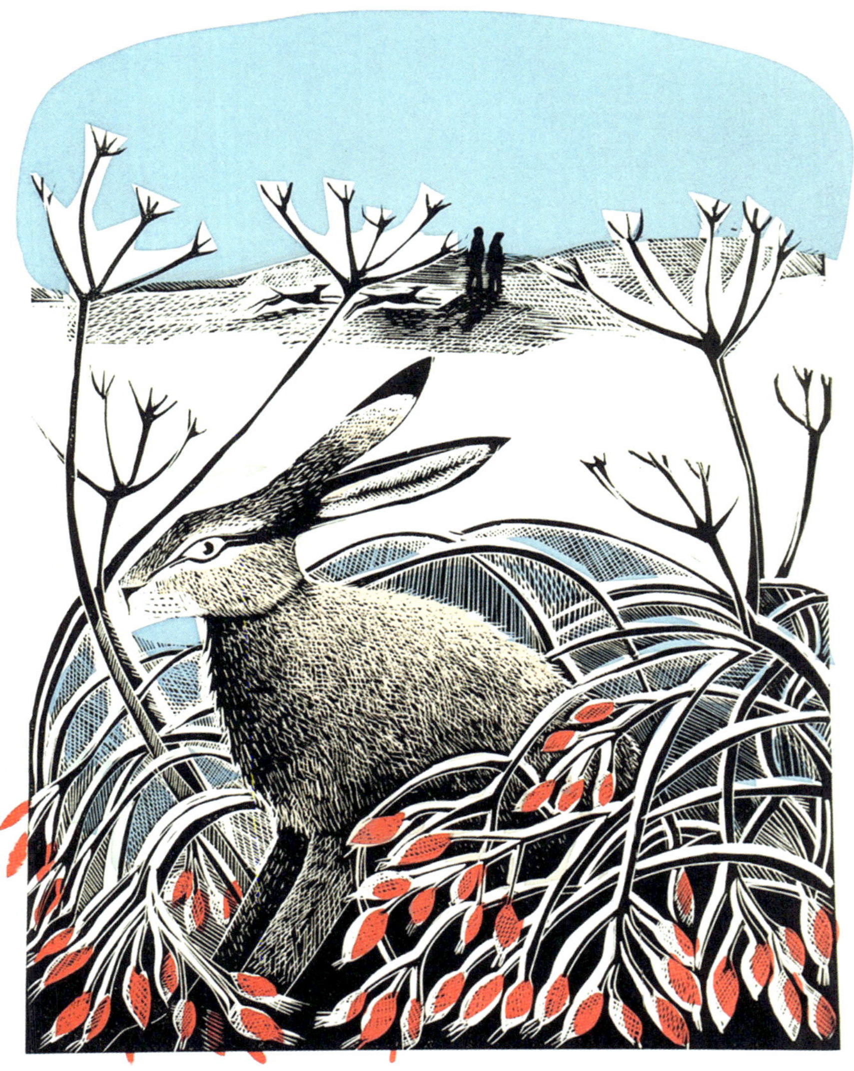

Winter Hare

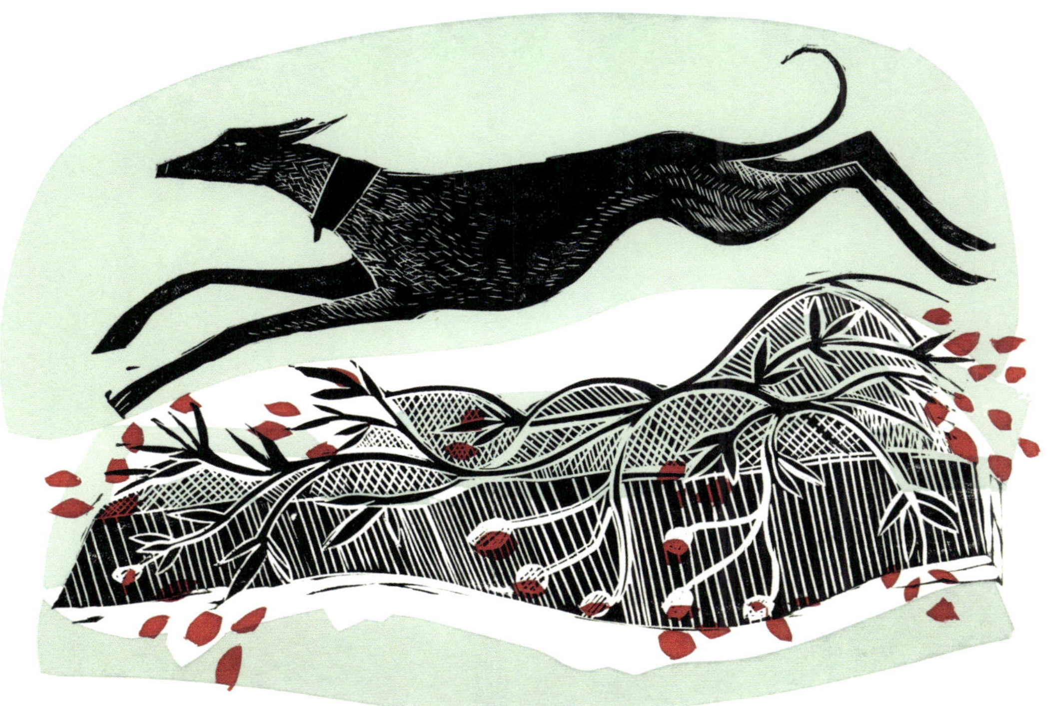

Evening Run

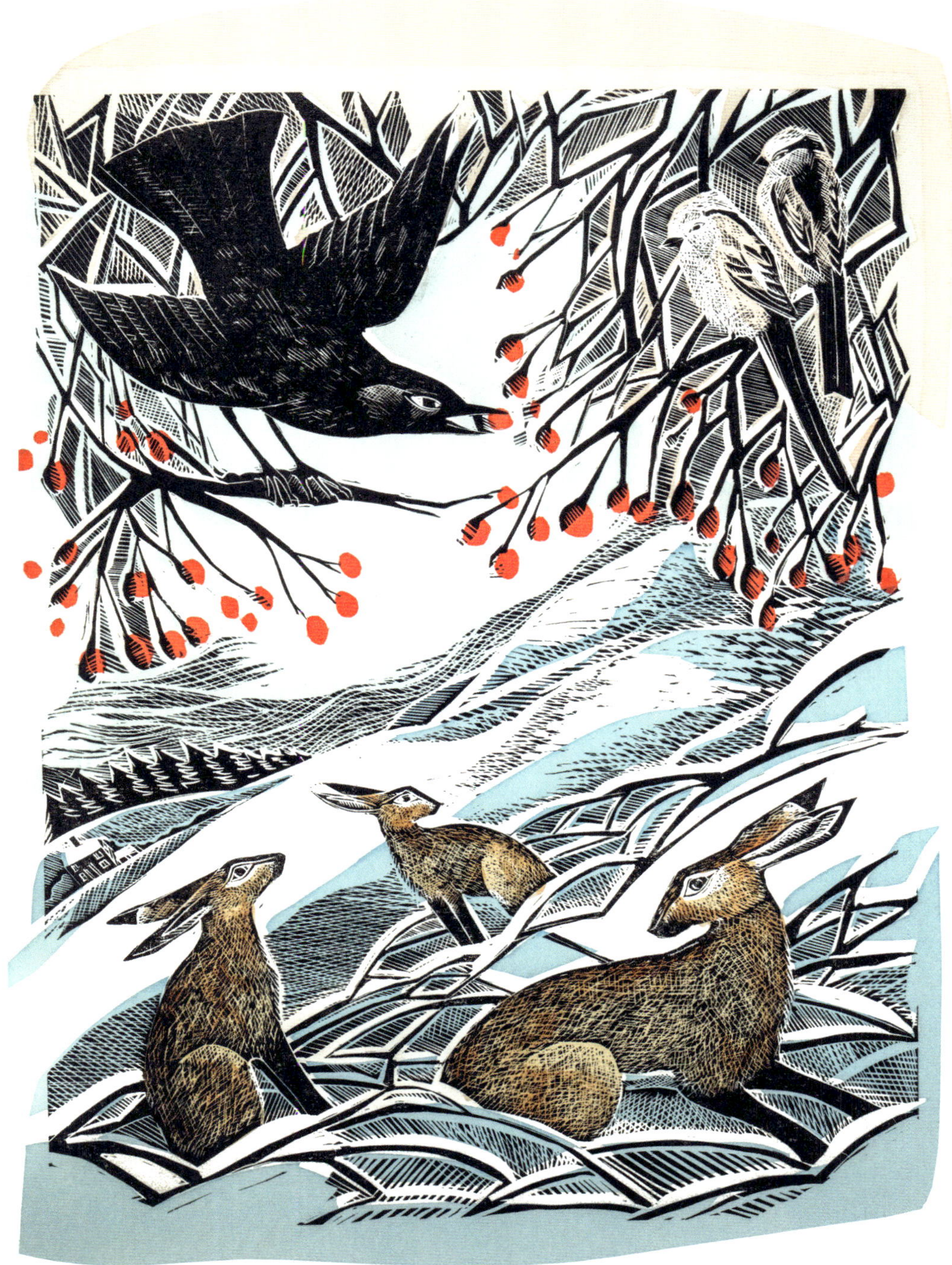

Hares in Conversation

There is a good population of hares in our area; we see them all year round, but a snow-covered field really does give you an insight into their behaviour. Walking through the fields after a heavy snowfall, it is easy to spot hare tracks. The tracks are very distinctive due to their large back feet and small front paws; they make the most beautiful criss-cross designs in the snow. If you are lucky you can follow a track to see the silhouette of a hare against a bright white field.

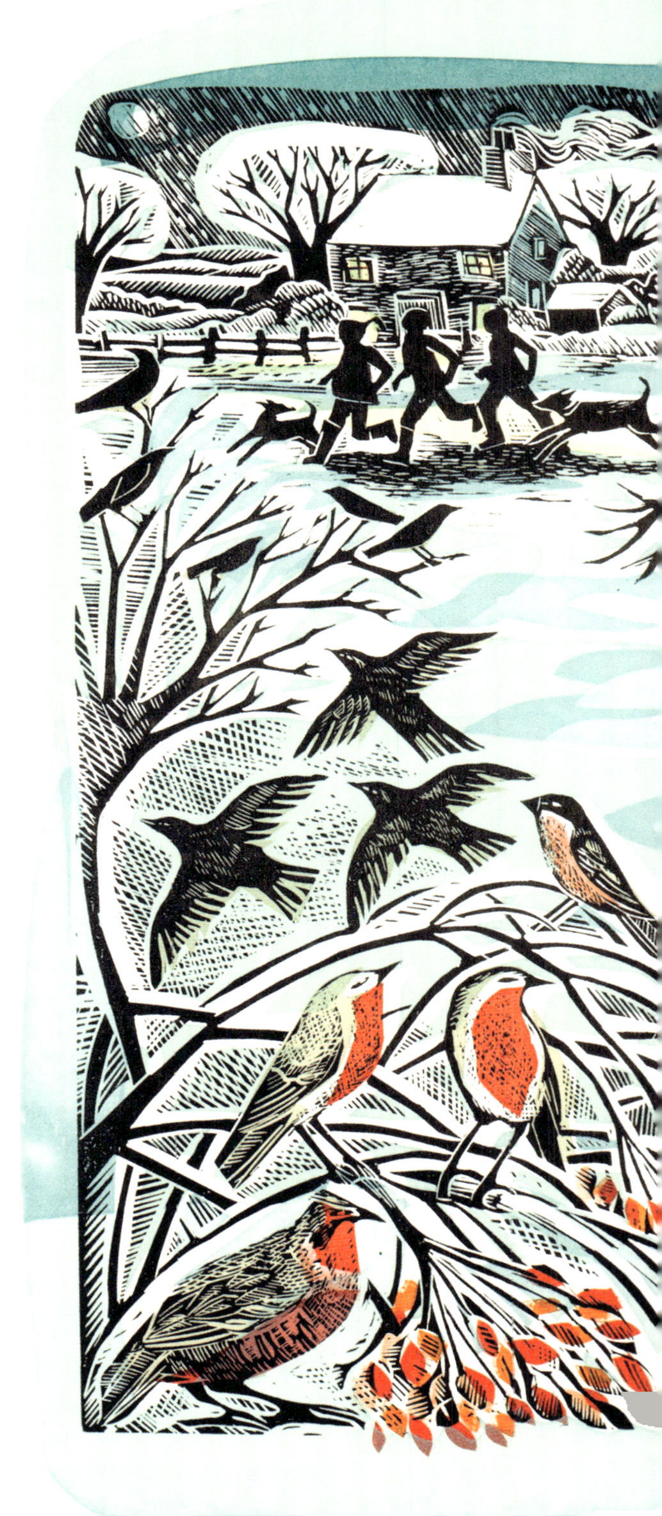

Winter Woodland

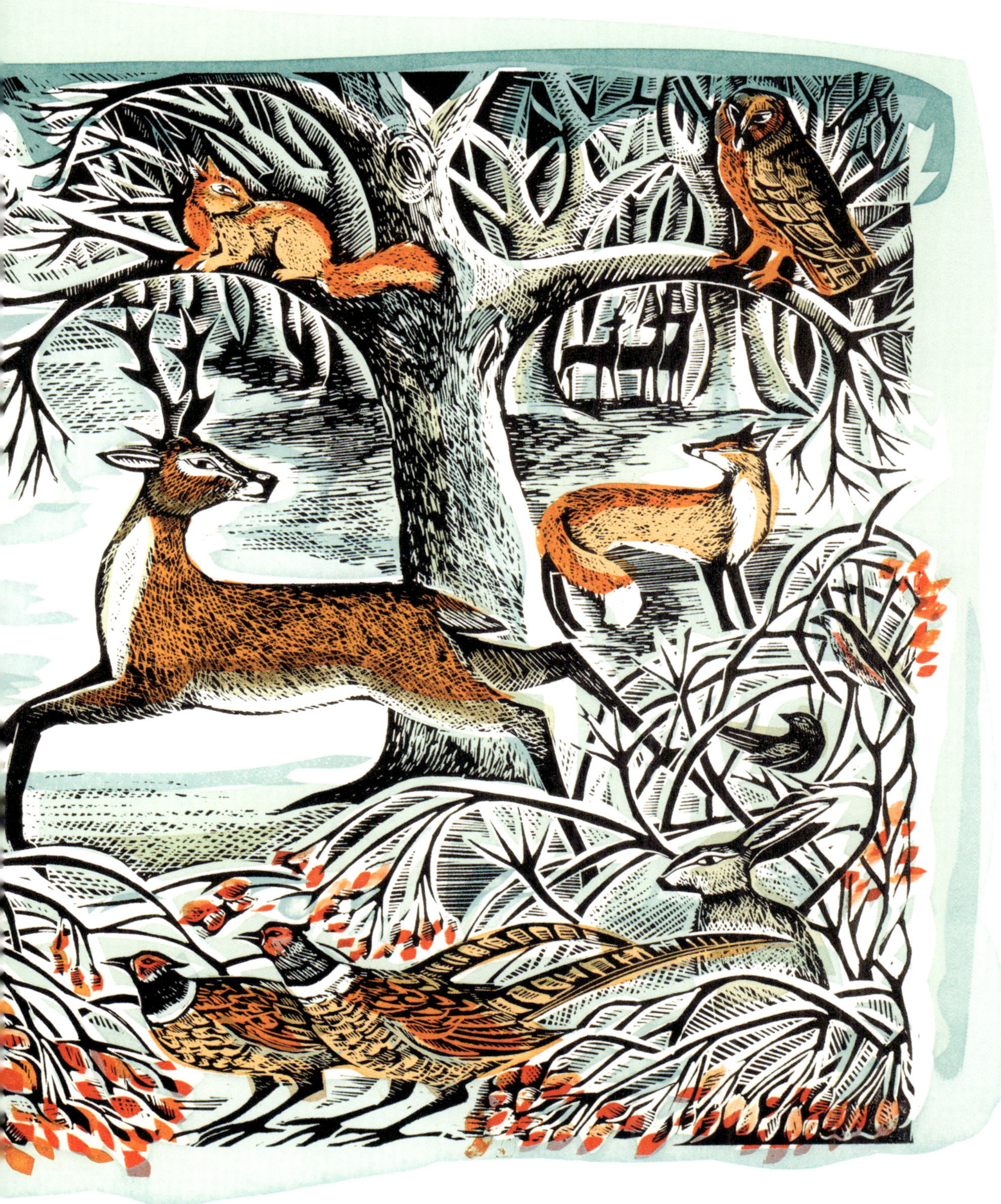

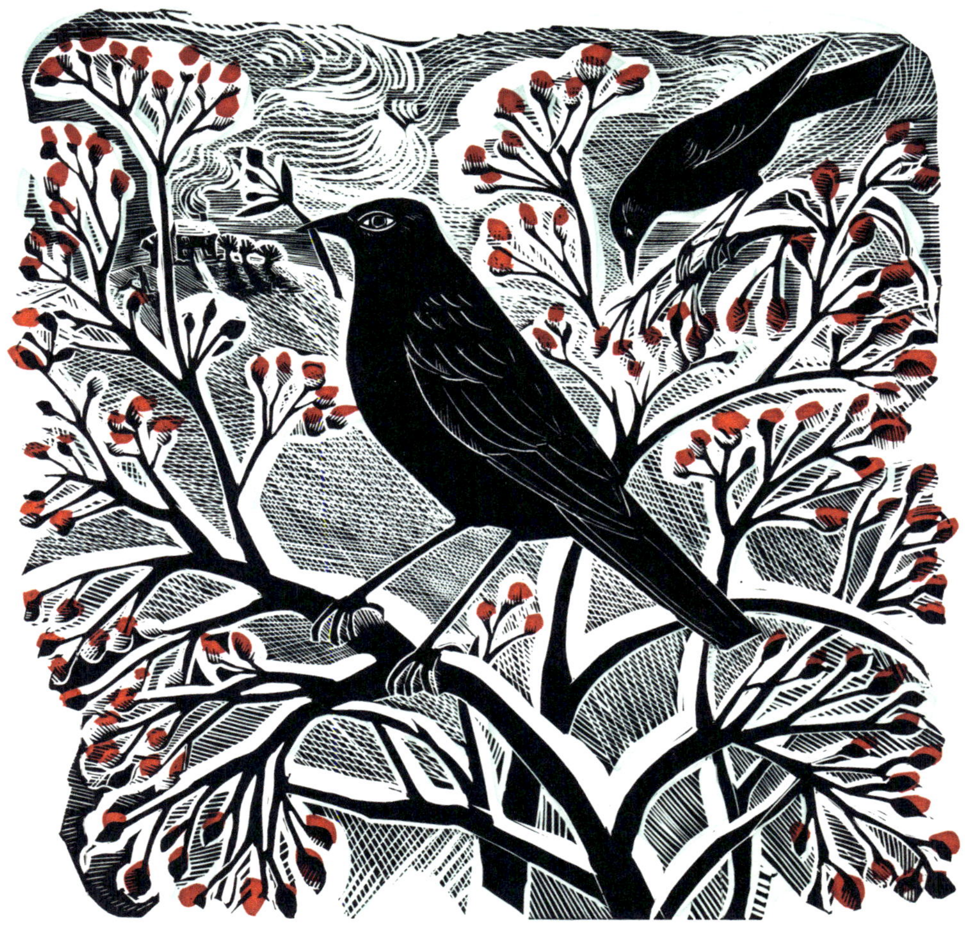

Blackbird and Berries

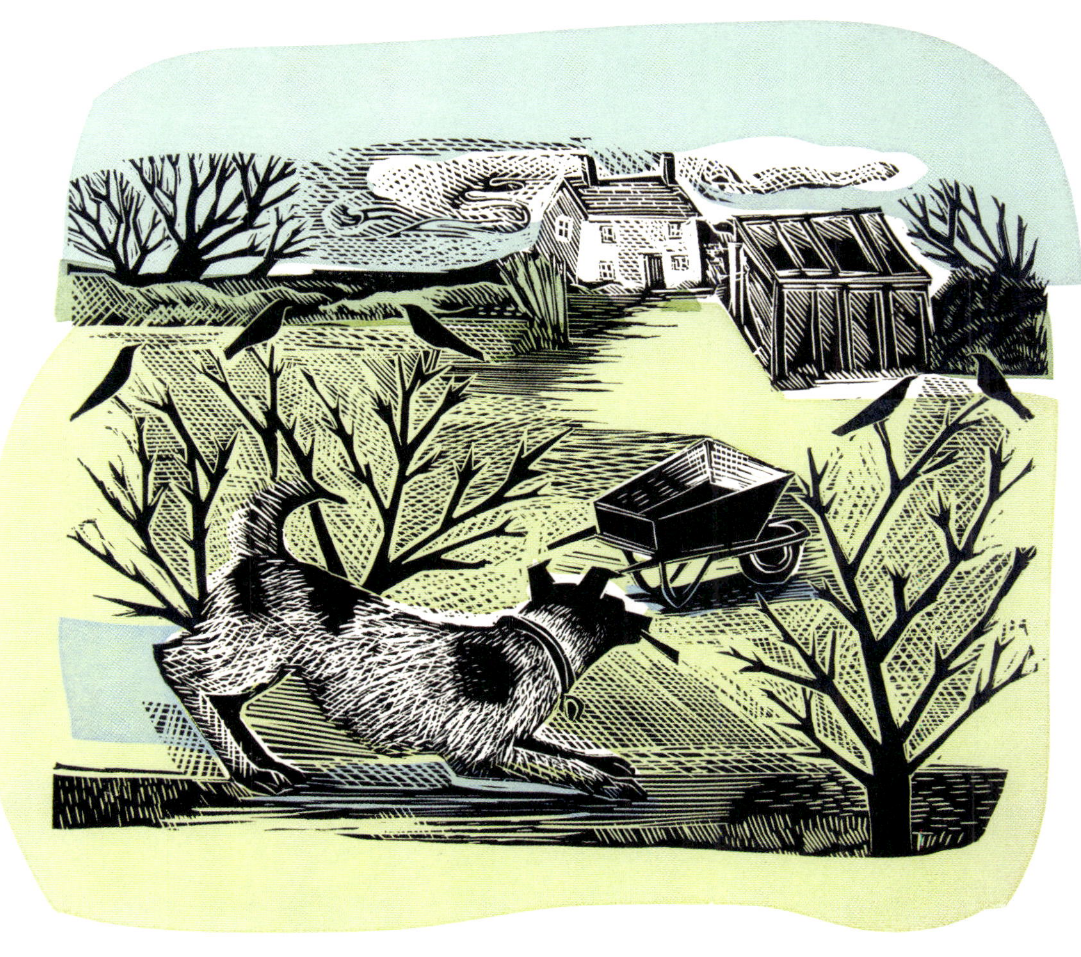

Barney and Stick

Holly Hedge

The hedgerows in winter are particularly beautiful but they are also of great importance. They give shelter to our native birds that stay throughout the winter rather than migrate. Long-tailed tits can often be seen topping the hedgerows, and they team up with others from the tit family. In winter there is a distinctive medley of calls that marks out a gang of blue, great, marsh, coal and long-tailed tits that have clubbed together to feed. The long-tailed tits are often in the garden on the bird feeder outside my studio windows. They really enjoy the fat balls and it is very important that these tiny birds take on enough calories to get them though the cold nights. Overnight, long-tailed tits will bed down together to conserve their energy. A thick shrub such as hawthorn is favoured, and individuals will huddle into a ball with their tails sticking out.

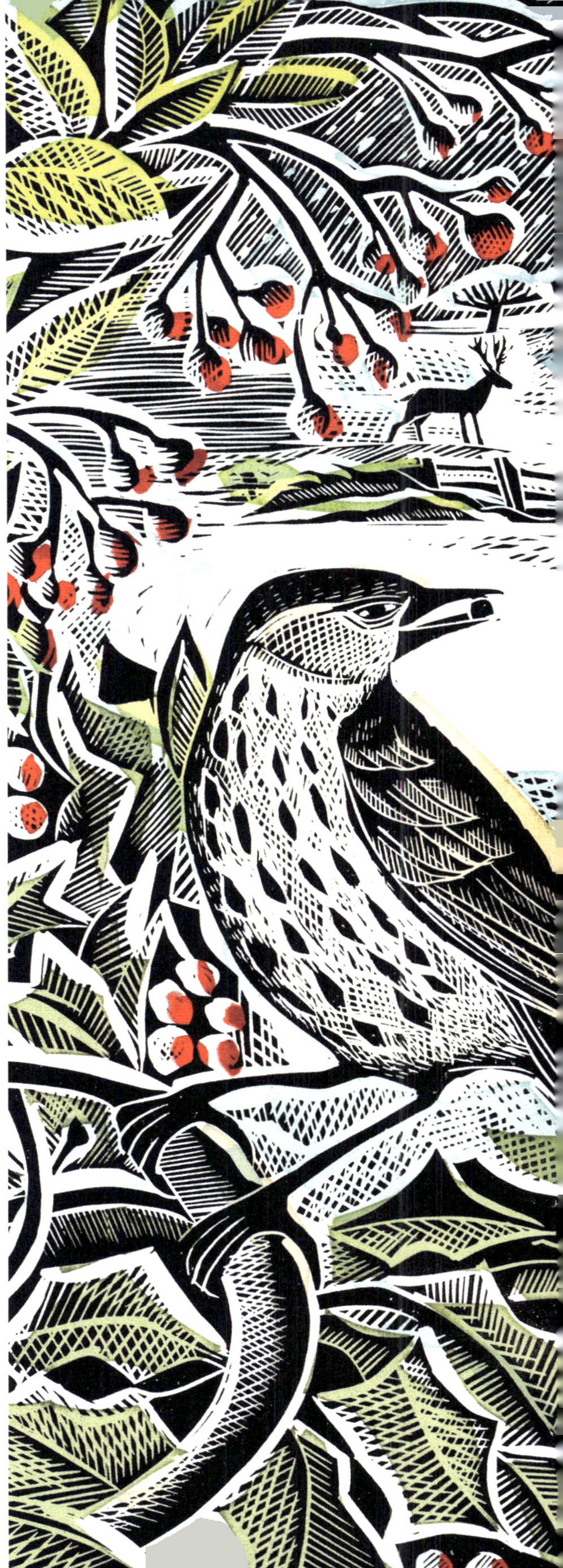

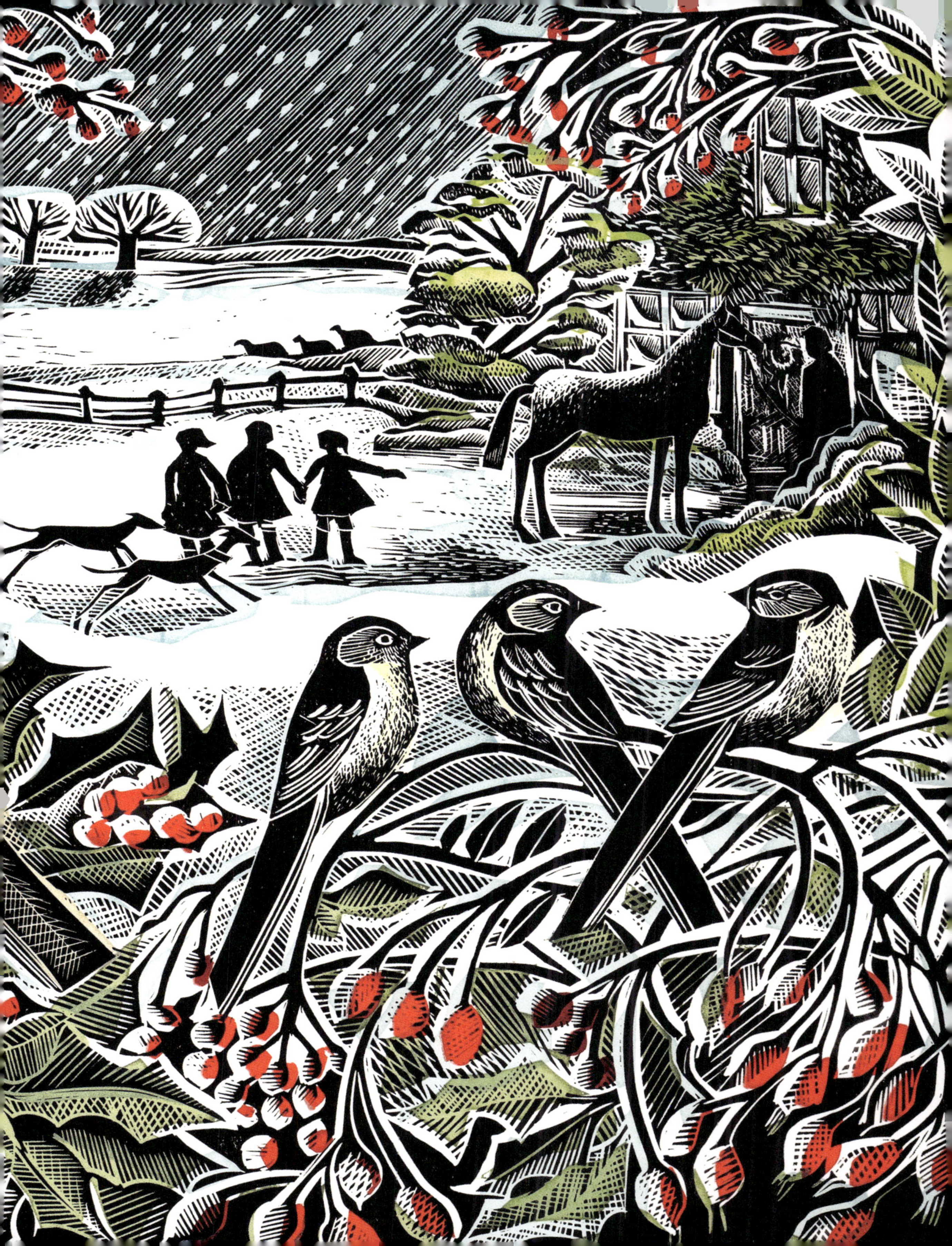

Seal Song

There are few more spectacular sights than seeing the grey seals pupping on the South Norfolk beaches of Winterton and Horsey, but I have to say it is a trip I will not willingly repeat. It was the most wonderful of sights, a huge expanse of beautiful sandy beach stretching out as far as the eye could see and covered with seals and their pups. But the behaviour of many of the other visitors was atrocious, truly shocking – putting both themselves and the seal pups in danger. They seemed to regard the seals not as wildlife but as some sort of amusement park entertainment, only there for selfies and fun. The beaches are patrolled by volunteers from a charity organisation, Friends of Horsey Seals, but on the day I visited there were just too many people for them to control. I found the experience very upsetting and it seemed to highlight the great distance there is between human understanding of nature and how to respect it.

It was a relief to get away from the chaos of the seal watchers to a different part of the beach. There in the sand dunes was a flock of snow buntings – I had never seem them before. These delicate little white and mottled brown birds migrate south in the winter, having spent the summer breeding around the Arctic. It was the most charming of sights as they flitted through the sand dunes.

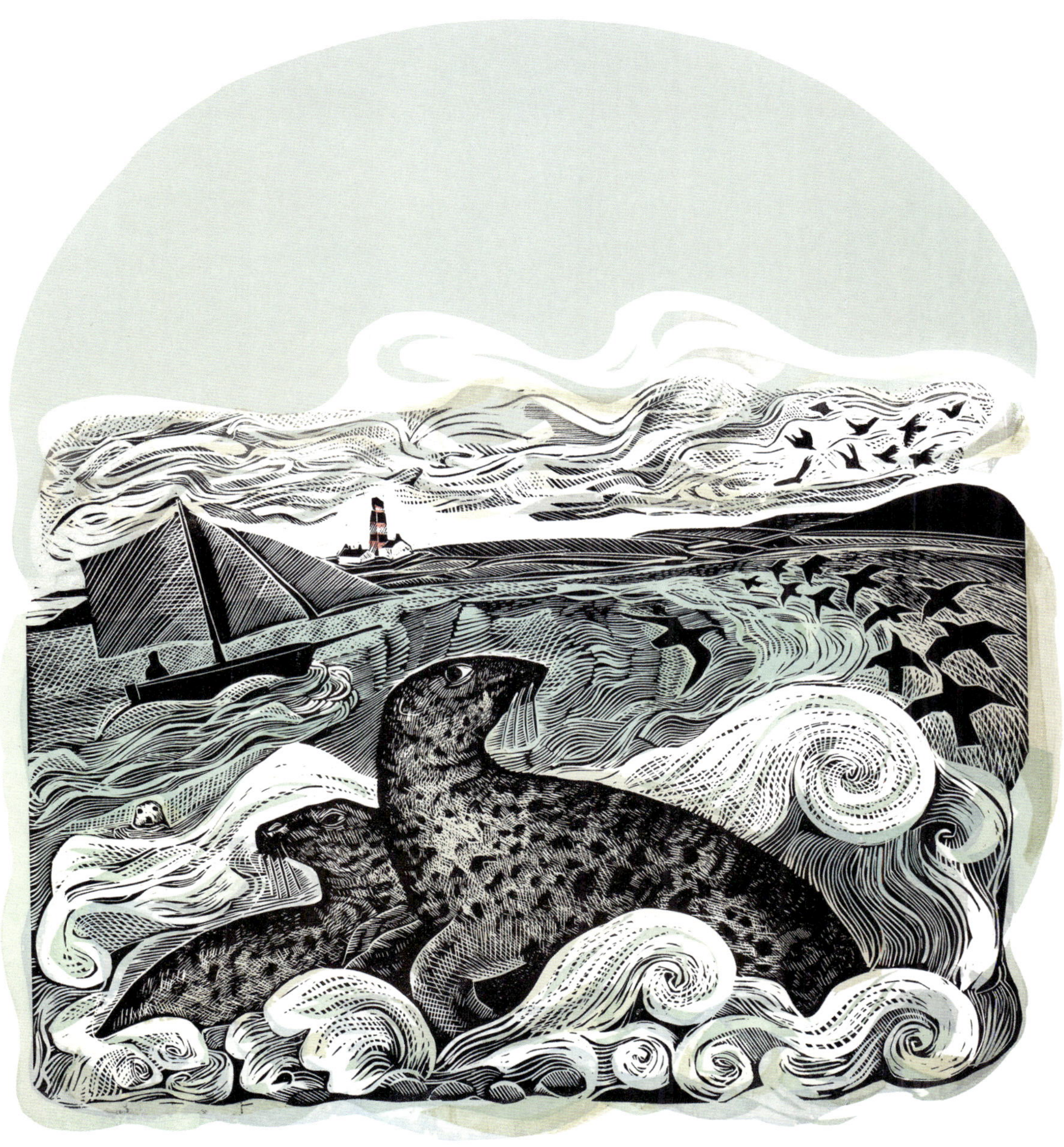

A Winter's Tail

Cornwall is a place I have visited many times, but I have only been to the Scilly Isles once. That was in the winter of 2016, and we stayed on St Mary but ventured out on the local taxi boats to the other islands. I loved all the islands, each had such a distinctive flavour of its own and each felt unique. This was February so everywhere was quiet, we would walk all day and hardly see another person. When we first arrived, I was very excited at the thought of visiting Tresco and its famous gardens. I had also heard that there could be a chance of seeing red squirrels. Twenty red squirrels first arrived on Tresco in 2013 – they came from the mainland in an experiment to see if they would settle and breed. It has been a great success story: they have thrived, increasing their numbers to over a hundred. Tresco is the home of the Abbey sub-tropical gardens, established in the nineteenth century by Augustus Smith. The temperate climate means it is possible to grow a huge range of plants from all over the world. In the summer season it is very busy but in February there were only a few other visitors. When we arrived at the garden we put our £5 each in the honesty box and entered the garden with bated breath looking for the squirrels. Within minutes we spotted two ginger dots, which turned out to be two red squirrels feeding close to the gate where we had just entered. We watched them entranced, not daring to move, but then as quickly as they had appeared they were gone. We didn't see them again, but that day will stay with me as I had always wanted to visit Tresco and to see red squirrels.

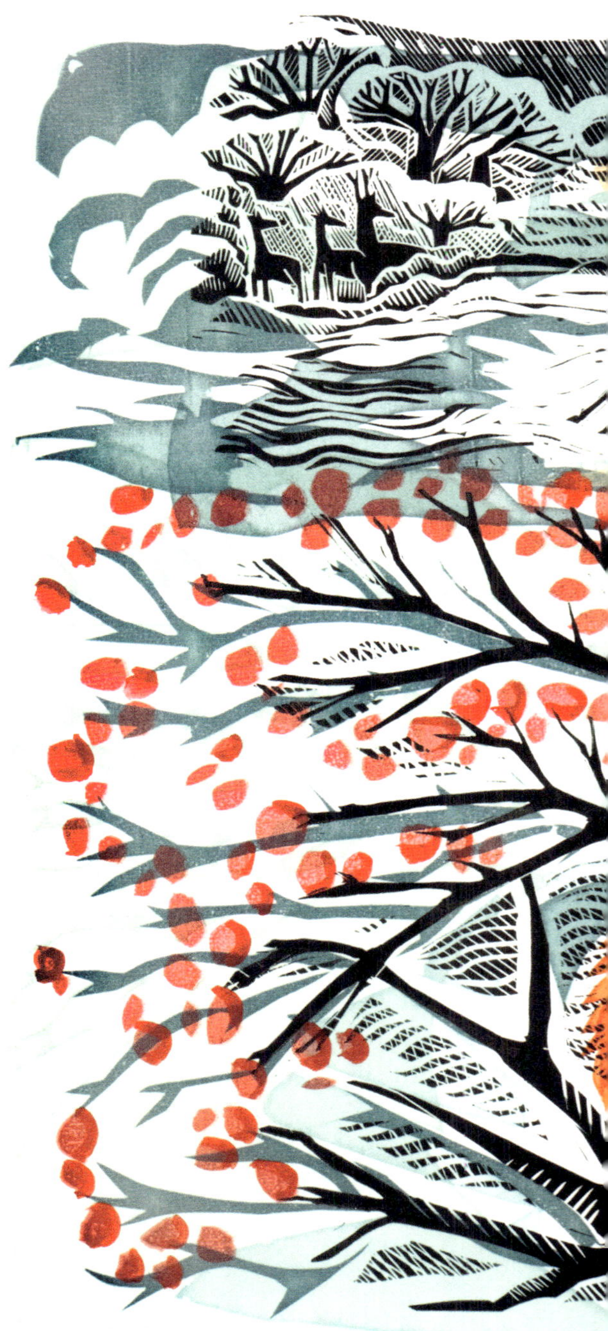

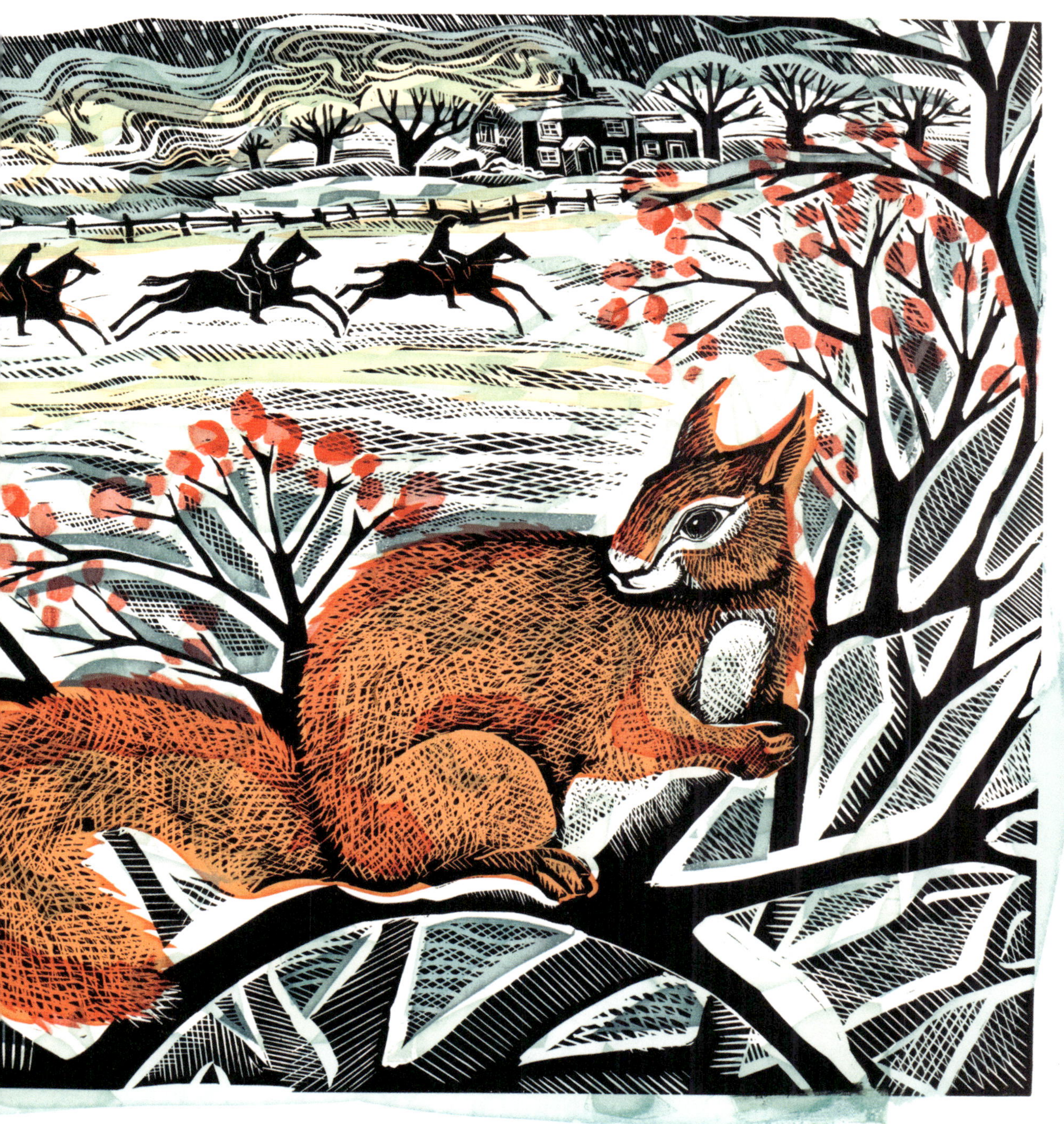

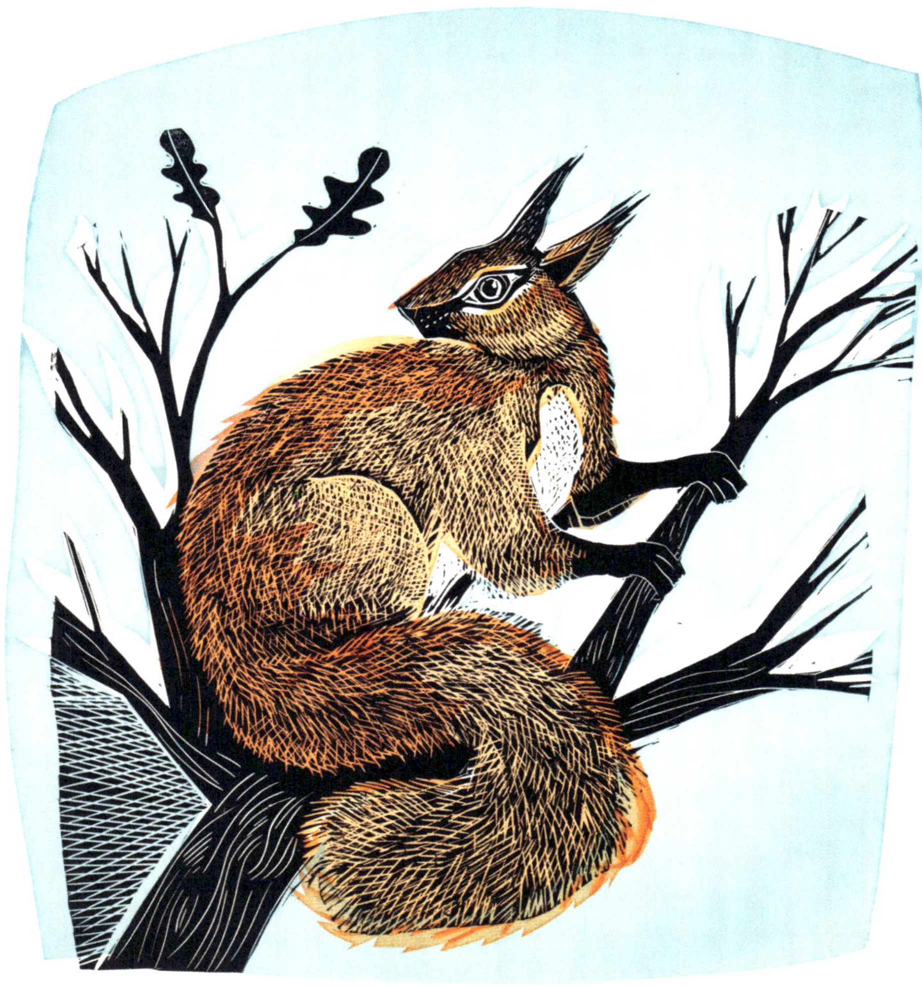

Winter Squirrel

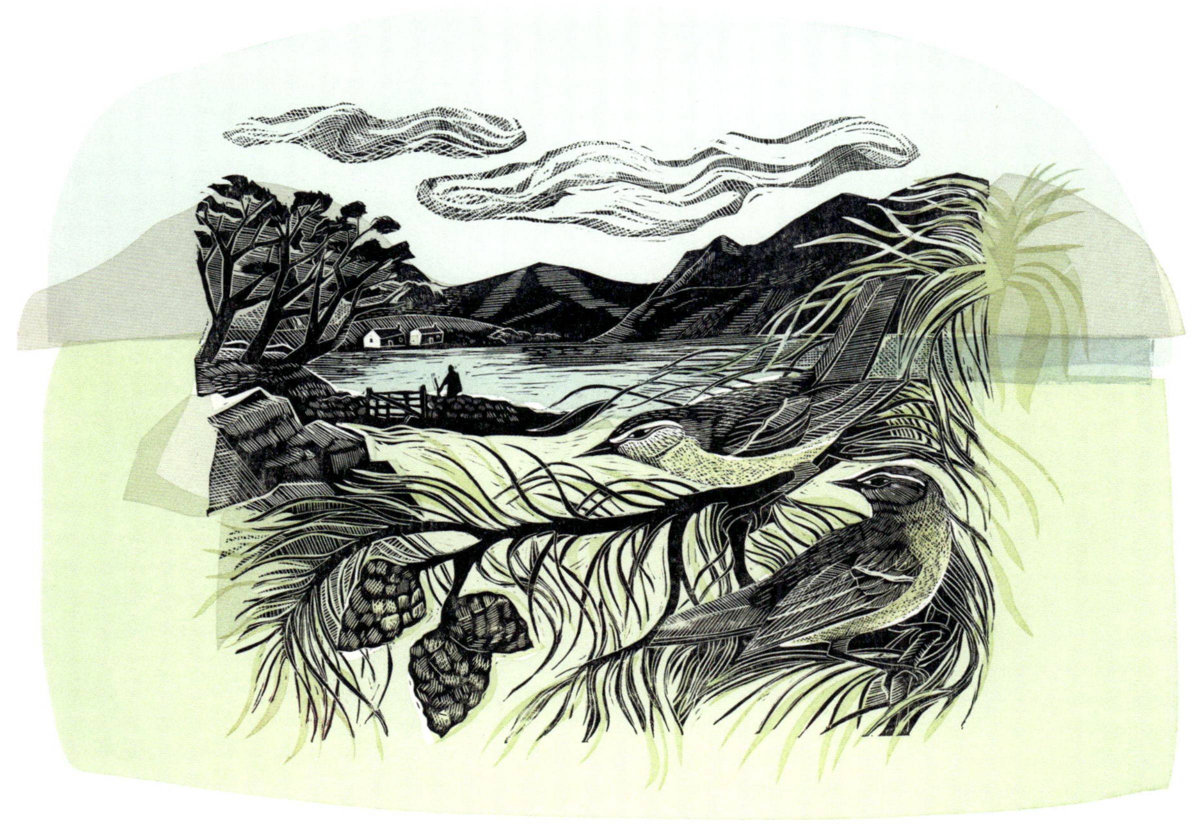

Highland Warbler

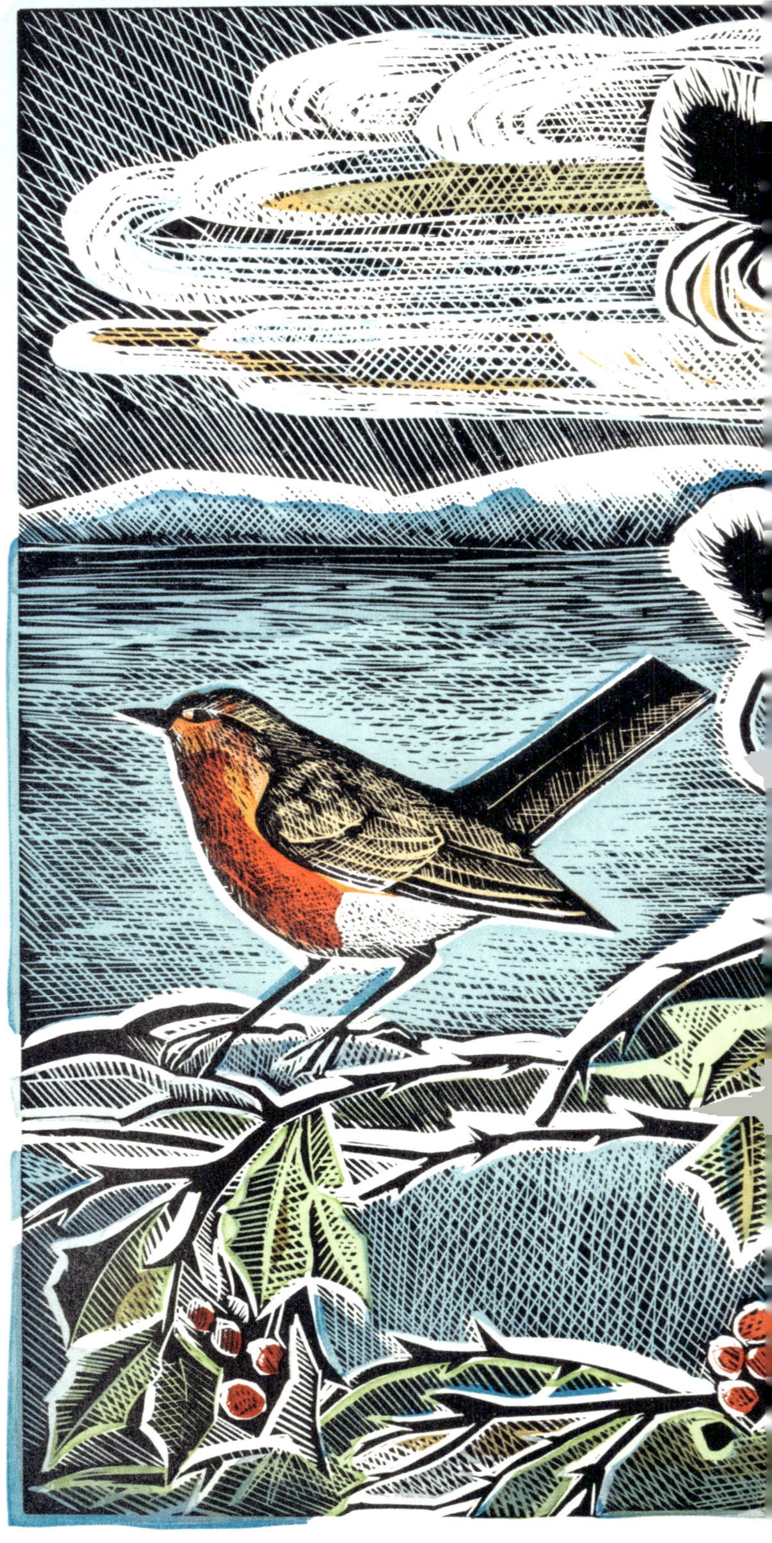

Scottish Robins

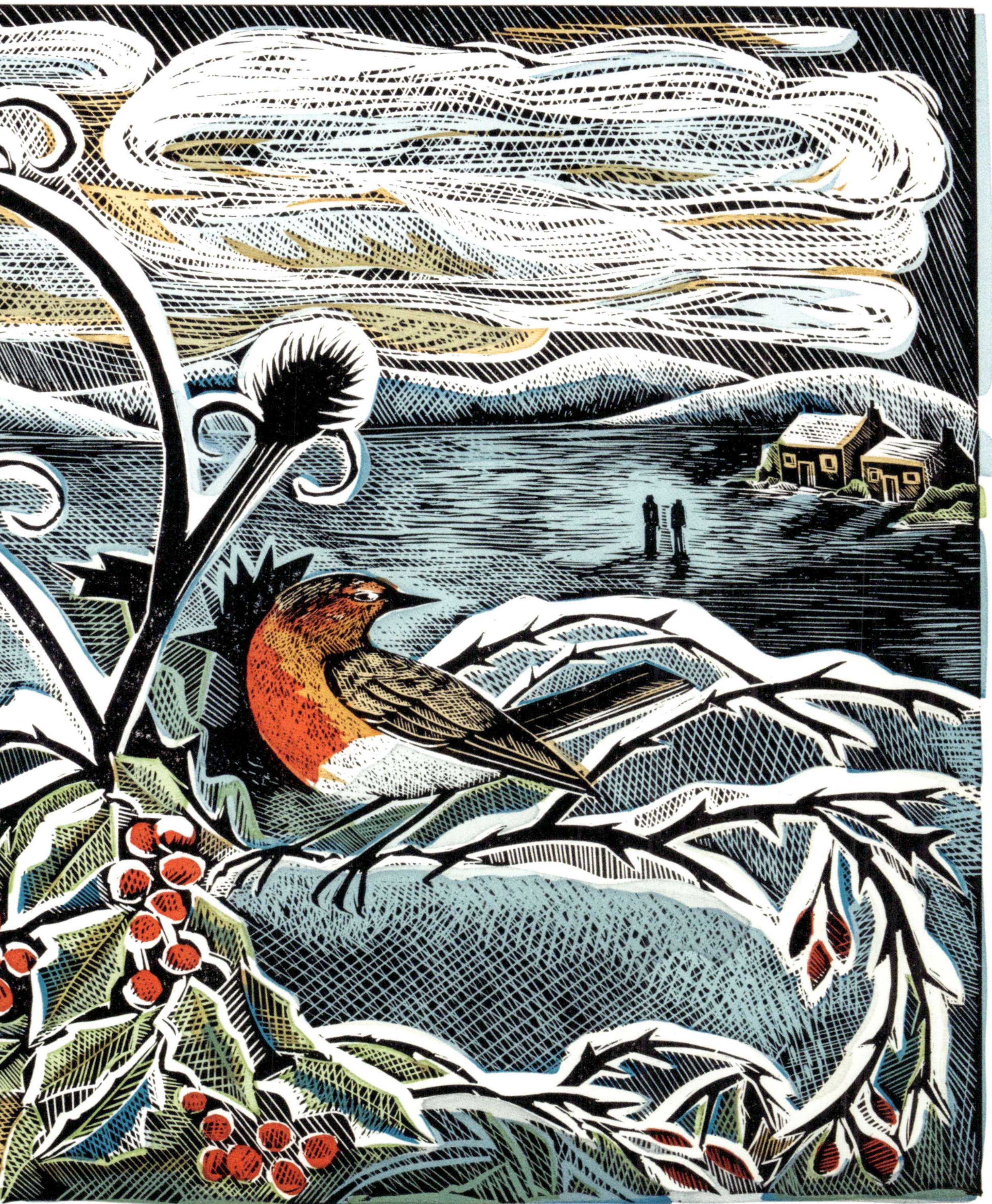

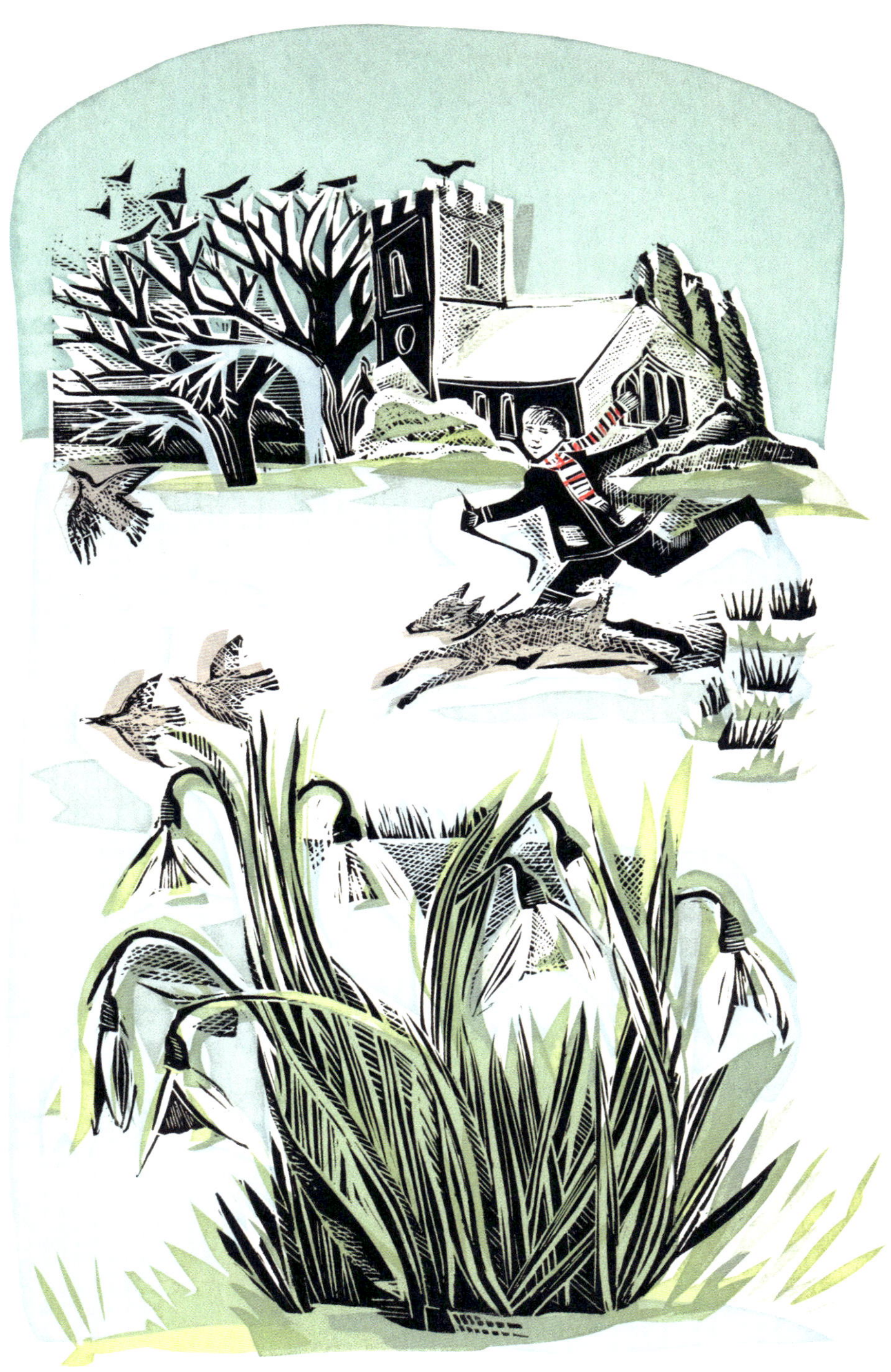

Winter Dog and Church

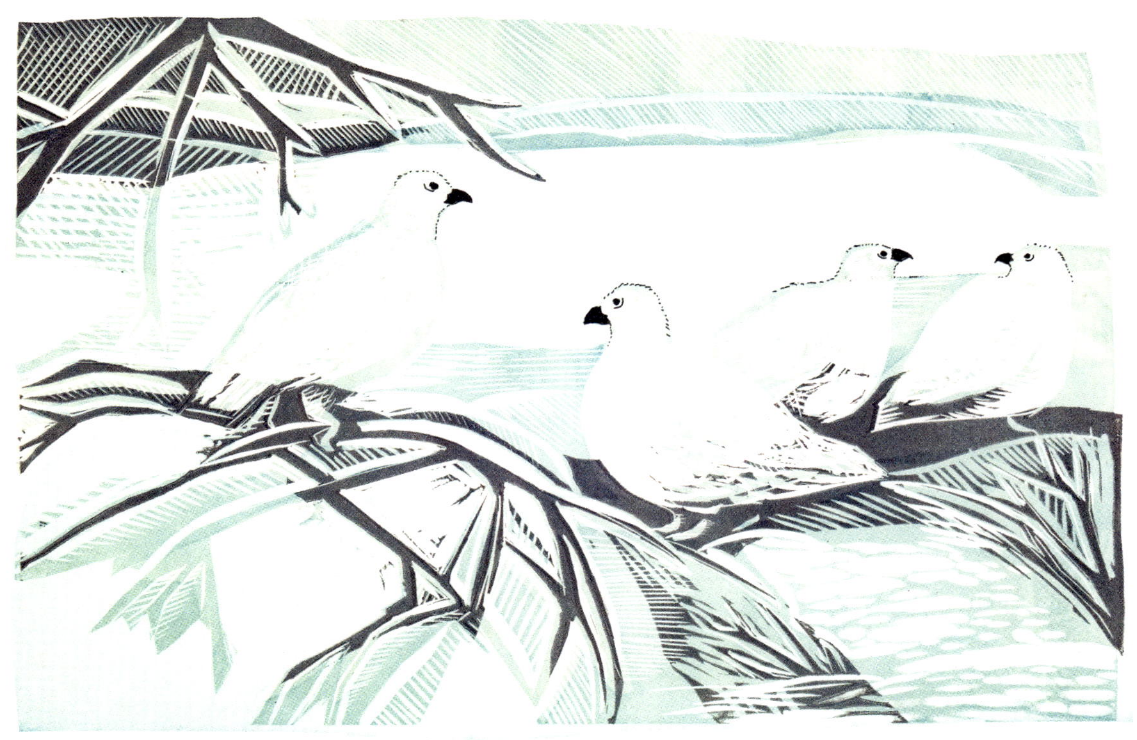

Winter Partridge

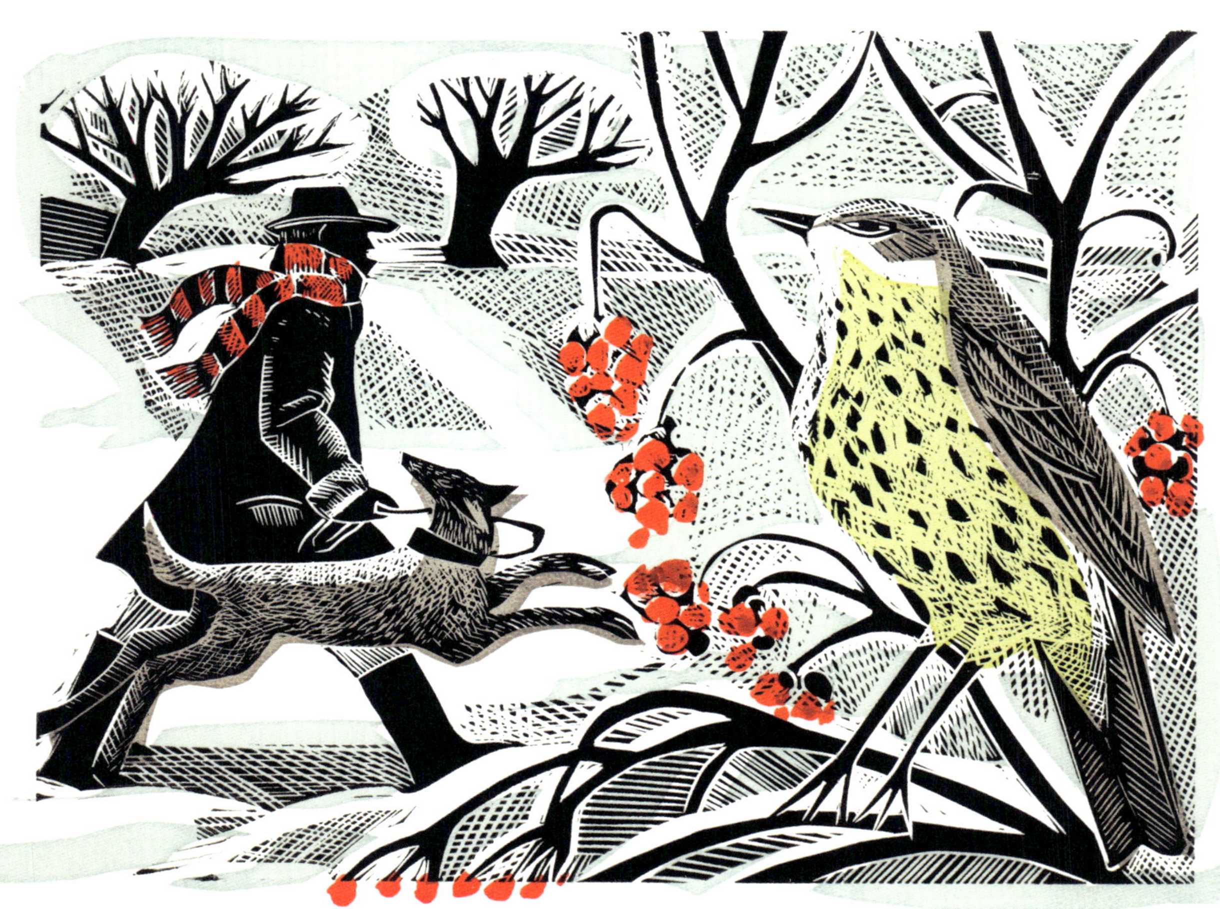

Winter Walk

The arrival of the fieldfares and redwings in Wing seems to bring the year full circle. These birds migrate from Scandinavia to overwinter in our fields and woods. They are markers that the days are growing shorter and the nights darker. For Mark and me these winter days bring their own cosiness. Every evening we have the ritual lighting of the wood burner; our house is small, so the heat soon spreads through the rooms. We are not the only ones to enjoy a winter fire as this is the time when our whippets, Amy and Slim, migrate full time to the sitting room – ensuring they are the ones soaking up the most heat.

Winter weather is no excuse for not getting to work when your place of work is only a short walk down the garden path. I work most days and usually have a number of different projects on the go at the same time. This can be illustrations for book covers, calendars, cards etc. Though I am often working on these projects from a set brief the inspiration for the designs is always rooted in the things that I have seen. It is the changing seasons, the birds and animals that I see on a daily basis that feed directly into my artwork. I consider myself very lucky to be able to express the joy I feel in nature and the things I see around me in the prints that I create. These illustrations are my attempt to portray a year unfolding.

Acknowledgements

For my husband Mark Dyas & our family.

With thanks to all our friends for their great support.

Special thanks to:

Nickie Gibson
Stuart Morris
Chris Large, FSG Design
Liz Oldfield, FSG Design
Dan Bugg, Penfold Press
Jo Crawford, photography
Chris Cordingly, Art Angel Publishing
Frances Bodiam, Flame Tree Publishing

Angela Harding trained in Fine Art at Leicester Polytechnic and went on to specialise in printmaking at Nottingham Trent University. She now lives in the small county of Rutland, and works out of the studio at the bottom of her garden in the village of Wing.

Angela has worked on the covers for a number of books: she created the image for the now-iconic cover of *The Salt Path*, her children's book for the RSPB, Birds, was longlisted for the Klaus Flugge Prize and her work is regularly featured in magazines like *Country Living*, *Countryfile* and *Gardens Illustrated*. She is the author of *A Year of Unfolding: A Printmaker's View* and *Wild Light: A Printmaker's Day and Night*.

Angela's unique and distinct style has become instantly recognisable to nature lovers and book lovers alike, gaining her a huge number of fans who flock to buy her merchandise, including calendars, cards, tea towels, tote bags and jigsaws.

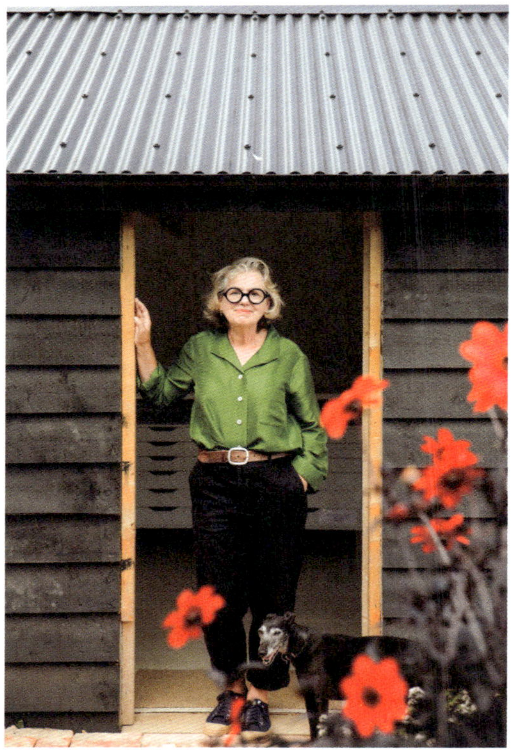

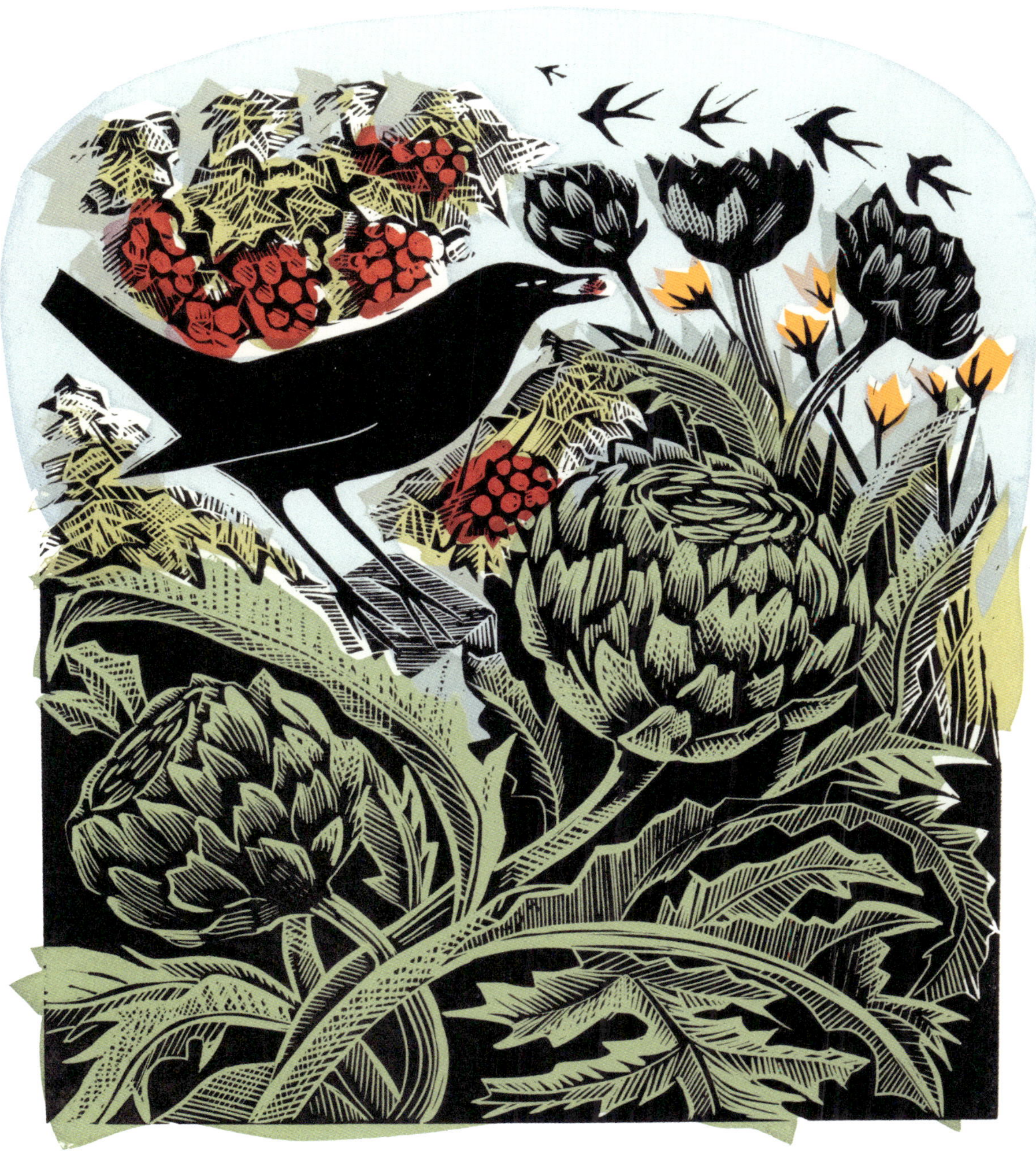

Blackbird Stealing Redcurrants

Early Spring

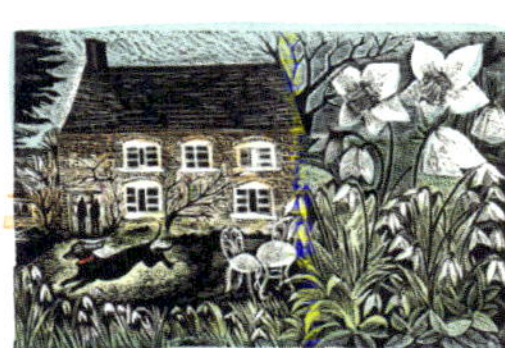
Gardener's Cottage p.20

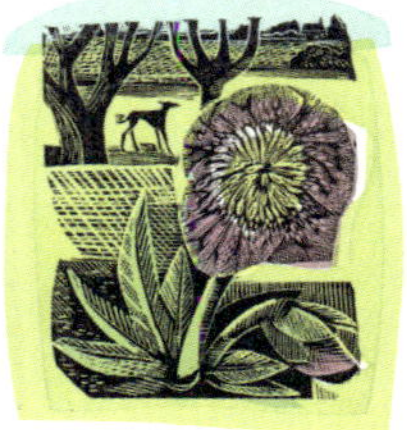
Hellebores and Hound p.23

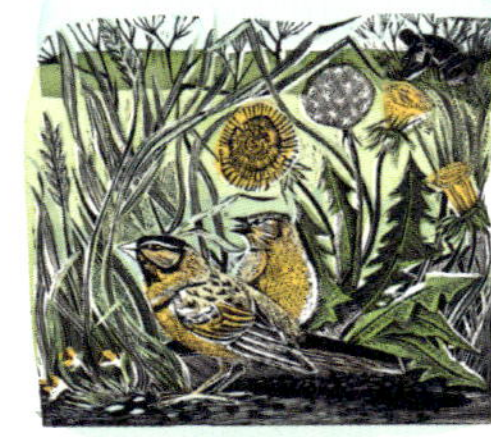
Wonders of Weeding p.24

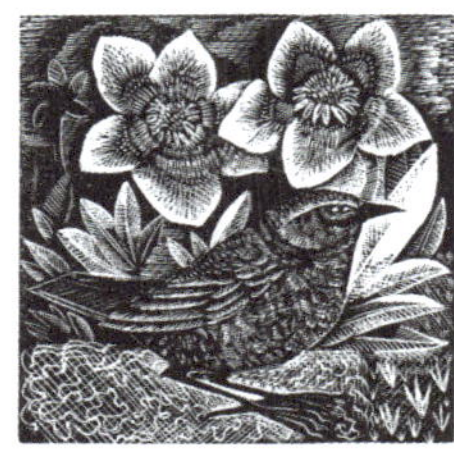
Dunnock p.26

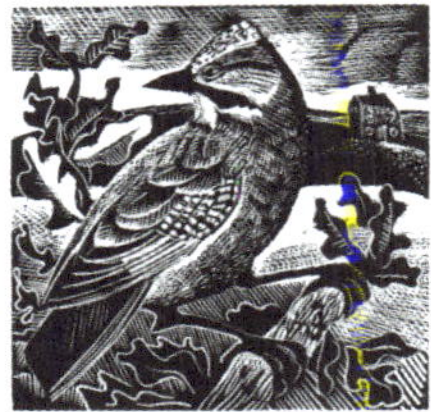
Jay p.26

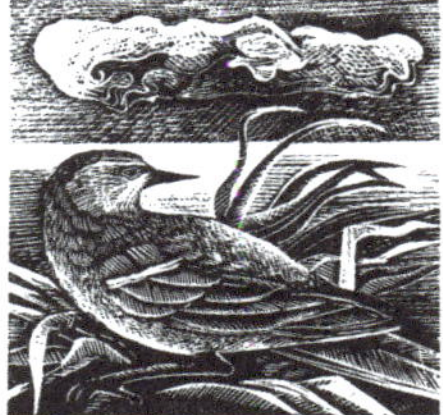
Warbler p.26

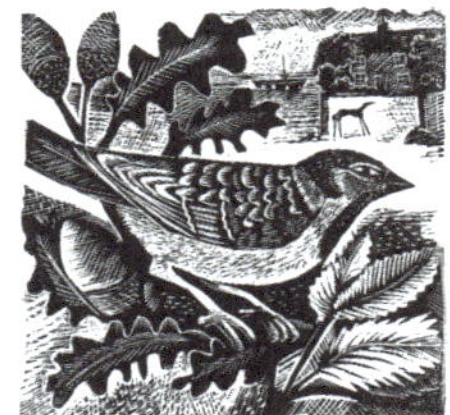
House Sparrow p.27

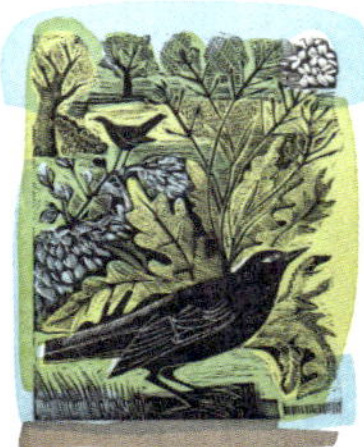
Spring Blackbird p.28

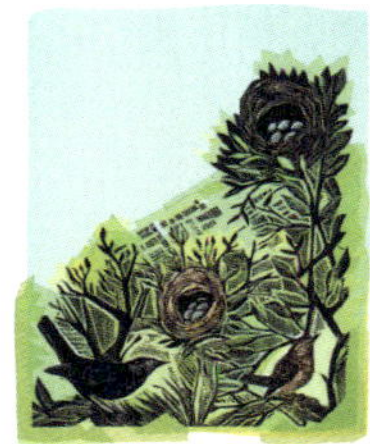
Spring Nests p.29

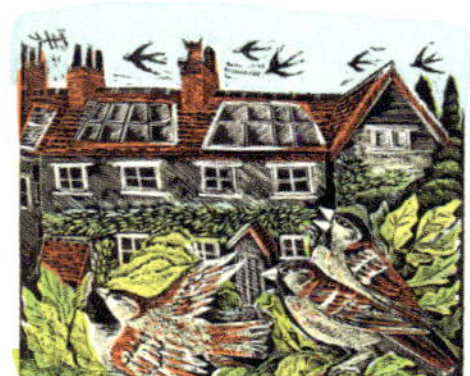
House Sparrows p.30

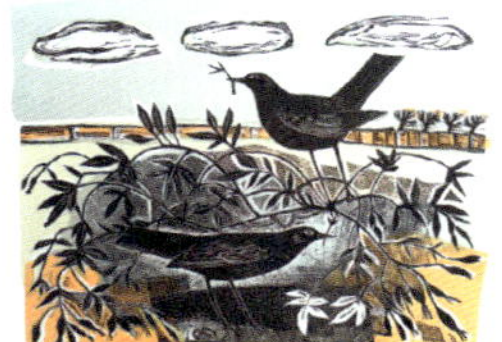
Early Nesters p.33

Blackbird and Rose Nest p.34

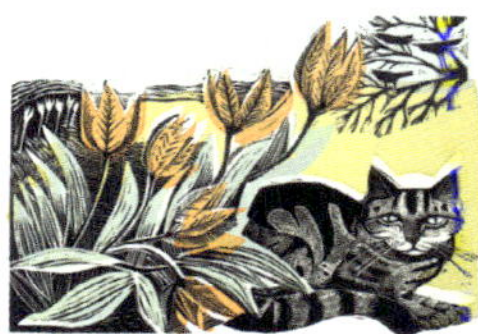
Cat Amongst the Tulips p.35

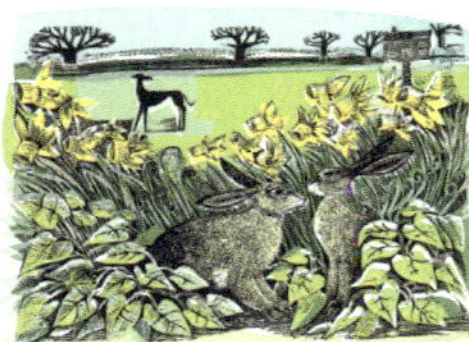
Look Out p.36

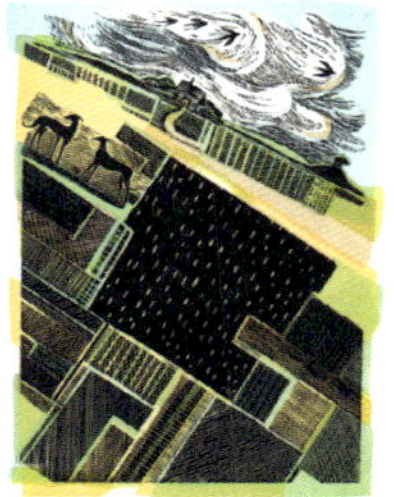
Spring Fields p.38

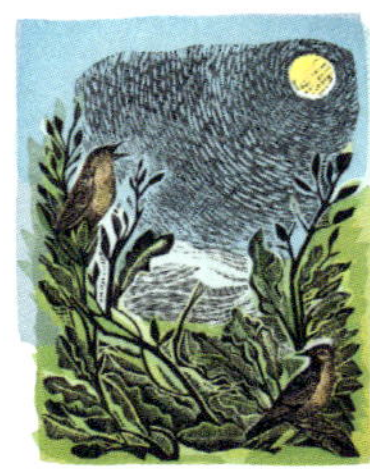
Spring Song p.39

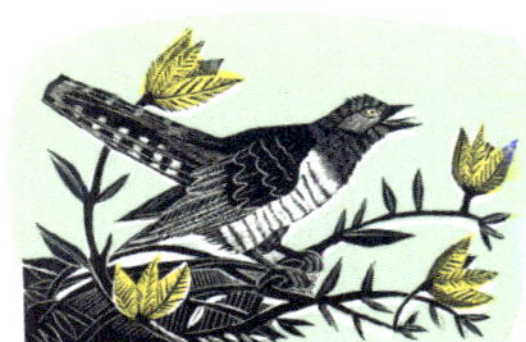
Cuckoo p.40

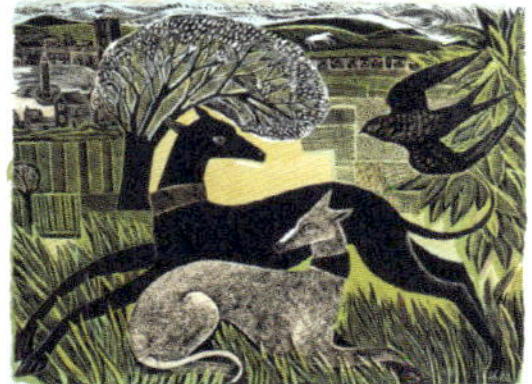
Two Yorkshire Whippets p.42

Spring

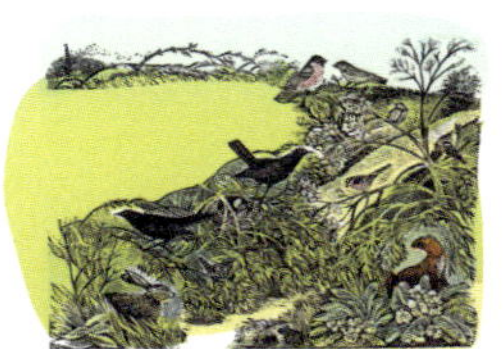
Spring Hedgerow p.49

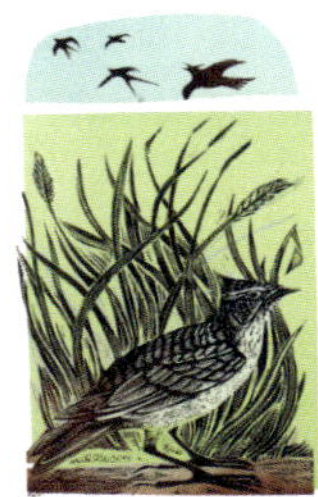
Skylark p. 50

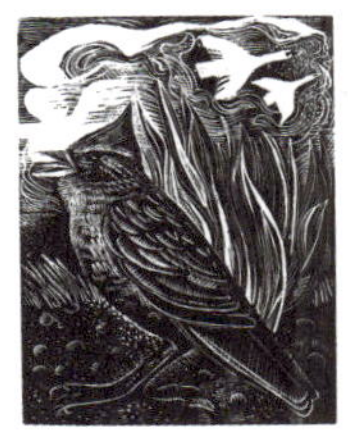
Skylark p.51

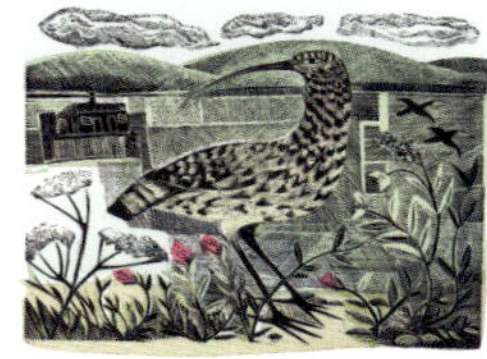
Shippen Curlew p.52

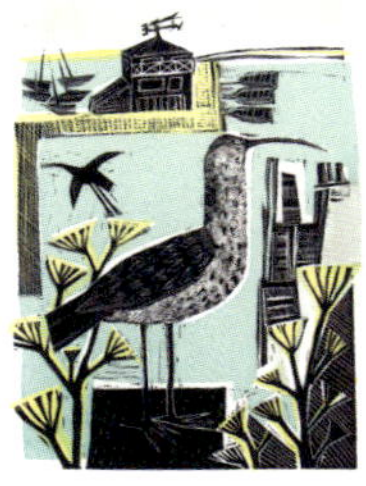
Curlew at Morston p.54

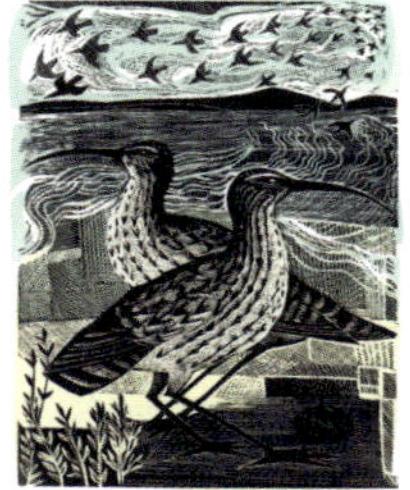
Two Curlews p.55

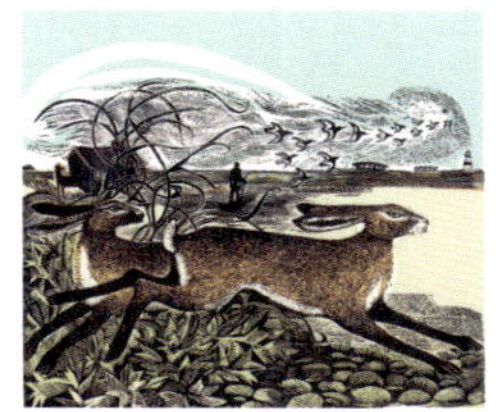
Orford Hares p.57

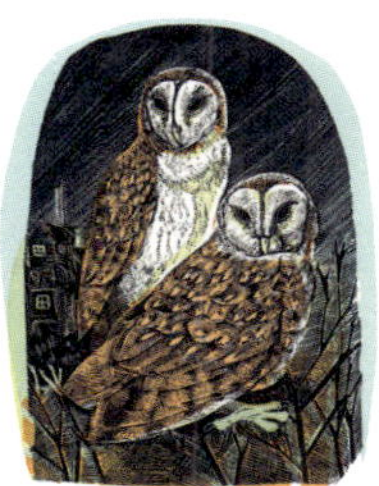
Barn Owls at Orford p.58

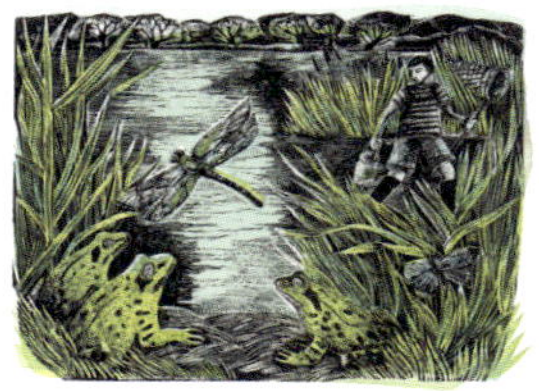
Frogs and Flax Dam p.60

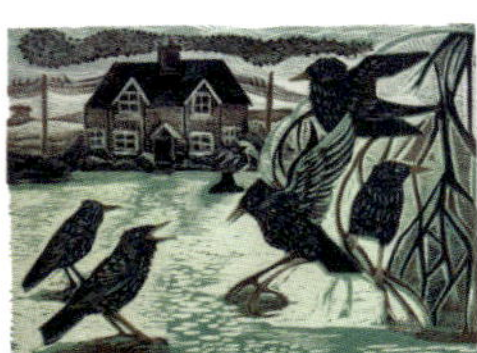
Spring Starlings p. 62

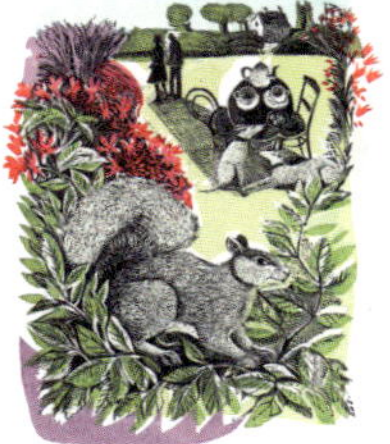
Visitors for Tea p.63

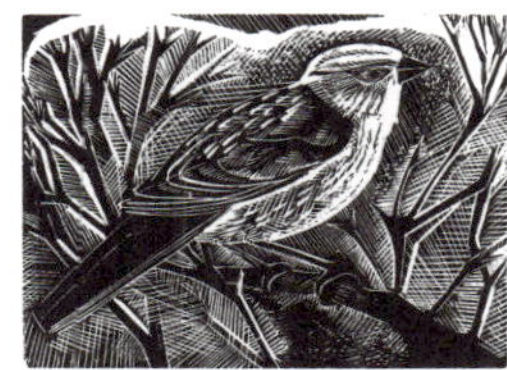
Yellowhammer p.64

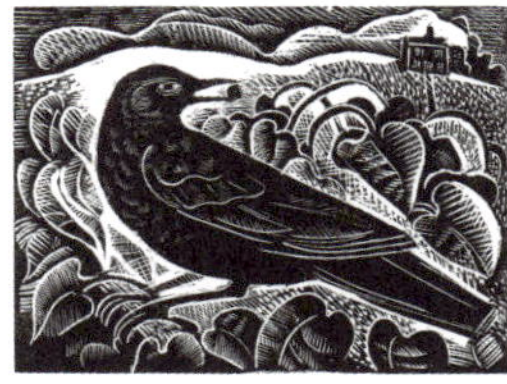
Blackbird p.64

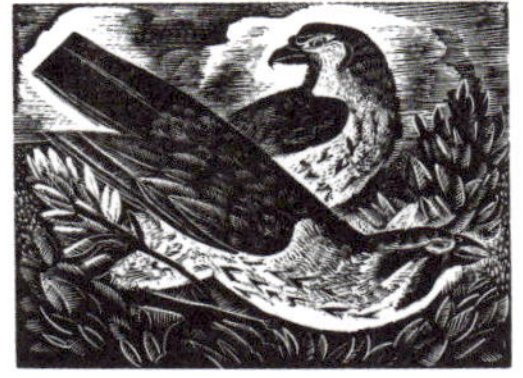
Two Falcons p. 65

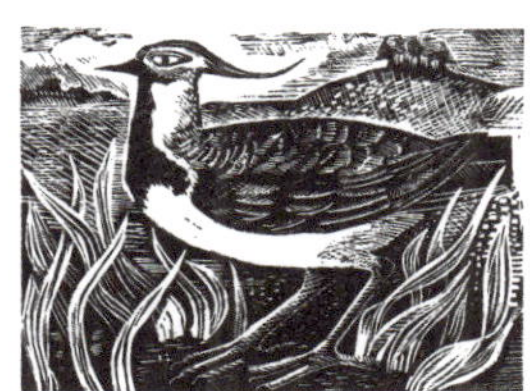
Lapwing p.65

Early Summer

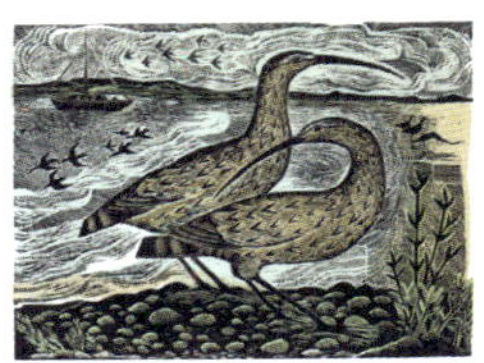

Two Curlews on the Deben p.71

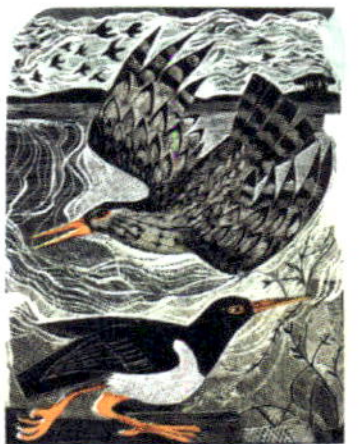

Redshank and Oystercatcher p.72

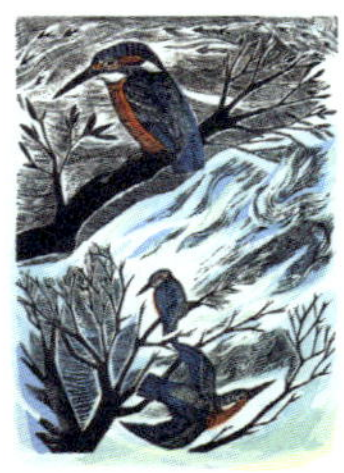

Suffolk Kingfishers p.73

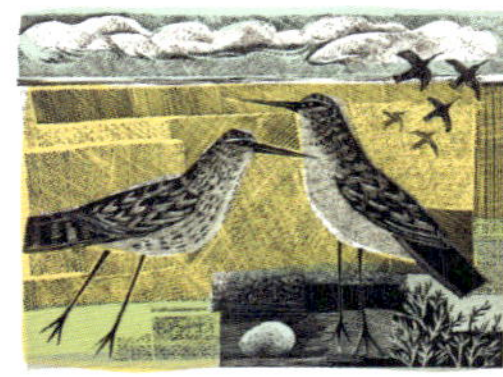

Norfolk Birds p.75

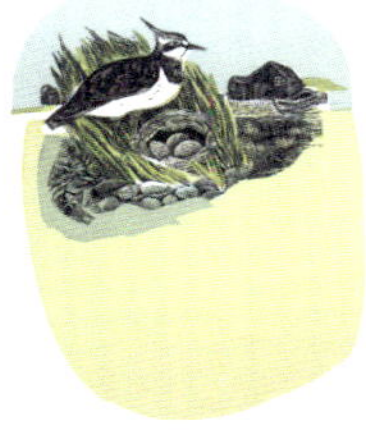

Lapwings Nesting p.76

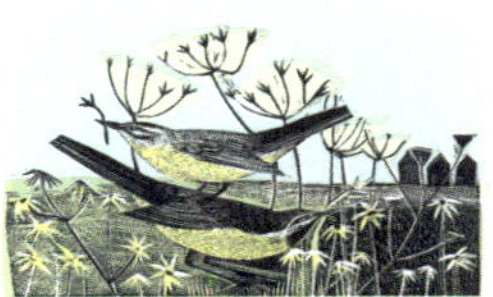

Wagtails and Daisy Fields p.77

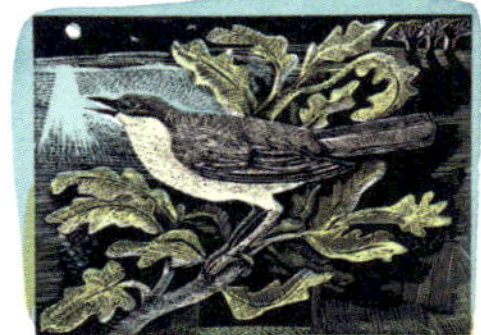

The Nightingale p.79

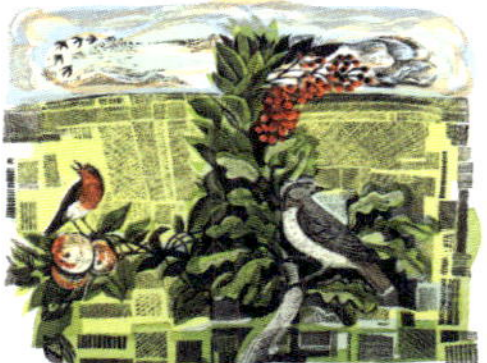

Keats's Nightingale p.81

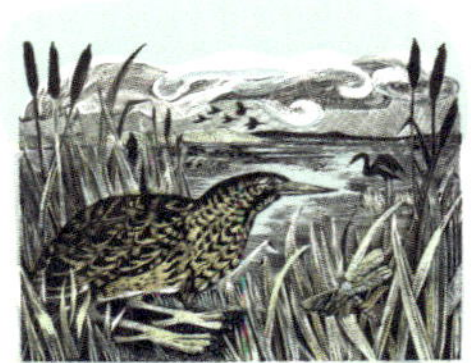

Bittern at Wetlands p.82

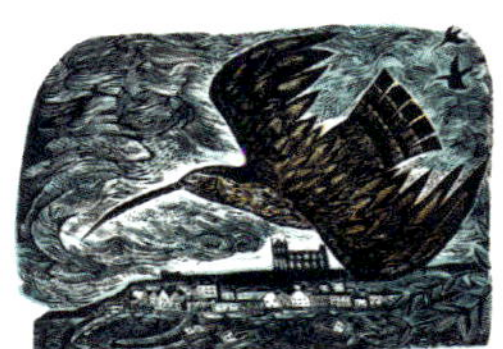

Curlew at Whitby p.83

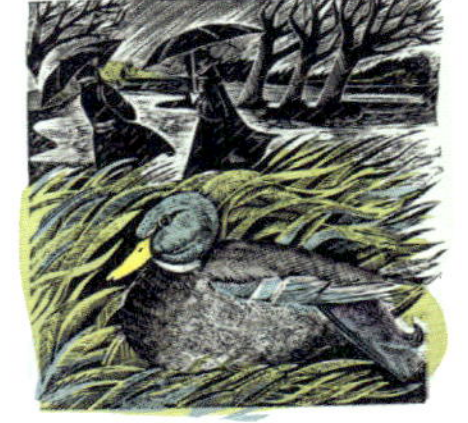

Rainy Days p.84

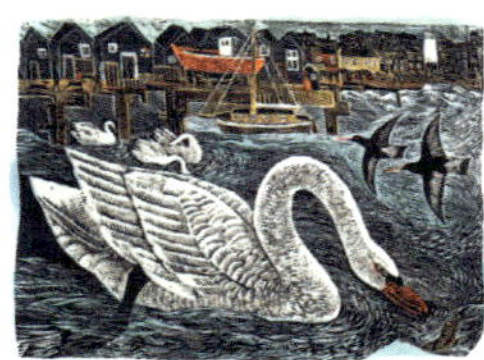

Southwold Swan p.87

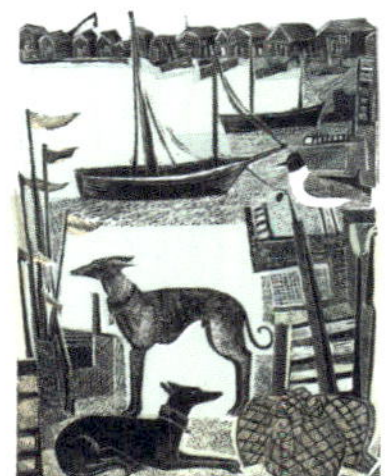

Harbour Whippets p.88

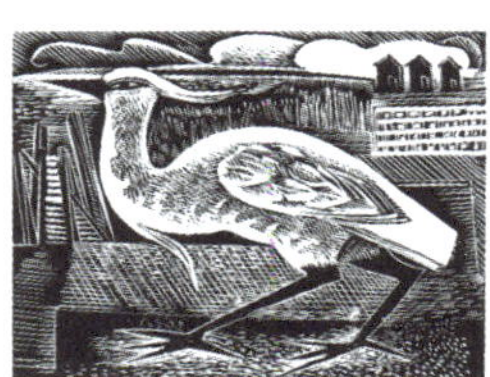

Egret p.89

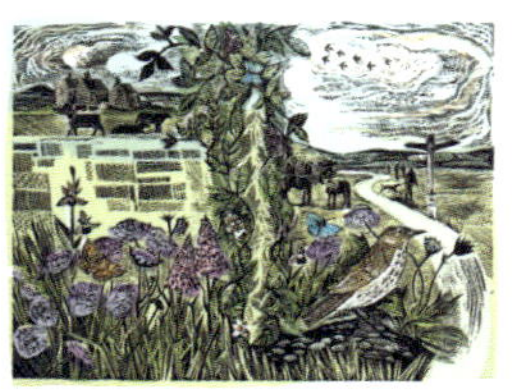

The Common p.91

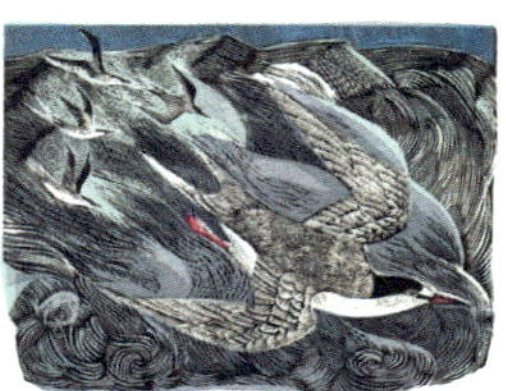

Terns at Sea p.93

Summer

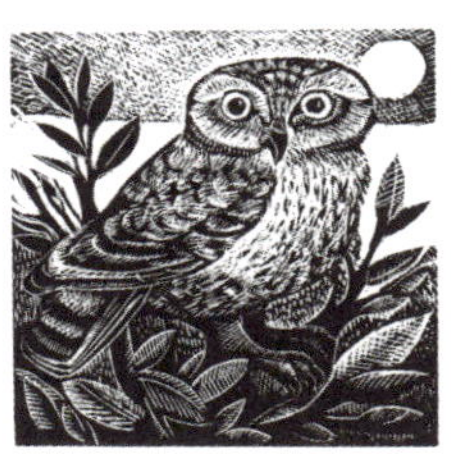
Little Owl p.98

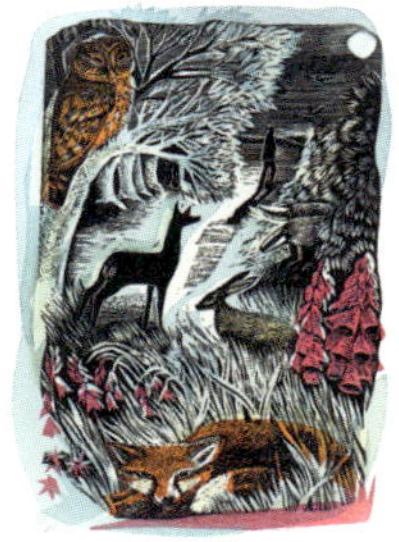
Moon Walk p.99

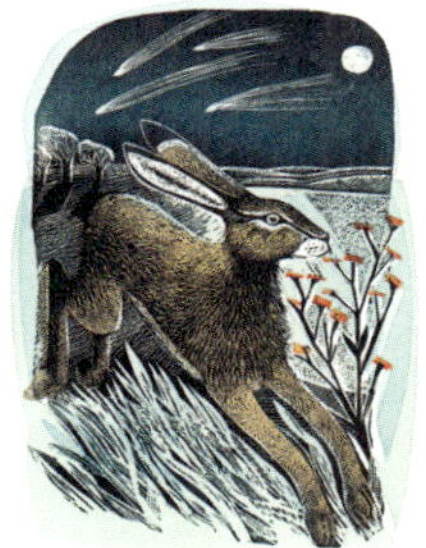
Shooting Stars p.100

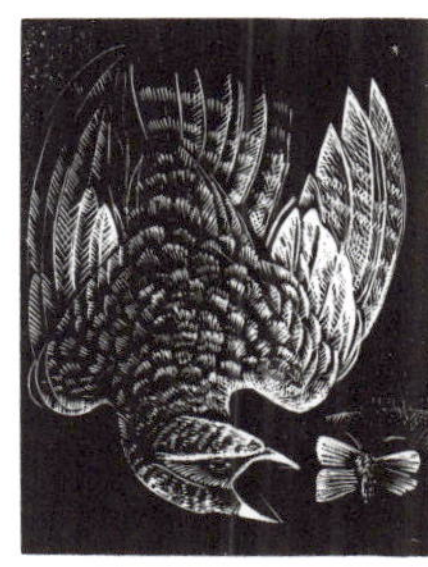
Nightjar p.101

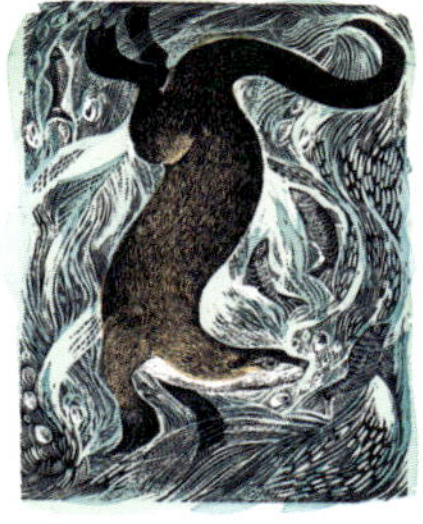
Fishing Otter p.103

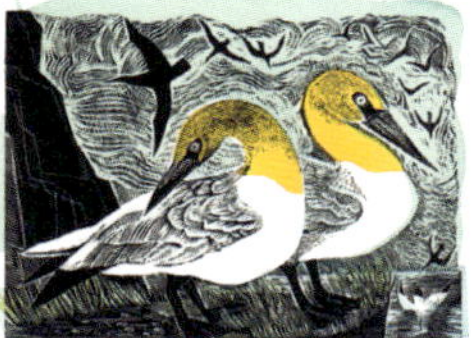
Two Gannets p.104

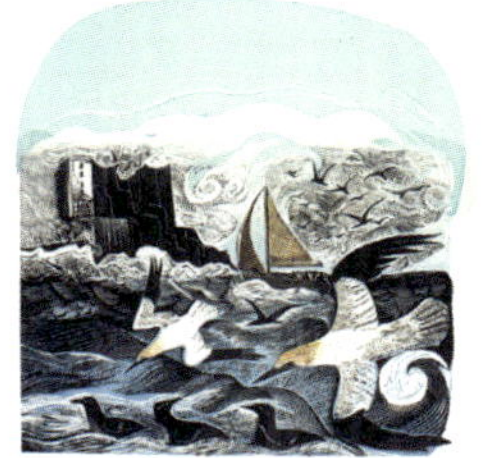
Gannets at Rathlin Island p.105

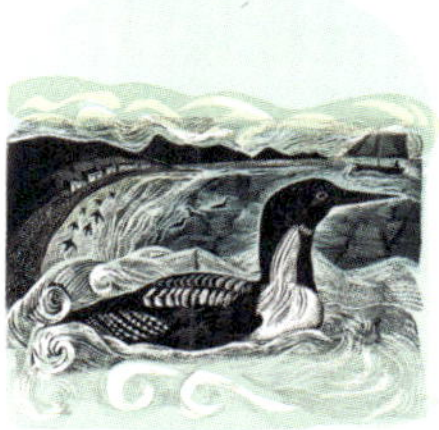
Black-Throated Diver p.106

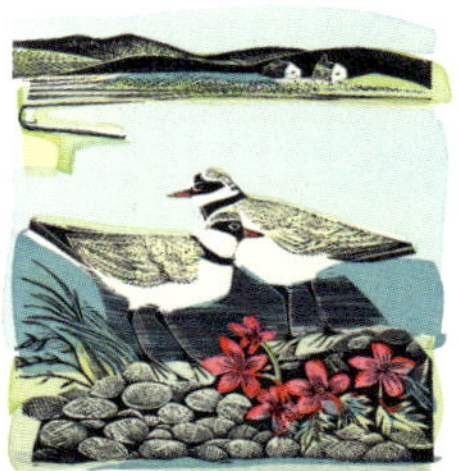
Plovers and Pinks p.107

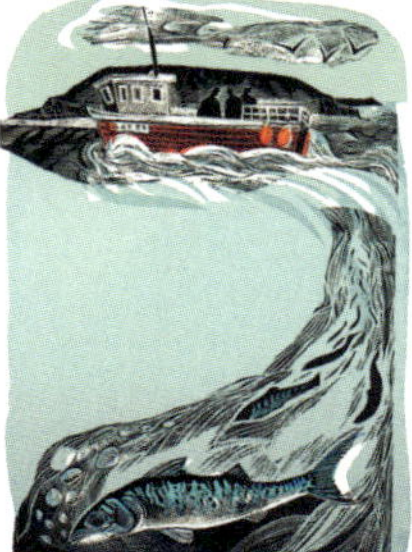
Mackerel and Boat p.108

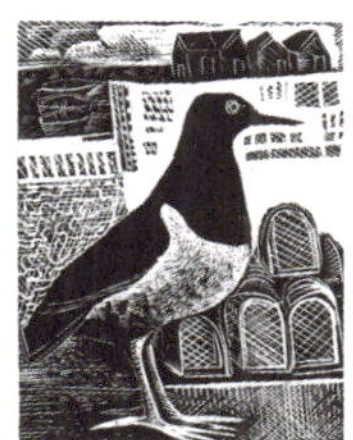
Oystercatcher p.109

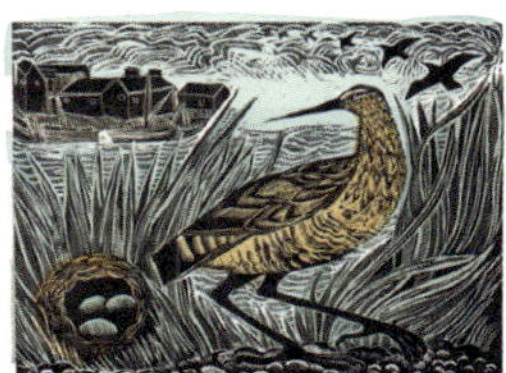
Snape Maltings p.111

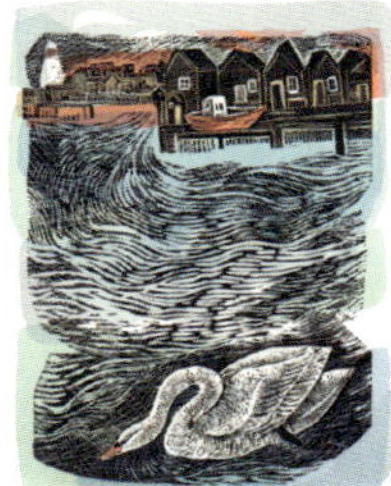
Summer Swans p.112

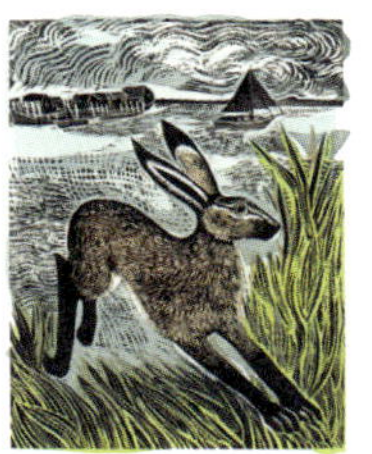
Young Hare p.113

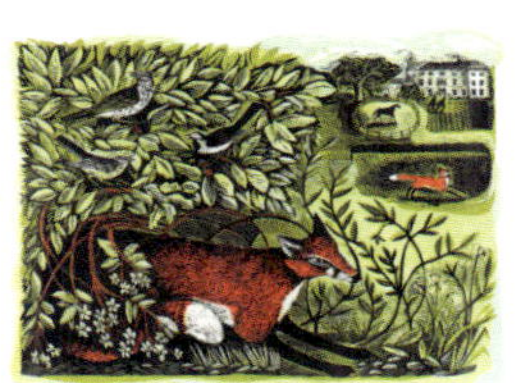
Summer Foxes p.115

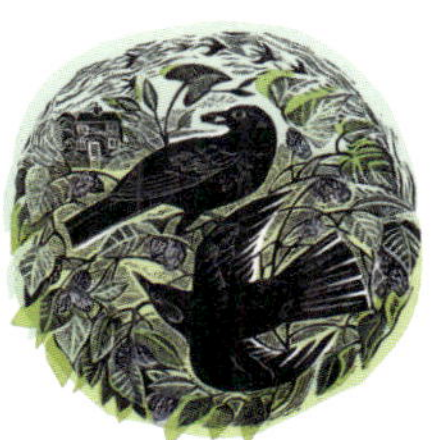
Blackbirds and Mulberry Tree p.116

Autumn

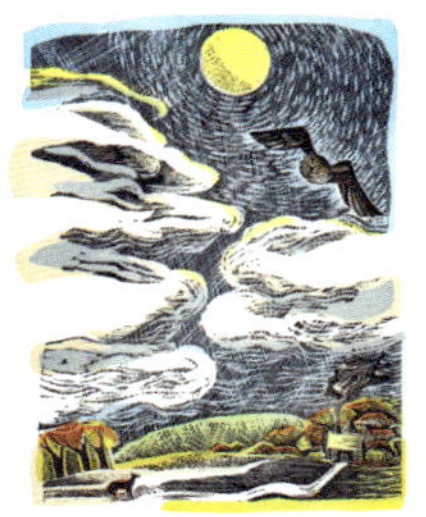
Autumn Flight p.122

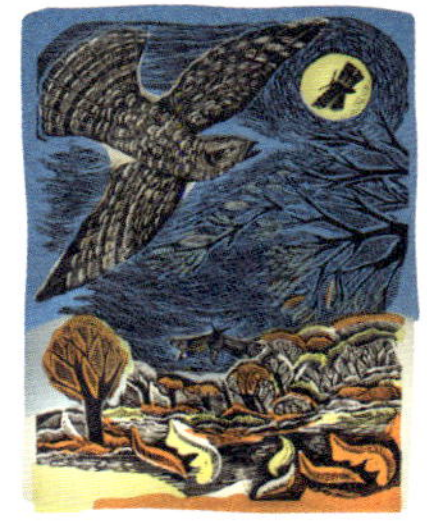
Autumn Nightjar p.123

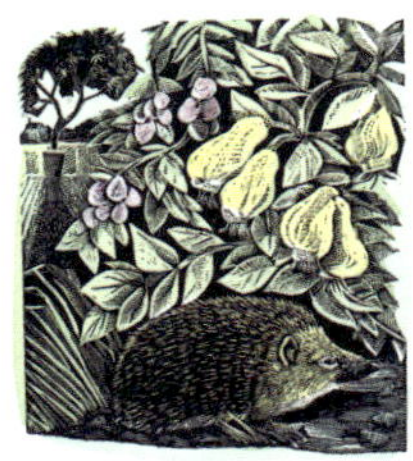
Hedgehog and Fruit p.124

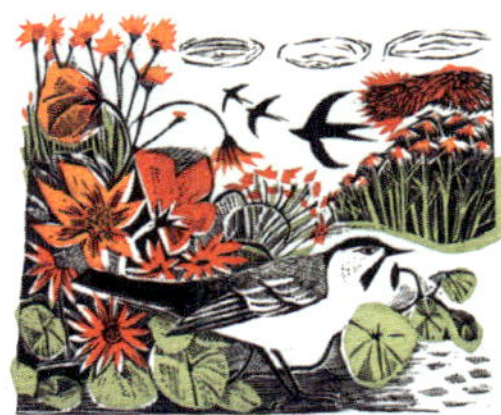
Heading Home p.126

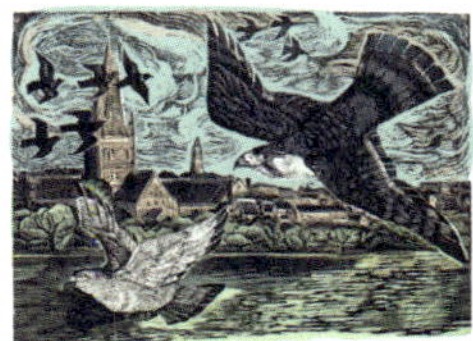
Peregrine and Pigeon p.127

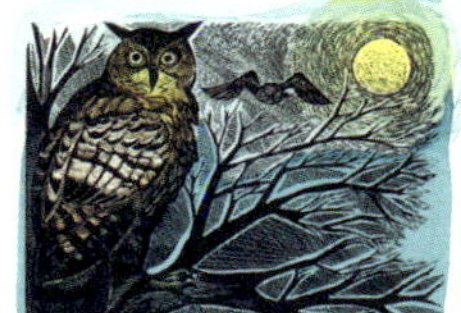
Owl and Moon p.128

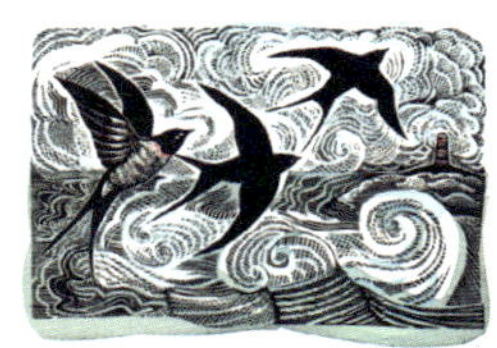
Swallows and Seas p.131

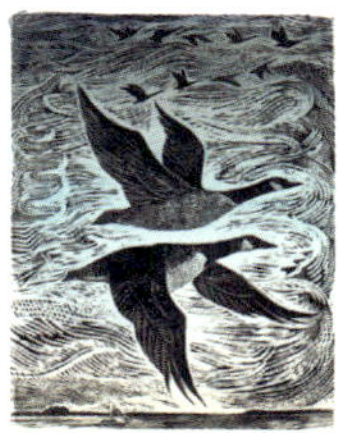
Canada Geese at the Butely p.132

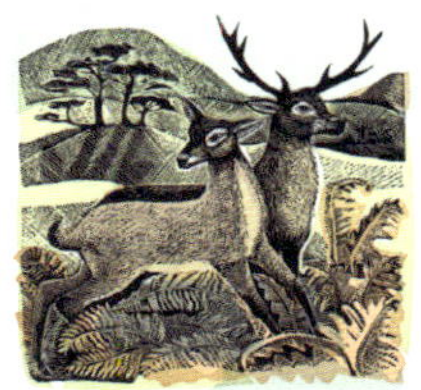
Deer in Bracken p.134

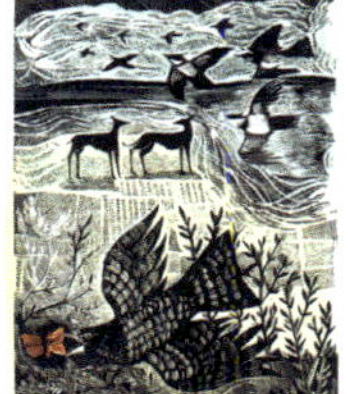
Nightjar and Sea p.135

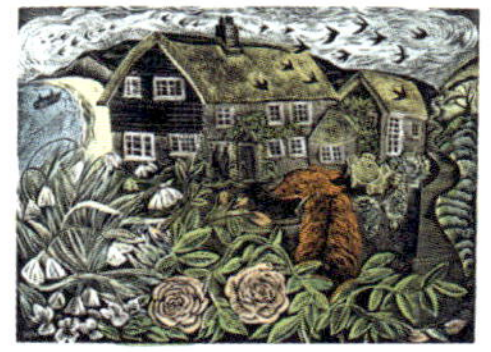
Rose Cottage p.137

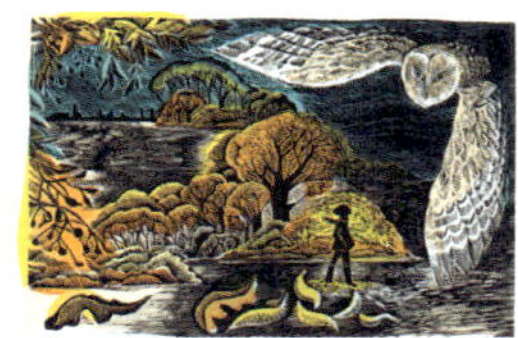
October Owl pp.138-139

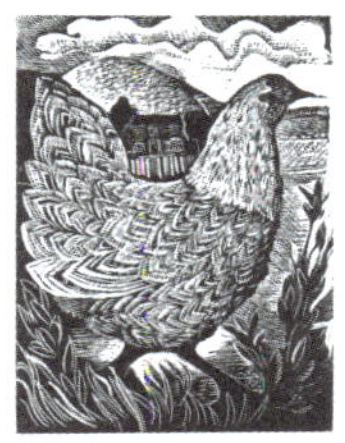
Chicken p.140

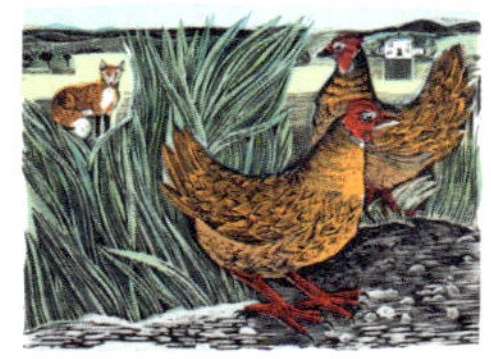
Autumn Chicken p.141

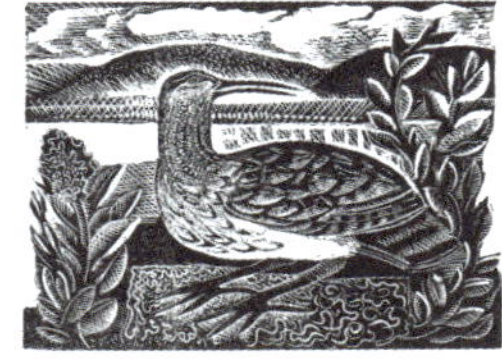
Whimbrel p.142

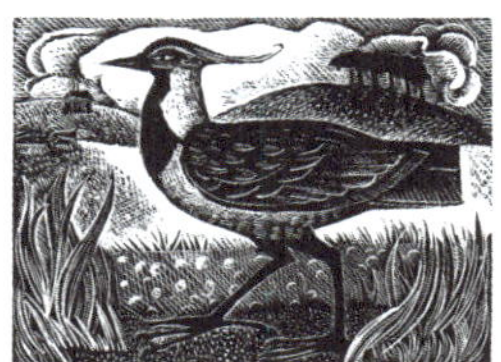
Varas Varas p.142

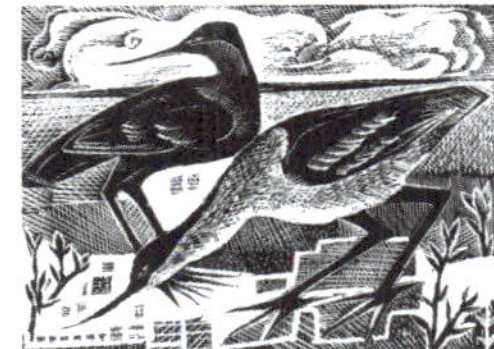
Avocets p.143

Winter

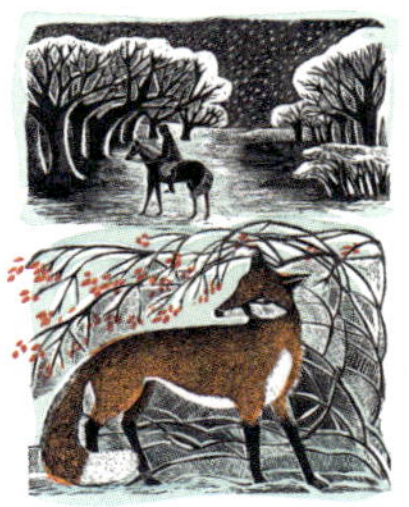
Stopping by the Woods p.148

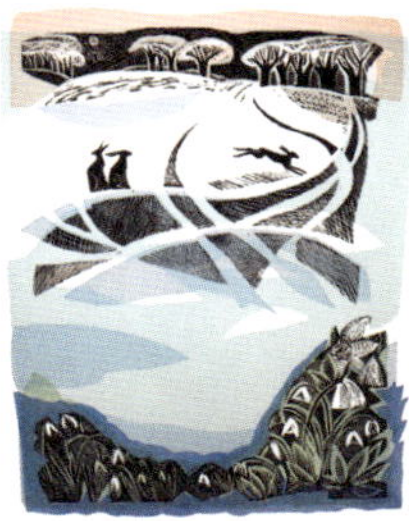
Winter Fields p.149

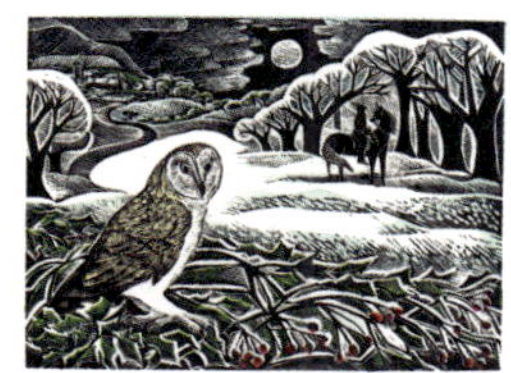
Winter Wood p.150

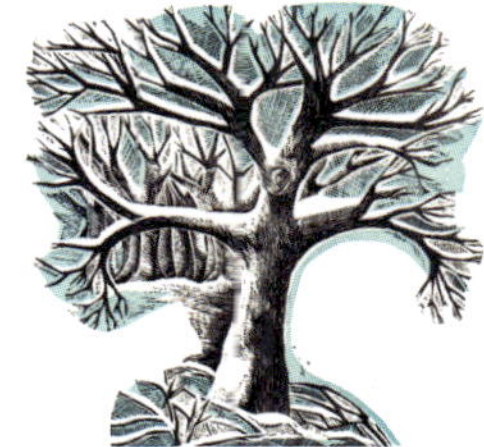
Winter Trees p.152

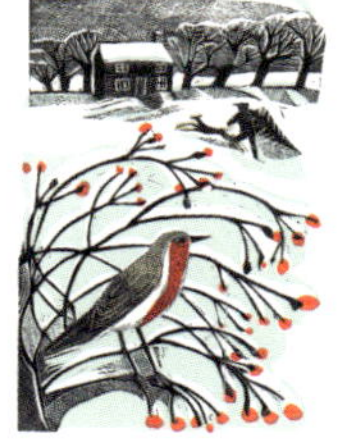
Bringing Back the Tree p.153

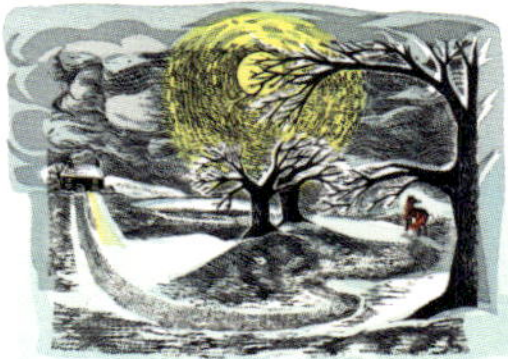
Winter Fox p.155

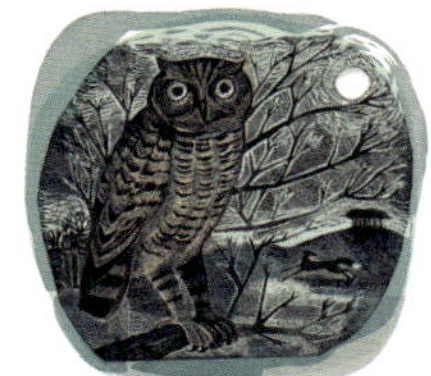
Owl, Hill and Fox p.156

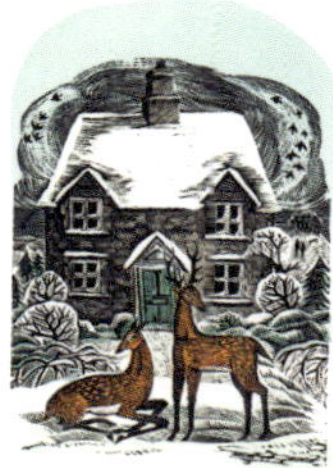
Winter Cottage p.157

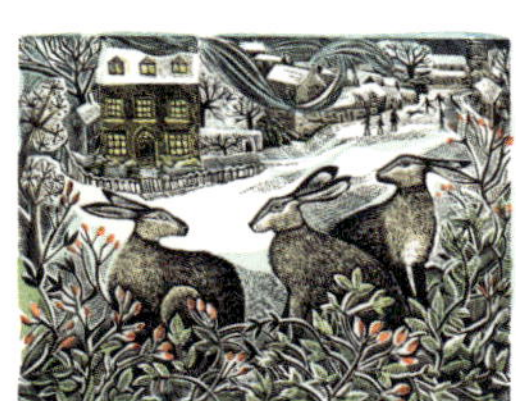
We Three Hares p.159

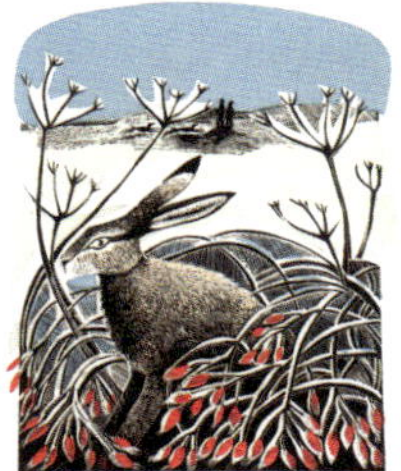
Winter Hare p.160

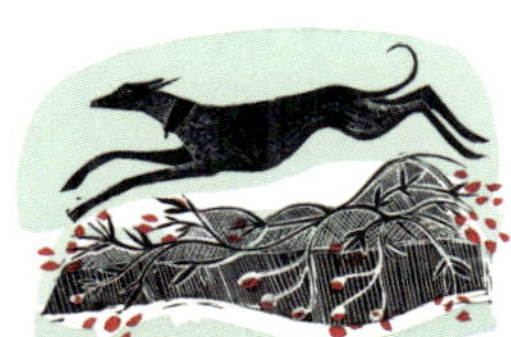
Evening Run p.161

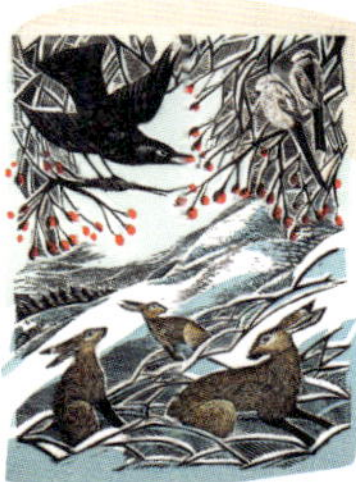
Hares in Conversation p.162

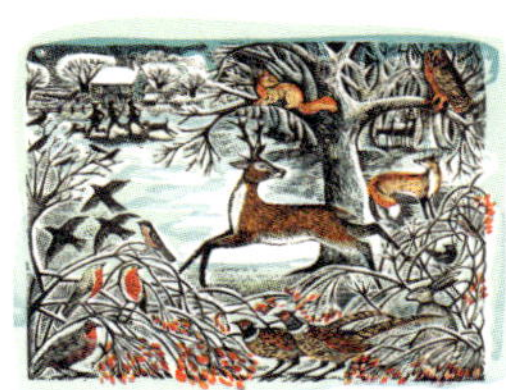
Winter Woodland p.165

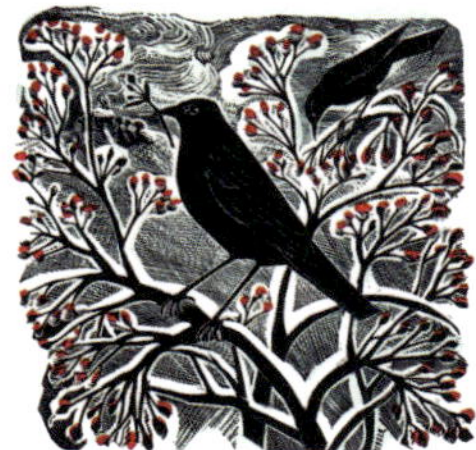
Blackbird and Berries p.166

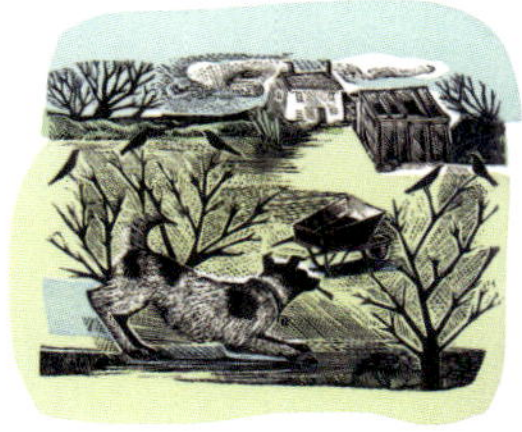
Barney and Stick p.167

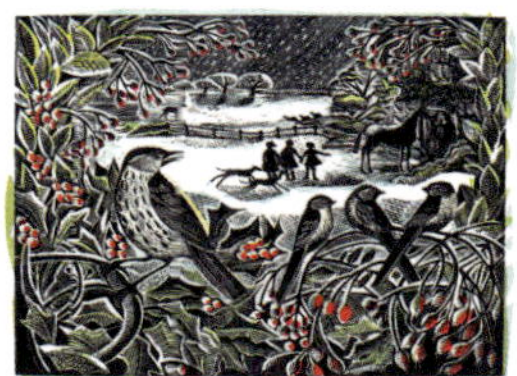
Holly Hedge p.169

Winter continued …

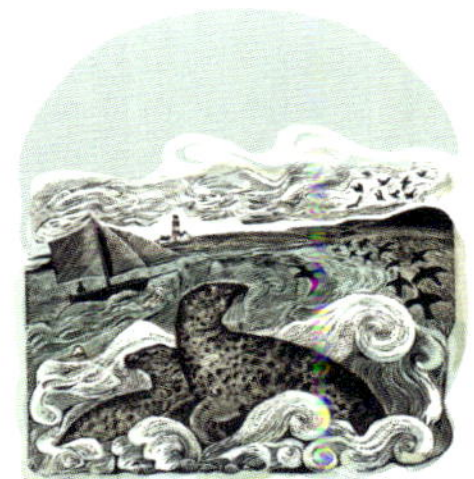
Seal Song p.171

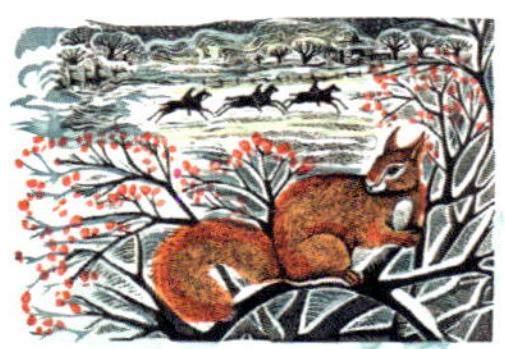
A Winter's Tail p.173

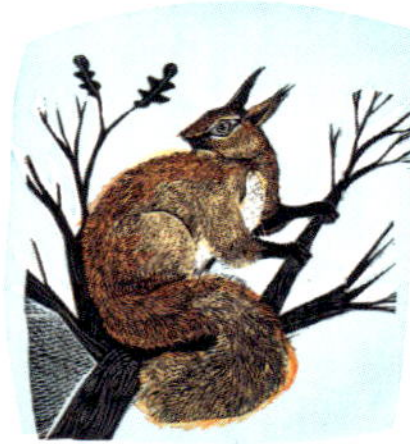
Winter Squirrel p.174

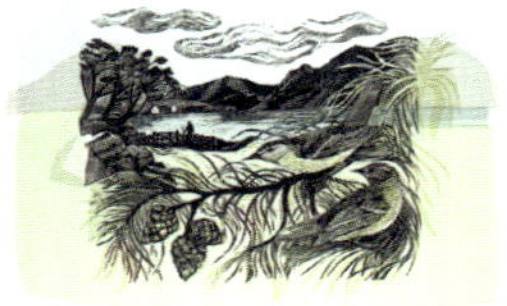
Highland Warbler p.175

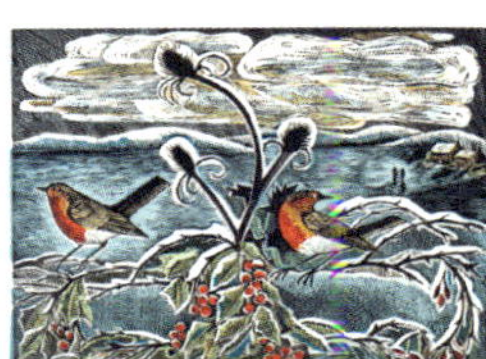
Scottish Robins p.177

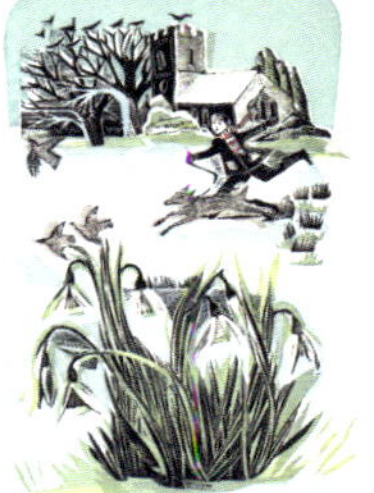
Winter Dog and Church p.178

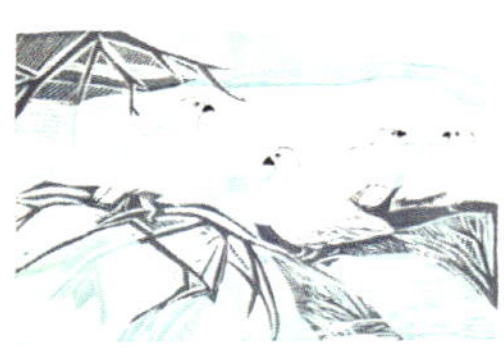
Winter Partridge p.179

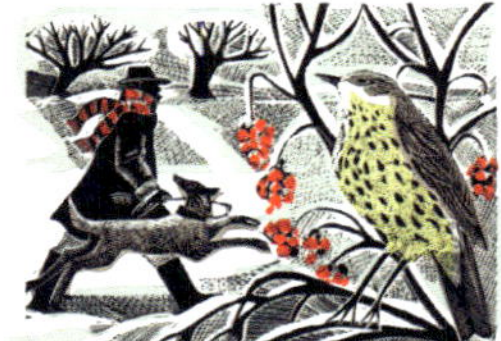
Winter Walk p.180

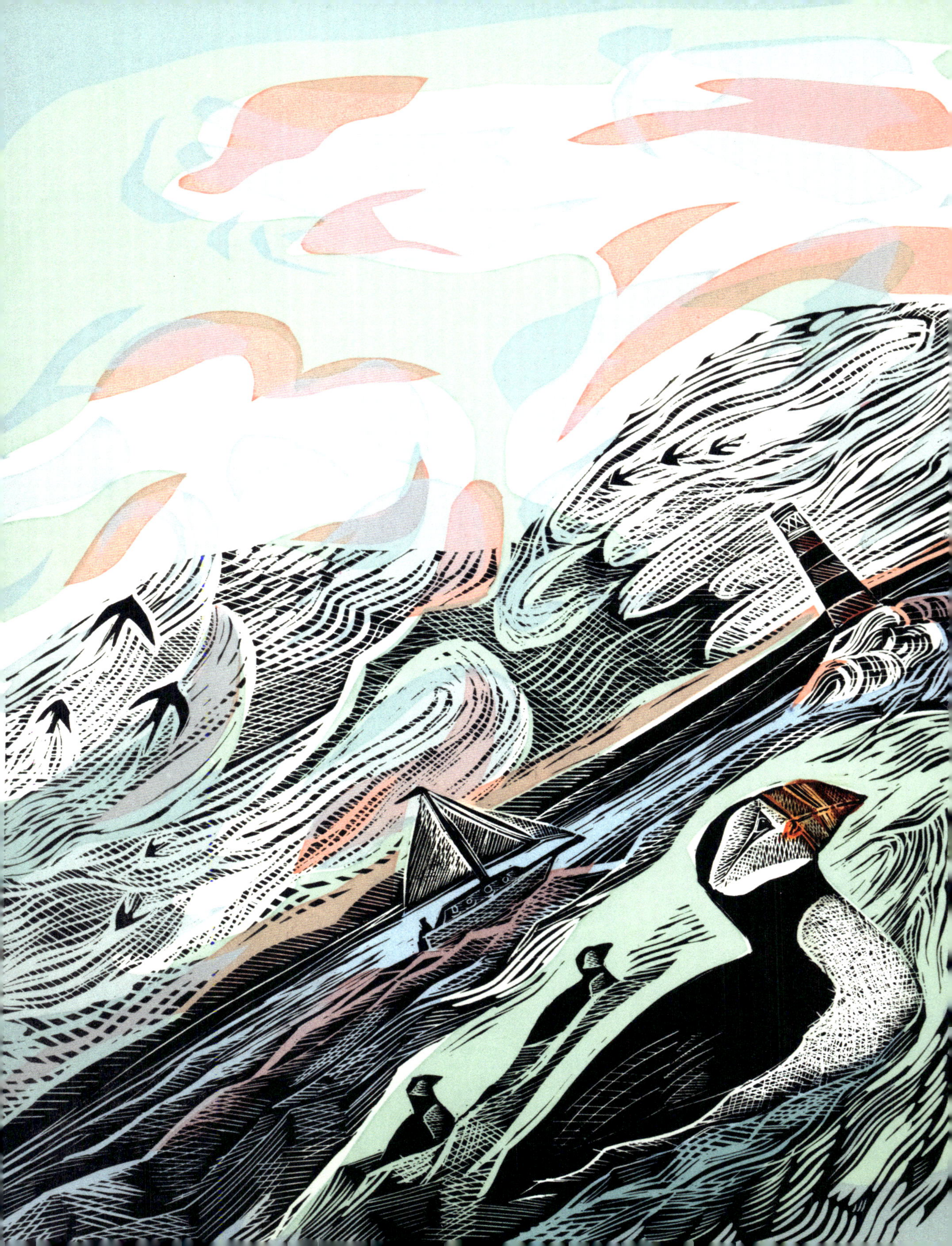

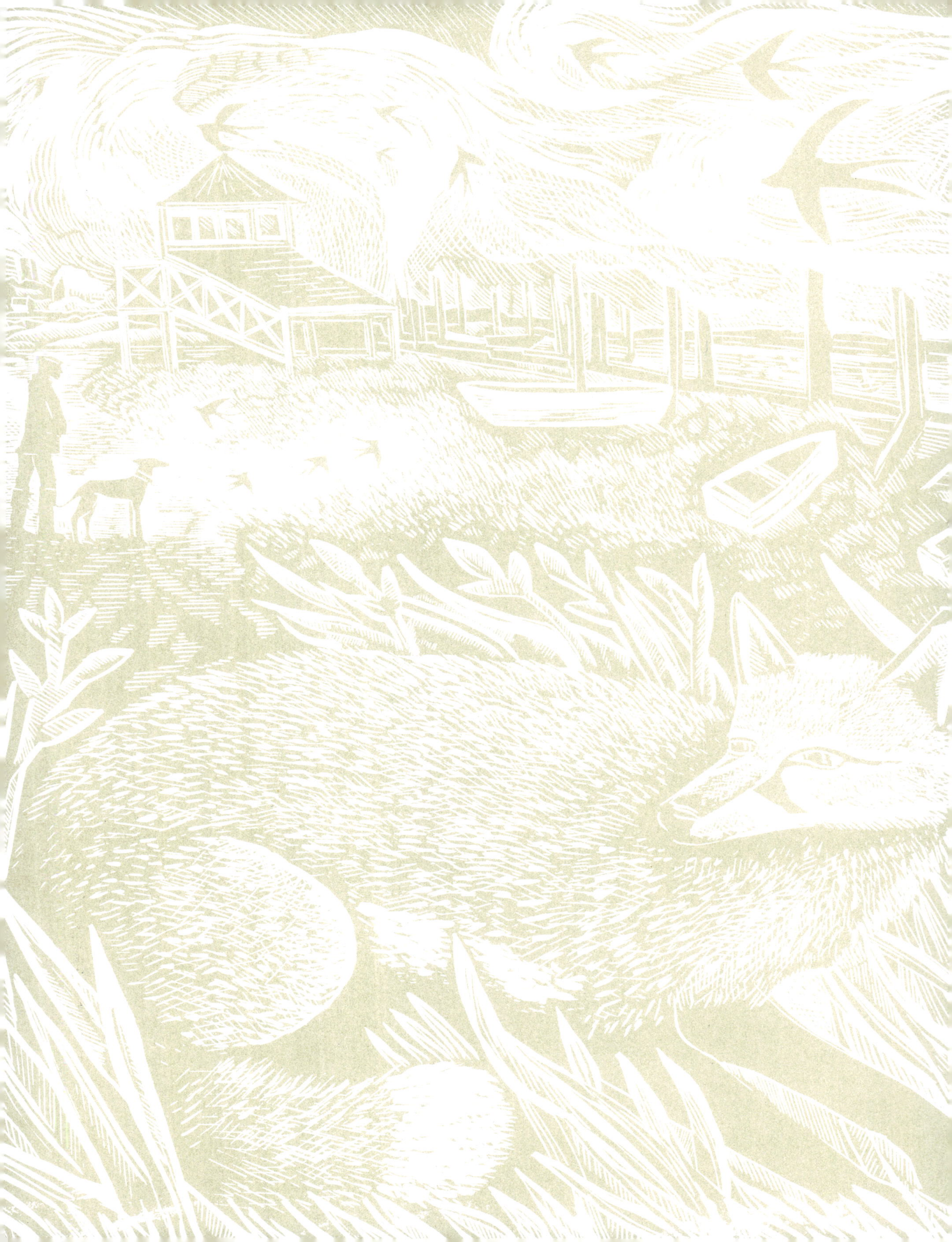